CONTEMPORARY SACRAMENTAL CONTOURS
OF A GOD INCARNATE

TEXTES ET ÉTUDES LITURGIQUES
STUDIES IN LITURGY
XVI

CONTEMPORARY SACRAMENTAL CONTOURS OF A GOD INCARNATE

edited by
Lieven BOEVE and Lambert LEIJSSEN

ABDIJ KEIZERSBERG
FACULTEIT GODGELEERDHEID

PEETERS

LEUVEN
2001

ISBN 90-429-1094-1 (Peeters-Leuven)
ISBN 2-87723-612-9 (Peeters-France)

© Uitgeverij Peeters, Bondgenotenlaan 153, B-3000 Leuven - 2001

TABLE OF CONTENTS

Lieven BOEVE – Lambert LEIJSSEN 7-8
Preface

PART ONE

THE SACRAMENTOLOGY OF LOUIS-MARIE CHAUVET

Stijn VAN DEN BOSSCHE 11-13
Introduction
Louis-Marie CHAUVET 14-38
Le pain rompu comme figure théologique de la présence eucharistique
Luk DEVOLDER 39-50
Do We Still Need Sacraments?
Kristiaan DEPOORTERE 51-62
From Sacramentality to Sacraments, and Vice-Versa
Lorelei F. FUCHS 63-73
Louis-Marie Chauvet's Theology of Sacrament and Ecumenical Theology: Connections in Terms of an Ecumenical Hermeneutics of Unity Based on a Koinonia Ecclesiology
Glenn P. AMBROSE 74-84
Chauvet and Pickstock: Two Compatible Visions?
Franklin PILARIO 85-101
'Gift-Exchange' in Sacramentology: A Critical Assessment from the Perspective of Pierre Bourdieu

PART TWO

FACETS OF SACRAMENTOLOGY

John C. RIES 105-109
Introduction

Section One: Discovering the Sacramentality of Sacraments

Kevin W. IRWIN 111-123
   Liturgical Actio – Sacramentality, Eschatology and Ecology
George S. WORGUL 124-136
   Root Metaphors and Sacramental Presence in a Postmodern Age
László LUKÁCS 137-153
   Communication – Symbols – Sacraments
Timothy J. CRUTCHER 154-165
   Personally Speaking: Reflections on Relational Thinking for the Ecumenical Sacramental Dialogue

Section Two: Exposing Eucharistic Faces

Gino MATTHEEUWS 167-175
   Presiding at the Eucharist: Sacrament of the Ecclesial Christ
Thomas J. SCIRGHI 176-189
   Preaching in a Postmodern Context
Jerry FARMER 190-204
   "Sunday Celebrations in the Absence of a Priest":
   A Postmodern Reading
Willem Marie SPEELMAN 205-217
   The Sacrament Is the Message:
   On the Mediation of Liturgy through the Electronic Media

Section Three: Re-imag(in)ing Sacramental Contours

Eugene C. MCDOWELL & Meghan F. FROEHLICH 219-232
   An Incarnational Approach to Eucharistic Participation:
   Anglican Reflection on the Real Presence of Christ in the Eucharist
Dorothy MCDOUGALL 233-241
   The Cosmos as Primary Sacrament:
   An Ecological Perspective for Sacramental Theology
Susan K. ROLL 242-255
   Baptism: New Thinking from Women-identified Perspectives
Jon PAHL 256-270
   God's Clothing: The Limits of Postmodernity & Living Waters
   God as Source, (Dis)Solution, and Delight

PREFACE

The variety of questioning, methods and answers presented in this volume all make manifest that 'thinking sacramentality' has become a crucial theme under theological discussion. The contemporary sacramentological question – how to think the divine and its mediation, i.e. the 'presence of God', in a intellectual context which is most critical of premodern and modern thinking patterns of doing so – clearly stands at the heart of theology's endeavours today. As a matter of fact, more than being the subject of a more narrowly focused 'sacramentology' or 'theology of the sacraments', today's reflection on the sacramentality of religious life, in its activity and its thinking, constitutes a critical and fecund point of departure for theology as a whole. In short, contemporary theology would seem to be profoundly 'sacramento-theology'. "As such, every expression about God, whether in word or deed, needs to be called sacramental and thus submitted to sacramento-theological reflection in as far as it is inscribed in, and gives form to – or better, realises and constitutes – the mutual involvement of human beings and God ."[1]

From the 3rd through the 6th of November 1999, scholars from various countries gathered in Leuven to participate in the second biannual 'Leuven Encounters in Systematic Theology' (LEST). This second Congress, entitled "Sacramental Presence in a Postmodern Context: Fundamental-Theological Approaches," was devoted to reflection on the conditions and possibilities for thinking the 'presence of God' in the present 'postmodern' context. This Congress has been part of the programme of a more extended research project, called 'Postmodern Sacramento-theology', sponsored by the K.U.Leuven Research Fund and the Fund for Scientific Research of Flanders (fwo-v). The subject under investigation in this project has also been selected for the programme of collaboration between the faculty of theology, K.U.Leuven, and The Netherlands School for Advanced Studies in Theology and Religion (Noster). Within the framework of this agreement, Noster co-sponsored the organisation of this Congress, in particular the Junior Scholars Conference (3 November 1999), which preceded the main Congress.

---

1. L. Boeve, "Post-Modern Sacramento-Theology: Retelling the Christian Story," in *Ephemerides Theologicae Lovanienses* 74 (1998) 326-343, p. 326.

This Congress also included the fourteenth biennial International Liturgy Colloquium of the Liturgical Institute of the Faculty of Theology, K.U. Leuven, in cooperation with the Abbey of Keizersberg. As usual, the texts of the Colloquium are published in the review *Questions Liturgiques – Studies in Liturgy* (nrs. 3/4, 2000 and 1, 2001). All texts of the main speakers and their respondents, along with a selection of other contributions at the Congress, are published in the series *Bibliotheca Ephemeridum Theologicarum Lovaniensium*.

The present volume consists of a collection of papers that were presented at the Conference and the Congress. By focusing upon differing facets of 'sacramentality', each contribution seeks to explore the "sacramental contours of a God incarnate" by bringing to light the vital role of 'sacramentality' in theological reflection as well as some of the aporias entailed in doing 'sacramento-theology' in the present postmodern context.

We sincerely thank mrs. Rita Corstjens, dr. Stijn Van den Bossche and dr. John Ries for the editorial assistance. We hope that this volume may stimulate further scholarly reflections on thinking sacramental presence in a postmodern context.

Lieven BOEVE   Lambert LEIJSSEN

PART ONE

THE SACRAMENTOLOGY OF LOUIS-MARIE CHAUVET

INTRODUCTION

At the second international conference in the series *Leuven Encounters in Systematic Theology* (LEST), organised at K.U. Leuven in November 1999, entitled 'Sacramental Presence in a Postmodern Context', one of the major referents was the Parisian sacramentologist Louis-Marie Chauvet, whose extensive study *Symbol and Sacrament* is certainly one of the most brilliant contributions to sacramentology since Vatican II, and is precisely taking its point of departure in the post-metaphysical thinking patterns that constitute the so-called post-modern era. As such, CHAUVET's contribution opens this volume. In this he not only resumes the main features of *Symbol and Sacrament* in a marvellous way, but he at the same time pursues these more deeply. After discussing the triangular relation between the 'meta-' of metaphysics, phenomenology and hermeneutics, he comes to the way in which the presence of Christ in the Eucharist can be conceived along these lines. Chauvet first makes clear what is at stake in the scholastic and Tridentine doctrine of transubstantiation, and evaluates this classic approach of the Lord's presence, including its major limitation which Chauvet calls 'the forgetting of the relation'. Then he introduces a phenomenological approach, taking the breaking of the bread as its focus. This leads him to thinking Eucharistic presence "in the mode of Openness," which shows itself in the breaking of the bread.

Subsequently, part one includes five contributions of theologians who also presented papers at the LEST II conference, in which they engage Chauvet's *Symbol and Sacrament*.

Luk DE VOLDER asks the question whether we still need the sacraments. There is strong resistance to the ritual and the sacramental in the Church today. The believer finds it hard to fit his/her personal beliefs and spirituality in with the liturgical-sacramental pattern as prescribed by the Church. De Volder seeks to resolve this pastoral problem of the seeming irrelevance of sacraments through the thought of Chauvet. Underneath this resistance there is in fact a refusal of mediation at work. De Volder then works through the main steps of Chauvet's thinking pattern, to demonstrate that faith is sacramental as such: as a Christian we always receive grace through *mediation*. The Church exists in the threefold mediation structure of Holy Scripture, sacraments and ethical testimony. In the specific sacraments, then, the Church finds its corporeality as the highest level of the symbolic order. So to agree to mediation – and God could not? appear otherwise – means to agree to sacraments.

Kristiaan DEPOORTERE pursues Chauvet's symbolic line of thought in a quite radical way. He seeks to broaden and dynamise the notion of sacramental presence. To do this, he begins by balancing the Greek *mysterion* and the Latin *sacramentum*, indicating their complementarity. While *mysterion* pertains to the participation of reality in the invisible salvific plan of God, *sacramentum* rather concerns the engagement of God, signified in the visible. Because these two cannot be completely separated, we should therefore pay more attention to the continuity between the sacramental(s) and the sacraments. Only then shall we understand major shifts in theology and pastoral practice today. In sacramentology, theologians now build on the symbolic structure that is opened in the distance between signifier and signified, and thereby overcome the previous onto-theological approaches. In ecclesiology, Christian identity must then be conceived in the triadic scheme of *kerygma*, *leitourgia* and *diakonia*, rather than be deduced from Mass attendance. In ministerial theology, we then face nothing less than a fusion of ordained and lay ministries. All of this leads Depoortere to a plea for a continuum of sacramentality, at the end of which appear the sacraments *stricto sensu*.

Sr. Lorelei FUCHS finds profound inspiration in Chauvet's sacramentology for ecumenical discussion. After working through the four parts of *Symbol and Sacrament*, she focuses on the *coincidentia oppositorum* encountered in Chauvet's thinking, which pertains to the givenness and creativity of sacrament. As such, graduality can replace the metaphysical black-and-white discussions hence forth, and this graduality can serve as a hermeneutical tool not only to find some *auream mediocritatem* between denominations, but also "to transcend confessional extremes of denominational retrenchment." Applied on the sacraments, the respective Catholic and Protestant emphases (*efficiunt quod figurant* versus *figurant quod efficiunt*) can approach each other: for there is *coincidentia oppositorum*. Finally, Fuchs applies the same idea to the ecumenical use of the biblical term of *koinonia*.

Glenn AMBROSE undertakes a critical comparison between Chauvet's *Symbol and Sacrament* and Catherine Pickstock's *After Writing: On the Liturgical Consummation of Philosophy*. According to Ambrose, both these authors take a similar point of departure: the postmodern agenda, with its critique of the sovereign subject, and its new emphasis on apophatic theology. But from there, Chauvet and Pickstock opt for quite different paths. Where Chauvet seeks to rely on a post-metaphysical setting,

Pickstock rather makes a plea for retrieving the pre-modern metaphysical tradition. Ambrose compares both authors on the level of their respective pedagogies of liturgy, their assessment of the legitimacy of a world outside Christendom, and the consequences of the implementation of their visions. Although he thinks that both points of view can challenge and enrich each other, his sympathies fall more with Chauvet, whose theology he deems more adequate for the Church(es) and the world of today.

Finally with Daniel Franklin PILARIO's contribution, we meet a real critique to Chauvet's thought, or at least to a part of it: Chauvet's elaboration of the *admirabile commercium* between God and humanity which we call 'grace'. Pilario begins by reviewing Chauvet's anthropological model for thinking this *commercium*: the model of the gift-exchange, borrowed mainly from Marcel Mauss and Claude-Lévi Strauss. But then Pilario applies the critique of Pierre Bourdieu to this model. Bourdieu unmasks the symbolic exchange as in fact leading to the same result as economic exchange: relations of power and oppression are installed. After an extensive analysis of Bourdieu's critique to the anthropological model, and after having applied this critique to Chauvet's theological use of the model, Pilario concludes that the model of gift-exchange is an inadequate theological model. It brings God present in the gift and thereby runs the risk of ideological abuse again. Here Bourdieu's critique to the model can help. In contrast to 'gracious existence' by an excessive gift which however turns also into excessive abuse of power, there is the 'contrast experience' as a different, but perhaps equally sacramental experience. This experience, Pilario concludes, is actually more in line with Chauvet's Heideggerian plea for the absence of God.

These six contributions concerning the use of symbol as a model for thinking sacrament(-ality) – diverse as they are – will undoubtedly stimulate discussion around Chauvet's position rather than bring concord. I am not sure that Chauvet would agree with each of the interpretations of his position, nor with what is suggested as the outcome of the application of his position on different domains. This proves that the project of *Symbol and Sacrament*, which is *A Sacramental Reinterpretation of Christian Existence* after we have lost the (metaphysical) presence of God, leads indeed into an adventure that leaves no area in theology untouched, and provokes many new adventures. But after all, is theology not the adventurous enterprise of the encounter between faith tradition and even a 'postmodern' or 'post-metaphysical' culture?

Stationsstraat 120
9850 Nevele-Landegem

Stijn VAN DEN BOSSCHE

LE PAIN ROMPU COMME FIGURE THÉOLOGIQUE DE LA PRÉSENCE EUCHARISTIQUE

Pour tenter de penser, comme y invite le présent Colloque, la présence eucharistique dans l'actuel contexte de «post-modernité», j'ai choisi d'attacher ma réflexion au rite de la fraction du pain. Avant d'en venir au sujet lui-même, je crois important de dire un mot de cette post-modernité. Je laisse de côté la question de savoir si cette expression est vraiment adéquate pour étiqueter l'époque actuelle. Je me contenterai de noter, à la suite de J. Baudrillard que «la modernité n'est ni un concept sociologique, ni un concept politique, ni proprement un concept historique. C'est un mode de civilisation caractéristique, qui s'oppose au mode de la tradition, c'est-à-dire à toutes les autres cultures antérieures ou traditionnelles (...) Comme elle n'est pas un concept d'analyse, il n'y a pas de lois de la modernité, il n'y a que des traits de la modernité. Il n'y a pas non plus de théorie, mais une logique de la modernité, et une idéologie»[1]. Il n'est pas question ici de s'étendre sur les «traits» qui caractérisent cette modernité. Il est pourtant indispensable d'en expliciter quelques-uns, puisque le discours théologique que nous tiendrons sur la présence eucharistique du Christ est nécessairement marqué par eux.

Ces traits sont désormais bien connus à partir des nombreux écrits des sociologues. Sans doute peut-on caractériser globalement l'actuelle (post-)modernité, comme le fait J. Baudrillard, par la manière dont elle valorise la nouveauté. Par différence avec les cultures traditionnelles, la modernité est «la tradition du nouveau», capable de faire «de la crise une valeur». Cette valorisation du nouveau, qui va jusqu'au «c'est bien, puisque c'est nouveau», n'est que la contrepartie de ce que le même Baudrillard appelle l'absence de référent, ou un philosophe comme J. Derrida, la dissémination du sens, héritière, dans le sillage de Galilée, Darwin et Freud, de la perte du centre. Précisons un peu. Qu'une pensée philosophique concernant de la dissémination du sens dans le pur «procès de signifiance» intra-textuel ait pu voir le jour n'est possible que parce que, selon la thèse heideggerienne du rapport entre l'Être et le Temps, nous sommes parvenus à un âge du «déploiement historial de la question de l'être» qui le permet. Bien entendu, cela ne signifie pas que cette pensée

---

1. J. BAUDRILLARD, Art. «*Modernité*» dans *Enc. Univ.* XV, 552 (1997).

serait nécessairement dominante dans les écoles philosophiques contemporaines, mais que toutes sont marquées de quelque manière par ce qui la marque et que l'on peut appeler, en un sens sur lequel il nous faudra revenir, la fin du mode de questionnement métaphysique, parce que cela appartient à l'air du temps et constitue même l'un des symptômes majeurs de ce temps. Or l'une des caractéristiques de cet âge «post-moderne» réside précisément dans l'effacement ou du moins le retrait des référents réels au bénéfice du «jeu formel du changement» (Baudrillard).

Ce retrait se vérifie à tous niveaux, et bien en-deçà des actuelles images virtuelles, lesquelles sont précisément l'expression paradigmatique de l'absence de référent réel. Ainsi, pour nous limiter à ces quelques exemples, les transactions commerciales se font par un pur jeu d'écriture et n'importe qui peut acheter n'importe quoi à n'importe qui moyennant carte bancaire, via Internet par exemple; ou bien encore, la «fermette» normande dont rêve le Parisien pour ses vacances n'a quasiment rien à voir, si ce n'est quelques murs anciens, avec la ferme réelle où le paysan normand a naguère trimé durant toute son existence; quant à la fête, on en parle d'autant plus qu'elle est plus éloignée de la fête «réelle» traditionnelle... La modernité accorde, de ce fait, beaucoup d'importance à ce que, dans *L'échange symbolique et la mort*, J. Baudrillard appelle le «simulacre»: simulacre d'habitat ancien, simulacre de contact direct et «sain» avec la nature, simulacre de fête, simulacre de culture, etc. L'important n'est pas la «substance» réelle de ces référents, mais le jeu de représentation qu'ils permettent, jeu qui n'est finalement que celui d'un pur système de signes où le référent n'est rien d'autre que le code lui-même. «The Medium is message»: la célèbre formule de Mac Luhan peut s'appliquer non seulement aux médias, non seulement au système de la mode naguère analysé par Roland Barthes, mais à l'ensemble des productions de la post-modernité. La pensée de la «dissémination du sens» est-elle d'ailleurs autre chose que la version philosophique radicale de ce jugement sociologique? Plus largement, ce que nous avons appelé la fin du mode de questionnement métaphysique n'est-il pas l'expression par excellence d'une société qui a cessé de trouver son fondement en «Dieu» ou dans la «Tradition» et qui doit s'ingénier constamment à faire du débat démocratique la clef de sa survie?

Cette brève analyse le rappelle: les changements culturels en cours sont profonds, si profonds que l'on en parle, à juste titre semble-t-il, comme d'une «mutation». Celle-ci touche au plus vif des «sujets», dans la mesure où elle affecte la matrice symbolique même où s'engendrent les normes et les valeurs. Cela pose évidemment une sérieuse question à la théologie, s'il est vrai que celle-ci, comme discours de la *fides quaerens intellectum*, a pour tâche d'exprimer à frais nouveaux, dans les catégories culturelles de l'époque, le mystère du Dieu révélé en Jésus-

Christ. Par rapport au sujet qui nous occupe, la question posée par cette mutation est particulièrement importante. Nous percevons immédiatement en effet que la confession de la présence du Christ dans l'eucharistie vient se heurter de plein fouet à ce que nous avons estimé être l'un des symptômes majeurs de l'actuelle modernité: la dissolution des référents proprement objectifs ou 'substantiels'. En effet, pour reprendre la problématique de S. Thomas, l'eucharistie a ceci de singulier par rapport à tous les autres sacrements que là où ces derniers se réalisent *in suscipiente*, et donc n'adviennent qu'*in ordine ad aliud*, à savoir relativement au sujet récepteur, elle se réalise, elle, *in ipsa materia* et *absolute*, donc avant même son usage par le sujet, puisqu'elle «contient le Christ lui-même» (III, q.73, a.1, ad 3) – ce pourquoi elle est fréquemment appelée «le sacrement par excellence» ou même, par antonomase, «*le*» sacrement, le «*saint*» sacrement. Rien donc de plus «objectif» que ladite «présence réelle», et rien, par conséquent, qui ne vienne heurter plus directement la culture contemporaine. La chose, à vrai dire, n'est pas nouvelle en soi: quand on se souvient des prouesses de pensée dont ont dû faire preuve les grands scolastiques du XIII° siècle par rapport à la présence eucharistique, que Thomas d'Aquin déclarait «plus miraculeuse que la création»[2], quand on se souvient de la sorte d'agnosticisme que professait le grand Pascal face à ce mystère qu'il confessait comme «le plus étrange et le plus obscur secret» du Dieu caché[3], on se dit en effet que la réflexion chrétienne n'a pas attendu notre époque pour percevoir dans celui-ci l'un des plus grands défis lancé à la raison croyante. Ce qui est nouveau en revanche est le fait que ce mystère vient heurter non seulement la raison «en général» comme dans les âges précédents, mais la forme culturelle de cette raison.

1. La triple détermination de la vérité[4]

Comment donc penser théologiquement ce mystère dans l'actuelle modernité? Ma proposition sera la suivante: il s'agit de croiser ce qu'indique la fonction «méta» de la métaphysique avec ce que Paul Ricœur appelle la greffe herméneutique de la phénoménologie. Si l'on voulait représenter visuellement cette proposition, on ferait un triangle dont les trois pointes représenteraient le «méta» de la métaphysique, la phénoménologie et l'herméneutique et dont la surface représenterait le champ de la vérité, laquelle ne peut aujourd'hui s'énoncer que selon la triple détermination

---

2. *Somme Théol.* III, q.75, a.8, ad 3.
3. B. PASCAL, *Œuvres*, Paris, Brunschvicg, 1914, 88-89.
4. Ce paragraphe s'inspire d'une conférence de Joseph CAILLOT intitulée «*Les dogmes entre histoire et vérité*», conférence publiée dans le Cahier «*Vérité et histoire en théologie*», Paris, Inst. Cath., Déc. 1996, p. 93-113.

que l'on vient de dire. Précisons que, bien entendu, les déterminations phénoménologique et herméneutique de la vérité ne viennent pas simplement s'ajouter à la détermination métaphysique: elles viennent affecter profondément celle-ci. Expliquons-nous.

1. Nous ne pouvons plus penser le mystère eucharistique dans le sillage de la théologie métaphysique ou de l'onto-théologie classique. Cela ne signifie cependant pas que le registre métaphysique de détermination de la vérité n'aurait plus rien à nous dire et devrait être jeté aux poubelles de l'histoire. J'ai appris de Heidegger notamment que «la métaphysique» comme profil de la pensée philosophique héritée d'Athènes n'est pas une erreur que l'on pourrait rayer d'un trait de plume «comme on se défait d'une opinion», mais la pente sur laquelle a été inexorablement entraînée la pensée occidentale à partir du moment où elle a oublié la différence ontico-ontologique de l'étant et de l'être, et que le fameux «dépassement» de la métaphysique ne signifie aucunement le rejet de celle-ci: il requiert au contraire que, ruminant longuement la tradition de pensée qui porte ce nom, on médite ce sur quoi elle se fonde à son insu, et qui est la pensée du «fondement stable», de l'*ousia*, de la présence pleine. Dépasser la métaphysique en la «déconstruisant», c'est être amené à dégager ce que Stanislas Breton a appelé «la fonction méta», terme à comprendre au sens de la «méta-phore», c'est-à-dire de ce qui n'est bien entendu qu'à condition d'être «porté par-delà» l'énoncé, un «par-delà» que les grands penseurs ont monnayé comme un exposant critique par rapport à leur discours sous le mode approximatif d'un *oion* grec ou d'un *quodammodo* latin. Ce «par-delà» a une double portée. D'une part, il rappelle que la force de la métaphysique est d'avoir toujours résisté à la réduction, soit subjectiviste, soit intra-textuelle, de la vérité: le réel, en d'autres termes, est toujours plus grand que nos discours et concepts et s'impose à eux dans ce qu'il convient alors d'appeler une «objectivité». D'autre part et en conséquence, il permet de lier l'ensemble de l'humanité sous l'instance «objective» de la vérité en une universelle communauté.

Cette objectivité et universalité de la vérité ne peut cependant plus être tenue sans le principe même d'une prise en compte des médiations concrètes dans lesquelles elle advient et se donne. L'être se déploie lui-même temporalement (*Sein und Zeit*) ou, pour le dire plus simplement, la vérité n'advient jamais autrement que dans des médiations historiques: «toute affirmation reste interne à un langage», a écrit en ce sens M. De Certeau. Or ces médiations, selon le terme de P. Ricœur, sont «longues». Elles le sont pour une double raison: nombreuses (linguistiques, historiques, psychologiques, sociologiques, etc.), elles requièrent un immense travail; consistantes ensuite, elles résistent à une facile dissolution et s'opposent ainsi au désir d'atteinte immédiate de la «Chose» qui habite chacun, désir qui, dans sa version métaphysique précisément, a pris la forme de l'«arraisonnement» du réel ou de cet ennemi le plus acharné de la pensée qui s'appelle «la rage de savoir».

Le patient passage par les médiations a ouvert la voie d'abord à la phénoménologie, ensuite à l'herméneutique. La première conserve très vif le souvenir de la fonction «méta», puisqu'elle part de la pensée que la vérité advient par donation transcendantale. Mais elle inscrit aussitôt cette fonction dans l'épaisseur des choses concrètes. L'être humain en effet, en raison même de l'intentionnalité de sa conscience, n'est à l'intérieur de lui-même qu'en étant toujours-déjà à l'extérieur, là-bas, près de l'objet. La vérité ne se donne à lui par conséquent que dans la médiation du «monde» jusque dans ses plus humbles contingences. Tout, pour rappeler ici certaines méditations de Heidegger, depuis une simple cruche ou un pont jusqu'à un temple grec ou une peinture de Van Gogh, s'offre à la manifestation de la vérité, c'est-à-dire à son déploiement en vue d'un «accomplissement» qui n'en est jamais l'achèvement. Et ce déploiement s'effectue au sein même d'un clair-obscur, d'une «éclaircie» (Heidegger) qui n'est jamais la pure lumière de la *theoria* grecque. La phénoménologie se bat donc avec l'opacité du monde. Mais elle s'y bat avec l'assurance de pouvoir en épiphaniser le vrai toujours en excès, excès qui empêche le penseur de pouvoir «arraisonner» le réel. Elle a donc affaire aux «médiations longues», celles des choses en l'occurrence.

L'herméneutique a également affaire aux médiations longues, mais celles du texte cette fois. On sait combien le dernier Ricœur a pu accorder d'attention à cette affaire, comme si chez lui la «greffe herméneutique de la phénoménologie» était relayée par une greffe «analytique» (au sens de la philosophie analytique du langage) de l'herméneutique. De ses débats avec le structuralisme, notamment dans *Le conflit des interprétations*, l'auteur a retenu notamment la nécessité de passer par le texte tel qu'il se donne dans sa positivité structurée: «une nouvelle époque herméneutique est ouverte par le succès de l'analyse structurale; l'explication est désormais le chemin obligé de la compréhension»[5]. Or, un texte est porteur de beaucoup plus que de l'intention de son auteur: débordant largement celle-ci, on y trouve en effet non seulement les particularités personnelles de l'auteur (son «style» et, plus profondément, l'histoire de son propre désir inconscient), mais aussi, de manière codée, tout son «monde» de tradition, de culture, d'intérêts sociaux, etc. Il en va de même du côté du lecteur (ou de l'auditeur): il lit le texte à partir, lui aussi, de son propre «monde», donc d'un lieu qui n'est pas neutre. Deux «mondes» se confrontent donc dans toute lecture de texte, ce pourquoi

---

5. P. RICŒUR, *Du texte à l'action. Essai d'herméneutique II*, Paris, Seuil, 1986, p. 123.

précisément est ouvert au lecteur un «autre monde possible». Tel est le fonds même de l'herméneutique selon Ricœur: «Se comprendre, c'est se comprendre devant le texte et recevoir de lui les conditions d'un soi autre que le moi qui vient à la lecture»[6]. Toute écriture ou toute lecture est ainsi «située»: à l'époque de S. Augustin, on ne lisait pas la Bible avec les mêmes lunettes culturelles qu'au Moyen Âge ou qu'en notre fin de XX° siècle: pour prendre un exemple qui a directement trait avec le présent propos, on ne découvrait pas, en tout cas pas immédiatement, de théologie de l'eucharistie dans le récit d'Emmaüs[7].

2. Dans ce contexte, penser théologiquement la présence du Christ dans l'eucharistie ne peut évidemment plus se faire à partir du seul point de vue de la substance métaphysique. Certes, la fonction «méta» qui est prioritairement en jeu sur ce terrain de pensée dit probablement quelque chose de fort important et que nous aurons à retenir. Mais cette détermination métaphysique de la vérité eucharistique ne peut tenir que si ladite fonction méta dont elle est porteuse est pensée du point de vue des deux autres déterminations que l'on vient rappeler. La détermination herméneutique doit faire apparaître la particularité culturelle des discours tenus sur le mystère eucharistique; la faire apparaître non seulement du point de vue de la visée et de l'argumentation, mais aussi et peut-être même surtout du point de vue du mode d'écriture théologique de l'époque et du «monde culturel» dont le texte est porteur. Entre, par exemple, l'écriture «métaphorique» des Pères (cf., par exemple, le célèbre «soyez ce que vous voyez» d'Augustin à propos du corps eucharistique), l'écriture démonstrative des grandes synthèses systématiques des Scolastiques et l'écriture narrative des théologiens actuels, grandes sont les différences de fond qui tiennent à la forme même. La tâche de l'herméneutique est précisément de faire apparaître, en traversant les textes dans la positivité de leur altérité historique et culturelle, que le même mystère eucharistique n'a été ni exprimé, ni pensé, ni vécu de la même manière selon les époques et les lieux. Il n'est évidemment pas question, dans cette modeste contribution, d'effectuer une telle tâche. C'est néanmoins dans cet esprit que nous commencerons par porter notre regard sur les discours scolastiques concernant la «présence réelle».

Après avoir ainsi évalué la distance qui nous sépare du discours classique à se sujet, nous serons conduit à tenter d'exprimer à nouveaux frais le mystère en question. Nous le ferons d'un point de vue phénoménologique en focalisant peu à peu notre attention sur le rite de la fraction du pain. Nous voudrions mettre au jour ce dont un tel rite est

---

6. *Ibid.*, p. 31.

7. Cf. P. PRETOT, *Les yeux ouverts des pèlerins d'Emmaüs*, dans *LMD* 195 (1993) 7-48.

porteur et tenter de penser le mystère de la présence eucharistique du Christ à partir de là.

2. La doctrine scolastique et tridentine de la transsubstantiation: herméneutique

2.1. «Substantia»

Rappelons, pour commencer, quelques idées, d'ailleurs bien connues, concernant le concept de «transsubstantiation». La première est que ce concept vise à tenir l'objectivité de la présence sacramentelle du Christ dans le pain et le vin affirmée par l'Église dans la liturgie (notamment dans le *corpus Christi* de la communion) tout en rejetant la réification de cette objectivité. Du point de vue historique en effet, ce concept (en usage dès le début du XII° siècle chez Alger de Liège) s'est développé par réaction contre l'ultra-réalisme du XI° et du début du XII°, où le corps du Christ était supposé adhérer de manière tellement immédiate à l'espèce du pain qu'il fallait un miracle de Dieu (un second, après celui de la transformation du pain et vin en corps et sang du Christ) pour maintenir le voile qui le cachait. Le présupposé était que, «normalement», on aurait dû le voir, ce qui d'ailleurs ne manquait pas de se vérifier à l'époque: les miracles eucharistiques abondaient alors[8]! Une telle immédiateté aboutissait logiquement à des affirmations de type «sensualiste» selon lesquelles le Christ est rompu par les mains du prêtre et broyé par les dents des fidèles. On comprend, sans pour autant l'excuser, la réaction de Bérenger de Tours, c'est-à-dire pourquoi, pour la première fois dans l'histoire, on en est venu à nier la *veritas* de la présence du Christ dans l'eucharistie. Il n'est pas étonnant non plus que la profession de foi de 1059 officiellement imposée à ce même Bérenger n'ait pu éviter des affirmations proches de l'ultra-réalisme. L'époque manquait manifestement d'outils conceptuels suffisamment affinés pour répondre adéquatement à la difficulté: comment affirmer, dans le sillage de la pratique liturgique de l'Église, la réalité de la présence du Christ sans gommer la médiation du *sacramentum* du pain et du vin? Le couple aristotélicien substance/accident fut à ce sujet du plus grand secours.

---

8. Cf. E. DUMOUTET, *Corpus Domini. Aux sources de la piété eucharistique médiévale*, Paris, Beauchesne, 1942. – Rappelons en outre que la théorie d'Isidore de Séville rattachant le terme de *sacramentum* à *sacrum secretum* était en vigueur à l'époque; ce n'est qu'au XII° siècle que celle d'Augustin (*sacrum signum*) reviendra en force. Alors que pour ce dernier, le *sacramentum* est d'abord un signe qui dévoile, pour Isidore au contraire, il est d'abord un voile (*tegumentum*) qui cache. Cette théorie ne pouvait évidemment que renforcer les représentations culturelles relatives aux «miracles eucharistiques» de l'époque.

C'est contre le «sensualisme» que l'on vient d'évoquer que la grande scolastique du XIII° s. utilise le concept aristotélicien de «*substance*». Cet *hypokeimenon*, traduit littéralement en latin par *sub-iectum* (qui deviendra quatre siècles plus tard le «sujet» cartésien) ou par *sub-stantia*, désigne, on le sait, la réalité dernière des choses, ce qui les sou(s)-tient dans l'unité. Elle n'est ni un 'ceci', ni un 'cela' (étendue, couleur, goût, etc.), lesquels sont des 'accidents'; même la localisation spatiale lui est étrangère: une substance n'est localisée que moyennant ses accidents. Elle n'est donc rien de ce qui affecte nos sens (vue, toucher, goût...). Elle est pure «puissance» à être «actuée» dans des accidents et n'*existe* qu'individuée en eux: *Subiectum comparatur ad accidens sicut potentia ad actum; subiectum enim secundum accidens est aliquo modo in actu* (I, q.3, a6). Le concept de «substance» est donc un concept d'intelligibilité des étants. Pour le dire le plus simplement du monde, il permet de comprendre pourquoi la table ou l'arbre, dont mon regard ne perçoit pourtant que la multiplicité des accidents, peut précisément être appelé «table» ou «arbre», c'est-à-dire être appréhendé comme formant une unité, unité qui est d'un autre ordre que les multiples accidents que j'en perçois. Ainsi, à travers le concept de transsubstantiation, c'est-à-dire de *conversio totius substantiae*, les scolastiques exorcisent toutes les représentations spatiales (notamment) puisque le Christ est présent au niveau de la seule substance, et non des accidents. Le corps eucharistique ne peut donc être ni divisé, ni multiplié, ni transporté, ni enfermé; seul le signe sacramentel (accident) peut l'être. Ce qui est localisé, c'est le signe, i.e. le Christ-en-sacrement, donc *in specie aliena*, et non le Christ ressuscité comme tel *in specie propria*. Et les espèces ne sont pas un voile qui le cache, puisque, glorieux, il est invisible; elles sont là au contraire, écrit Thomas, «pour que ce soit en elles qu'on voie le corps du Christ» (donc «*in specie aliena*»), «et non pas dans son aspect propre» (III, q.75, a.6).

Cette problématique de la substance aristotélicienne avait le grand avantage, sur le plan spéculatif, de permettre de penser l'*esse* eucharistique du Christ dans tout son réalisme sans être victime, comme dans la problématique antérieure, d'une représentation d'immédiateté qui envahissait si directement la médiation du *sacramentum* qu'elle l'écrasait en quelque sorte. Sur le plan de la théologie de la liturgie par ailleurs, elle s'opposait à toute représentation du Christ, à partir des rites de la messe, comme humilié en se faisant pain, comme esclave en obéissant à la parole du prêtre, comme brisé lors de la fraction du pain, comme enfermé dans la prison du tabernacle, comme atteint par l'âme sacrilège qui le reçoit, etc, était en effet rejetée; de ce point de vue, la question, aussi fameuse à l'époque de la scolastique qu'elle nous paraît oiseuse aujourd'hui, *quid sumit mus?* est extrêmement significative[9]. Sur le plan pastoral enfin, la théologie de la transsubstantiation permettait aux chrétiens de comprendre pourquoi le fait de recevoir deux hosties ou seulement une demie lors de la communion ne procure ni avantage ni désavantage au plan spirituel! Une hymne comme celle du *Lauda Sion*, due à S. Thomas d'Aquin, était précisément chargée d'expliquer et d'inculquer cela à tous[10].

2.2. Apories

Une telle théorie n'en était pas moins confrontée à au moins deux apories. La première porte sur le concept lui-même de «transsubstantiation», dans la mesure où il signifie *conversio totius substantiae*. Les scolastiques n'ont pas manqué de percevoir une contradiction interne dans cette expression. Car qui dit «conversion» dit passage ou transformation d'une substance en une autre, ce qui rejette toute idée d'annihilation de la première substance ou de substitution de la seconde à la première: le pain «devient» (*ginetai, fit*) corps du Christ, il n'est pas anéanti. Or, selon la physique de l'époque, il n'existe pas de conversion de *toute* une substance en une autre: quand le feu transforme le bois en cendre, pour prendre une image employée à ce propos par Thomas, il demeure toujours quelque chose du bois. Dès lors, n'a-t-on pas affaire à une «création», puisque seule cette dernière consiste en l'apparition d'une totale nouveauté? Pas davantage, puisque la création, comprise au sens strict, ne se conçoit que *ex nihilo*. On se voit donc obligé de croiser deux concepts contradictoires sur ce point. Plus importante encore est la seconde aporie, d'ailleurs bien connue: comment des accidents peuvent-ils subsister sans leur *sub-stantia*, leur *sub-iectum*, leur sujet d'inhésion? Ici, Thomas tord consciemment le cou à l'aristotélisme. Il s'épuise alors en quelque sorte à montrer que le premier des accidents, à savoir la quantité, peut être donné par Dieu comme substitut de la substance du pain aux accidents qui, eux, demeurent.

2.3. Herméneutique

Le discours de Thomas est typiquement scolastique. Certes, des différences existent, sur ce sujet comme sur bien d'autres, entre lui et ses prédécesseurs ou ses contemporains scolastiques (Bonaventure, par exem-

---

9. Pour un survol rapide des principales positions théologiques à ce sujet, voir A.M. ROGUET, tome II du traité de l'eucharistie de S. Thomas dans la collection «Revue des Jeunes», Paris – Tournai – Rome, 1967, p. 339-340. – Cf. P.M. GY, *La liturgie dans l'histoire,* Paris, Cerf, 1990, p. 258-259.

10. On peut se demander au passage si, quoi qu'il en soit de la beauté de cette hymne, on n'a pas affaire ici à une dérive didactique de la liturgie.

ple)[11]. Mais tous participent du même modèle théologique, modèle lui-même à comprendre à partir du «monde» de l'époque. Rappelons à ce propos que l'époque est à la clarification et à la précision. Soutenue par une démographie pleine, une économie prospère, un urbanisme renaissant, des écoles de théologie florissantes, elle fait preuve d'un optimisme foncier envers les capacités de la raison dont Dieu a doté l'homme. Les nouveaux *scolares*, socialement solidaires des bourgeois et de leur désir d'émancipation, et intellectuellement ouverts aux disputes des grammairiens et logiciens de Chartres ou de Laon, mettent en oeuvre ce qui «fut tout le projet de ce XII°) siècle: la foi s'élaborant en science»[12], grâce notamment à la technique raffinée de la *quaestio*. La «mentalité symbolique» (id.) de l'âge roman demeure certes vivace, mais elle est peu à peu maîtrisée et ordonnée. On élabore alors de constructions théologiques systématiques avec la même audace et le même souci de clarté que les cathédrales gothiques (E. Panofsky). C'est sous l'effet de cet impératif culturel assurément nouveau que naît, pour la première fois, le besoin, inconnu jusqu'alors, de préciser, par exemple, la «différence spécifique» et le nombre des sacrements proprement dits.

Une nouvelle écriture théologique apparaît donc, opposée à l'«ancienne» théologie monastique, laquelle n'était au fond qu'«une pièce de l'office divin» (Chenu). Elle n'a même pu se constituer qu'en s'arrachant à la trop grande prégnance de la liturgie, au risque de perdre, comme cela se produira à la fin du Moyen Âge, son lien vivant avec cette dernière et de dériver ainsi vers la pure spéculation. Certes, quand Thomas d'Aquin commente les Écritures, il demeure proche de la *lectio divina* et de la liturgie: il ne craint pas alors de jouer avec les métaphores et de faire sa part à la typologie si prisée autrefois par les Pères. Dans ses ouvrages systématiques en revanche, son discours apparaît comme entièrement conçu et conduit comme une logique formelle, comme une *scientia*.

Le discours de la scolastique requiert évidemment d'être herméneutiquement compris à partir de ce monde culturel particulier. La concentration de toute la réflexion sur la *substantia* est à comprendre comme la manière, pour l'époque, de penser à nouveaux frais le mystère de la présence eucharistique, et de le penser dans sa radicalité mais en coupant court aux graves impasses de la théologie antérieure (celle, par exemple, de Pierre Damien ou de Lanfranc), c'est-à-dire à toute représentation réifiante du mystère. Il faut voir dans l'espèce de crispation de l'époque sur la *substantia* l'expression de ce que j'ai appelé précédemment un impératif culturel: la nouvelle classe des *magistri* ne pouvait assurément plus vivre sans élaborer en ce domaine comme en d'autres un nouveau

---

11. Cf. P.M. GY, *La relation au Christ dans l'eucharistie selon S. Bonaventure et S. Thomas d'Aquin*, dans *La liturgie dans l'histoire*, p. 247-283.
12. M.D. CHENU, *La théologie au XII° siècle*, Paris, Vrin, 1956, p. 329.

discours. En ce sens, écrire c'est vivre. Il n'en demeure pas moins que l'on ne saurait réduire ce discours à la particularité de son lieu culturel. Le fait d'ailleurs que, même revu au concile de Trente en fonction du couple «substance/espèces» pour éviter à l'Église de se lier officiellement à un système philosophique particulier, ce type de discours ait été dogmatiquement adopté est évidemment important à cet égard. Finalement, herméneutiquement compris, le discours scolastico-tridentin de la conversion de la substance du pain et du vin en corps et sang du Christ interpelle le théologien actuel sur au moins deux plans: d'une part, en ce qu'il exprime la radicalité de ce que croit l'Église en cette affaire; ensuite, en ce qu'il donne à penser à propos des rapports entre théologie et liturgie.

– «Radicalité», d'abord. En effet, le discours examiné signifie la transformation de la réalité dernière du pain et du vin, exprimée alors par le terme de substance; mais exprimée, on l'a rappelé, au prix d'une sorte de monstruosité philosophique: des accidents qui subsistent sans leur substance. Le terme de «monstruosité» que je viens d'employer est volontairement repris à l'analyse célèbre que P. Ricœur a faite du péché originel dans *Le conflit des interprétations*[13]. Il y montre en effet comment ce concept est «désespéré», puisqu'il «combine montrueusement» volonté et nature, mettant du volontaire (le «péché») dans de l'involontaire (un état acquis par nature)[14]. Mais il ne manque pas non plus de saluer la magistrale entreprise augustinienne sur ce point: Augustin a tenté avec une audace étonnante sinon de résoudre l'aporie de l'origine du mal, du moins de l'affronter et de la penser de telle sorte qu'elle ne soit attribuée ni à une *Anankè* ou à un *Fatum* extérieur, celui-ci prît-il le visage de Dieu, ni inversement à la seule responsabilité de l'homme. Ce faisant, il rejoignait tant bien que mal la double intentionnalité du langage métaphorique mis en oeuvre dans le mythe adamique de la Genèse: dédouaner Dieu de toute responsabilité quant à l'origine du mal sans attribuer pour autant celle-ci à la seule volonté de l'homme, puisque le serpent était déjà là; d'autre part, rendre compte ainsi de la contradiction qu'éprouve l'être humain dans son expérience du mal-faire: contradiction entre la nécessaire imputation de ce mal à son auteur, ce qui engage sa responsabilité éthique, et le sentiment que pourtant ce mal n'a pas été simplement voulu, mais qu'il est l'effet d'une sorte de loi qui déborde chacun jusqu'à lui faire s'écrier parfois: «c'est plus fort que moi!» (cf. Rm 7). En définitive, le concept ou plutôt le «pseudo-concept» augustinien de «péché originel» est «plein d'une ténébreuse richesse analogi-

---

13. P. RICŒUR, *Le péché originel. Étude de signification*, dans *Le conflit des interprétations*, Paris, Seuil, 1969, p. 265-282.
14. *Ibid.*, p. 281.

que»[15]. Il n'est pas sûr que son inventeur[16] ait su ou pu reconnaître la part d'obscurité que retenait la clarté de son concept. Pour éviter de faire chuter celui-ci du côté du savoir et donc de retomber dans une attitude «quasi gnostique», il aurait fallu qu'il le reconduise vers les images symboliques du mythe adamique d'où il l'avait tiré. On ne peut cependant que saluer le geste de pensée qu'il a tenté. Il est des apories ou des mystères qu'il faut avoir le courage de penser, alors même que l'on sait d'avance qu'ils défient toute réponse. Celui de l'origine du mal appartient à ces questions qui valent pour elles-mêmes, pour le chemin qu'elles font faire au penseur, et non pour le savoir auquel elles seraient censé conduire.

N'en irait-il pas de la sorte, *mutatis mutandis*, en ce qui concerne le concept, philosophiquement intenable lui aussi, de transsubstantiation? Le concile de Trente a d'ailleurs été prudent à cet égard, qui déclare ce concept convenir *aptissime* à l'expression de la foi de l'Église. Le superlatif ne doit pas tromper: il signifie tout aussi bien que, par conséquent, d'autres conceptualisations sont théoriquement possibles, à condition de respecter la radicalité de ce qui est en jeu dans le préfixe «trans-» et que S. Thomas a pensé avec des concepts aristotéliciens. Par conséquent, une bonne lecture herméneutique nous conduit à penser qu'il est théologiquement possible, à cette condition, de formuler autrement le mystère de la présence eucharistique. Le «trans» (comme le «meta» des Pères grecs: *metaballô; metaruthmizô, etc*) a une fonction d'avertisseur indiquant, comme le feu clignotant d'un phare, la direction à ne pas perdre de vue.

— La seconde interpellation porte sur le rapport entre le discours théologique et la *célébration liturgique*. Si Thomas d'Aquin a déployé de tels efforts pour approcher critiquement le mystère eucharistique, c'est en vue de rendre compte de l'acte de langage prononcé lors de la communion: «Le corps du Christ - Amen», lui-même écho du «ceci est mon corps» du récit de l'institution. Cela signifie que, même pour ce type de théologie, la liturgie demeure un lieu majeur de référence. Il faut bien reconnaître cependant que la scolastique n'a pas fait de celle-ci un lieu proprement théologique: ne s'est-elle pas d'ailleurs constituée, ai-je rappelé précédemment, en prenant ses distances par rapport à elle? L'acte de langage «le corps du Christ» n'est donc pas pris à proprement parler comme texte liturgique mais comme énoncé théologique. Le contexte rituel dans lequel il trouve place n'est pas pris en considération comme

---

15. P. RICŒUR, *Le péché originel*, p. 277.
16. Rappelons qu'Augustin est l'inventeur non seulement de l'expression mais aussi de son contenu, lequel a été reconnu pour l'essentiel par l'Église dès le concile de Carthage de 418.

ayant une pertinence par rapport à la signification théologique de l'énoncé. La sémantique, en d'autres termes, est jugée totalement indépendante de la pragmatique. Du même coup, rien ne vient détendre en quelque sorte l'atmosphère de la réflexion intellectuelle: le concept se durcit au maximum, sans aucune faille, sans renvoyer aucunement au «texte» liturgique (paroles, gestes, matériaux, etc.) dans lequel il prend naissance et où il aurait pu retrouver la souplesse des métaphores. En disant cela, je n'entends pas disqualifier le concept comme tel, mais rappeler que, comme dans la problématique du péché originel développée par Ricœur, le concept, si indispensable qu'il soit, doit être pris pour un moment de la réflexion théologique et être renvoyé aux symboles rituels où il trouve place pour éviter de se figer en pseudo-savoir.

J'ai parlé précédemment de «contexte rituel». En fait, la ritualité est bien plus qu'un simple «con-texte» accompagnant le texte liturgique. Elle est constitutive de la textualité même de ce texte, puisque celui-ci (l'expression «le corps du Christ», en l'occurrence) n'existe pas pour être lu «à plat» dans un bureau comme un texte dogmatique, mais pour être mis en œuvre dans la célébration. L'énoncé est ici inséparable de son énonciation rituelle (adresse au communiant, ton de voix, geste, posture..). La ritualité constitue donc véritablement le «pré-texte» du texte, la page en quelque sorte sur laquelle le texte est écrit. Du point de vue herméneutique, cela signifie que si la vérité, de manière générale, ne peut être déliée de la médiation textuelle dans laquelle elle advient (cf. le célèbre «expliquer plus pour comprendre mieux» de Ricœur), la vérité particulière concernant la présence eucharistique ne peut être énoncée hors de la textualité même de l'énoncé liturgique évoqué. C'est précisément vers cet acte rituel que nous allons nous tourner dans un instant; pas avant, toutefois, d'avoir évoqué ce qui paraît constituer la limite majeure de la problématique scolastique de la transsubstantiation.

2.4. Limite majeure

Ce passage par la pratique symbolique de la célébration est d'autant plus important qu'il s'oppose à la limite majeure de la problématique scolastique: l'oubli de la relation. Expliquons-nous. L'hérésie de Bérenger, au XI° siècle, avait créé un véritable traumatisme dans l'Église. Pour éviter tout risque de rechute dans cette direction, on a commencé à souligner si fort le rapport entre le corps eucharistique du Christ et son corps historique et glorieux qu'on en est venu à distendre le lien entre ce même corps eucharistique et le corps ecclésial du Christ, lien qui avait, au contraire, été fortement mis en relief naguère par les Pères (puisque l'Église était alors considérée comme la *veritas* du «corps mystique eucharistique»). La distension prend même l'allure, selon le P. de Lubac, d'une «césure meurtrière»[17]. Par différence avec le corps du Christ réellement présent dans le pain/vin (*res significata et contenta*, dit-on au XII° siècle), le corps ecclésial n'est plus que la *res significata et non contenta* (P. Lombard). Ainsi, «la réalité ultime du sacrement», à savoir l'unité du corps ecclésial, «celle qui en était autrefois la chose et la vérité par excellence, est expulsée du sacrement lui-même». Certes, les grands scolastiques n'oublient pas qu'elle en demeure la finalité: le simple fait que l'expression de *corpus mysticum* soit passée, à la fin du XII°, de l'eucharistie (corps en «mystère») à l'Église est significatif à cet égard; d'ailleurs, selon la doctrine commune des grands scolastiques, l'unité de l'Église, par le lien de la charité, n'est-elle pas la *res* ultime de l'eucharistie? Mais le corps ecclésial du Christ n'appartient plus désormais au «symbolisme intrinsèque» de l'eucharistie. Par conséquent, «on pourra désormais passer (celui-ci) sous silence sans nuire à l'intégrité du sacrement»[18].

On comprend dès lors que le rapport à l'Église soit pratiquement oublié dès que la réflexion se concentre sur l'analyse de la présence elle-même et son *quomodo*. On isole alors celle-ci comme un en-soi, en la pensant sur le seul registre de la «substance». On met ainsi entre parenthèses le *ad* qu'implique la notion même de présence (*ad-esse*) au profit du seul *esse* substantiel... Ce *ad* d'ailleurs, comme expression d'une relation, n'appartient-il pas, de même que la notion de «*praesentia*»[19], aux accidents? De toute façon, même si l'expression de *praesentia corporalis* est bien admise par les scolastiques, le vocabulaire de la «présence» était beaucoup moins familier alors qu'aujourd'hui et n'avait pas la force que lui ont donnée, depuis, le surgissement de la subjectivité et la phénoménologie. Le lexique alors accoutumé à propos de l'eucharistie était celui de l'*esse*, voire de l'*existere*.

Il en va de même au concile de Trente. Celui-ci retrouve certes la veine patristique, dans sa *Doctrine sur la très sainte eucharistie* (1551), en rappelant que l'eucharistie «est le symbole (symbolum) de cet unique 'Corps' dont le Christ est 'la tête'» (ch.2), ou encore qu'elle est le *signum unitatis*, le *vinculum caritatis*, le *symbolum concordiae* (ch. 8). Mais ces expressions augustiniennes ne viennent qu'au terme d'une doctrine dont l'essentiel a été exprimé auparavant et comme appel à l'unité des chrétiens divisés plutôt que comme expression théologique de la présence eucharistique du Seigneur. De toute façon, le symbolisme augustinien,

---

17. H. DE LUBAC, *Corpus mysticum. L'Église et l'eucharistie au Moyen Âge*, Paris, Aubier, 1944.
18. *Ibid.*, p. 280-283.
19. P.M. GY, *La liturgie dans l'histoire,* p. 242: «Cette notion [de praesentia corporalis] gêne S. Thomas, parce qu'elle lui paraît liée à une localisation», donc aux accidents.

qui avait si longtemps irradié la théologie de l'eucharistie, avait largement perdu sa force[20]. Dans les textes tridentins en effet, il ne fait guère le poids par rapport aux quatre *contineri*, aux trois *esse* ou *vere esse* ayant pour sujet «le corps et le sang du Christ», ainsi qu'aux trois *existere* ayant le Christ pour sujet, que l'on rencontre dans les ch. 1, 3 et 4 et les canons 1, 3 et 4: toute l'attention est centrée sur l'affirmation de la présence réelle, dont découlent d'abord, au ch. 5, la vénération due au saint-Sacrement (même s'il y est dit que le Christ a institué l'eucharistie comme nourriture), puis, aux ch. 6 à 8, la communion. La visée antiprotestante de Trente est certainement pour quelque chose dans cette insistance; mais, si important qu'il soit, cet élément conjoncturel n'explique pas tout: c'est, plus profondément, l'«archéologie» même du savoir et l'«épistèmè» théologique qui expliquent cette concentration. Par ailleurs, s'il est vrai que le concile est demeuré «jusqu'au bout prisonnier» de la «problématique dualiste» séparant le «sacrement» (présence réelle) (1551) du «sacrifice» (efficacité «propitiatoire» de la messe) (1563)[21], il lui était difficile de penser la présence eucharistique du Christ comme «être-pour», puisque cet « être-pour » est l'expression du don «sacrificiel» qu'il a fait de sa vie; il lui était difficile, du même coup, de la penser dans son rapport intrinsèque à l'Église.

3. La fraction du pain: approche phénoménologique

Là où la théologie métaphysique de S. Thomas écartait l'action liturgique et donc la relation à l'*ecclesia* de la réflexion sur la présence substantielle du Christ dans l'eucharistie, l'approche phénoménologique s'inscrit au contraire d'emblée dans ce champ. Je précise que si j'ai choisi ce rite plutôt que, par exemple, celui de l'élévation, c'est pour deux raisons très simples: la première est que l'élévation est née précisément en lien avec la théologie de la transsubstantiation et en vue, au moins indirectement, de renforcer celle-ci; la seconde est que, du point de vue de l'histoire de la liturgie, le rite de la fraction du pain apparaît, aussi bien par son antiquité que par son symbolisme (cf. p. ex. 1 Co 10,16), comme un rite sacramentel de premier rang, ce qui n'est pas du tout le cas de l'élévation.

3.1. L'être-pour (adesse) est constitutif de l'être sacramentel (esse)

a. Le rite de la fraction du pain prend place à un certain moment de la célébration eucharistique. Ce moment est à prendre en considération. Car on pourrait imaginer qu'il ouvre celle-ci comme il ouvrait le repas juif et qu'il continue de ce fait de désigner, par synecdoque, l'ensemble de la

---

20. Cf. A. DUVAL, *Des sacrements au concile de Trente*, Paris, Cerf, 1985, p. 55-56.
21. *Ibid.*, p. 72.

liturgie eucharistique, comme on le voit avec la *klasis tou artou* du corpus lucanien. Ou bien, il pourrait être exécuté durant le récit de l'institution lors des paroles «il le rompit», possibilité qui conforterait la théologie du prêtre agissant *in persona Christi*. Il n'en a jamais été ainsi dans aucune des grandes familles liturgiques, mais il y a lieu de penser que la tentation a dû en être forte, puisque l'on voit certains manuscrits du Moyen Âge prescrire au prêtre à ce moment de «feindre» la fraction (*fingat frangere* ou quelque chose de ce genre)[22], et que, de toute façon, le prêtre à cette époque imitait le Christ prenant le pain dans ses mains et levant les yeux au ciel avant de prononcer le «ceci est mon corps». L'exécution de la fraction à ce moment aurait d'ailleurs été en cohérence avec la théologie de S. Thomas, puisque celui-ci va jusqu'à déclarer qu'au moment où il prononce les *verba Christi*, le prêtre n'agit plus *in persona ecclesiae* mais seulement *in persona Christi*[23]; Thomas presse ainsi au maximum le rapport du prêtre au Christ: il l'interprète, si l'on reprend les catégories de la sémiotique de C.S. Peirce, comme relation d'«image» (la photo par rapport au réel) et pas seulement par conséquent comme relation de «diagramme» (la carte de géographie par rapport au terrain) ou comme relation d'«indice» (la girouette par rapport au vent)[24]. Malgré tout, Thomas ne semble même pas envisager l'hypothèse de la fraction dans le récit de l'institution. Pour le dire en des termes qui n'étaient pas ceux du Moyen Âge, «mémorial» n'est point «mime», et s'il est vrai que le récit de l'institution est central dans la prière eucharistique c'est parce que, la chose est bien connue, les quatre verbes techniques qui y désignent les actions de Jésus à la Cène structurent l'ensemble de la liturgie de l'eucharistie, depuis la présentation des dons («il prit le pain») jusqu'à la communion («et le leur donna»), en passant par la prière eucharistique («prononça la bénédiction») et la fraction du pain («le rompit»). Dans cette logique, cette dernière ne saurait évidemment prendre place qu'après la prière eucharistique.

---

22. Voir R. POTHIER, *La fraction du pain*, Mémoire de l'Institut Supérieur de Liturgie, Paris, 1990.

23. ST III, q. 82, a. 7, ad 3. Cf. B.D. MARLIANGEAS, *Clés pour une théologie des ministères: in persona Christi, in persona Ecclesiae*, Paris, Beauchesne, 1978, p. 118-122.

24. En fait, les catégories d'«image» et de «diagramme» sont regroupées par Peirce dans celle d'«icône». En bonne théologie catholique, le rapport entre le représentant (prêtre) et le représenté (Christ) n'a pas besoin d'être pensé sous le mode de l'«image». Le «diagramme» et même l'«indice» suffisent. En revanche, la relation de «symbole (au sens de Peirce, c'est-à-dire le rapport entre un objet et le signe linguistique, tout arbitraire, qui le représente) semble insuffisante. On devine l'intérêt de ces perspectives pour «détendre» la théologie catholique à ce sujet, notamment dans la question de la représentation du Christ par une femme. Cf. L.M. CHAUVET, *La fonction du prêtre dans le récit de l'institution à la lumière de la linguistique*, dans *Revue de l'Institut Catholique de Paris* 56, Oct.-Déc. 1995, p. 41-61.

b. L'intelligence théologique de la présence eucharistique du Christ selon les chrétiens est nécessairement affectée par le fait que le rite de la fraction est situé juste avant la communion, donc vers la fin de la messe. Il apparaît ainsi comme le fruit d'une dynamique célébratoire dont je voudrais rappeler rapidement les principaux éléments.

– D'abord, si nous regardons *l'ensemble de la célébration,* nous observons que cette dynamique va de la constitution de l'assemblée comme Église («Le Seigneur soit avec vous»: le Christ qui vient-en-présence dans l'eucharistie est donc celui qui préside l'assemblée; il ne tombe pas des nues...), en passant par la table de la Parole («Acclamons la Parole de Dieu»: le Christ qui vient-en-présence dans l'eucharistie est donc celui qui parle à son Église dans les Écritures), vers la table de l'eucharistie («Ceci est mon corps livré pour vous»). Cela nous indique déjà que la présence eucharistique ne peut être comprise que comme la cristallisation sous mode visible de la Parole: *sacramentum est quasi visibile verbum* (Augustin).

– Concentrons maintenant notre attention sur la *prière eucharistique.* Deux traits principaux sont à relever. Premier trait: la présence eucharistique advient au sein d'une prière dont le mouvement va de la mémoire du passé en action de grâce vers la mémoire de l'avenir en supplication eschatologique. Dans cette perspective, comme l'a relevé naguère C. Perrot dans un article devenu célèbre, la présence eucharistique ne peut être comprise qu'à partir d'une «double distance entre l'hier du Golgotha et l'avenir de la Parousie»: son rapport à la Parousie l'empêche d'être réduite à une simple évocation historique de la croix qui assimilerait le repas chrétien aux rites funéraires grecs; son rapport au passé du Golgotha l'empêche de demeurer sur le registre de la pure attente juive; et l'écart entre les deux barre sa vérité même de présence du trait de l'absence, ce qui empêche de la concevoir comme une présence «pleine», à la manière gnostique[25]. Cela rappelle que, du point de vue de la tradition ancienne, dont la liturgie continue e se faire l'écho, la catégorie de «mémoire» est beaucoup plus importante que celle de «présence, et que, du point de vue proprement chrétien, celle-ci demande à être comprise à partir de celle-là.

Second trait: cette présence est indissociable de l'épiclèse. Celle-ci, du moins dans la forme achevée qu'elle a acquise depuis la fin du IV° siècle, notamment dans la tradition antiochienne, a une structure théologique qui est la suivante: que l'Esprit sanctifie le pain et le vin pour en faire le corps et le sang du Christ, *afin que* ceux qui y participeront par la

---

25. C. PERROT, «*L'anamnèse néo-testamentaire*», dans *Revue de l'Institut Catholique de Paris* 2, avril 1982.

communion soient rassemblés (par le même Esprit) en «un seul corps». Lorsque, comme dans les prières eucharistiques de Vatican II, cette épiclèse est double (avant et après le récit de l'institution), elle dédouble ce que l'épiclèse unique de la tradition antiochienne exprime en une seule prière[26]. Ce lien avec l'épiclèse ne rappelle pas seulement que le «corps» sacramentel du Christ est «corps spirituel», donc non représentable; il souligne aussi, et ce point est particulièrement important pour notre réflexion, que si l'eucharistie est bien le corps personnel du Christ, c'est en tant que celui-ci est, selon la très juste formule de J.-M. Tillard, «en acte de vivification de son Corps ecclésial par l'Esprit-Saint. Elle donne le corps personnel mais dans le lien indissoluble qui l'unit au Corps ecclésial»[27]. Impossible dès lors de penser ce corps «en soi», indépendamment de l'Église! En tant que corps réalisé par l'Esprit, le corps eucharistique n'advient que pour faire l'Église réalisée elle aussi, selon le troisième article du Credo, par le même Esprit. Il en résulte, comme les Pères l'ont si fréquemment souligné que, selon le vocabulaire augustinien, celui qui n'est pas dans la communion vivante du corps ecclésial reçoit rituellement (*sacramentaliter*) le corps du Seigneur, mais ne le reçoit pas «spirituellement» (*spiritaliter*): sa communion est sans fécondité; elle est même pour sa condamnation (cf. 1 Co 11). «Il ne faut pas dire que mange le corps du Christ celui qui n'est pas dans le corps du Christ»[28].

– Focalisons enfin sur le *récit de l'institution* lui-même. La double parole sur le pain et le vin n'y dit pas seulement le corps et le sang, elle les dit comme don «pour» (*hyper*). Elle ne les dit pas «*absolute*», mais «*relative*». Cet être-relatif, explicité par le «prenez et mangez-en (ou buvez-en) tous», est d'ailleurs visibilisé par le double geste de «rompre» et de «donner», gestes qu'il faut considérer comme des «paroles incorporées». En outre, le matériau lui-même est l'indicateur de cette relation de don. En effet, nous y reviendrons dans un instant, il appartient à l'«être-essentiel» du pain et du vin d'être pour leur incorporation par

---

26. Ce faisant, Vatican II s'est situé dans le sillage de la tradition alexandrine. D'autre part et surtout, il a voulu éviter de créer à nouveau des difficultés au sujet du «moment de la consécration», que la tradition latine situe dans le récit de l'institution, alors que la tradition syrienne le situe après l'épiclèse consécutive au récit de l'institution. On peut regretter que, de ce fait, aucune prière eucharistique de Vatican II n'ait adopté ce second point de vue, dont on sait qu'il est tout aussi légitime.

27. J.M. TILLARD, *Chair de l'Église, chair du Christ*, Paris, Cerf, 1992, p. 64.

28. AUGUSTIN, *Cité de Dieu* XXI, 35. – Les Médiévaux, qui connaissaient bien Augustin, n'avaient pas oublié cette vérité. Par exemple Bonaventure: «Celui qui veut s'approcher dignement du corps du Christ doit le manger spirituellement pour ainsi le mâcher (*masticet*) par la réflexion de la foi et le recevoir par la ferveur de l'amour. Par là, il ne transforme pas le Christ en lui, mais c'est plutôt lui-même qui est projeté dans son corps mystique» (*sed ipse potius traiiciatur in eius mysticum corpus*) (*Breviloquium* VI, 9,6).

l'être humain. Du point de vue phénoménologique, l'intentionnalité de «présence» transpire en quelque sorte de la figure que forment cet ensemble d'éléments verbaux, gestuels et matériels. Cela indique que le «pour» relationnel est constitutif de la présence du Christ comme telle. Ce «pour» n'en est pas une simple dérivation accidentelle et seconde, ni une simple finalité extrinsèque. Ce point est évidemment capital: l'«*esse*» eucharistique est constitutivement un «*adesse*». On ne peut par conséquent jamais mettre ce «ad» entre parenthèses, pas même durant l'analyse du comment de la présence.

– Ceci ressort peut-être avec plus de force encore du sein de la séquence rituelle en trois temps que forme la fraction du pain avec, juste en amont, le signe de paix échangé entre les participants et, juste en aval, la démarche de communion. Mais nous reviendrons sur ce point dans notre dernière partie.

3.2. La cruche et le pain

Si l'on demande, un peu comme le fait Heidegger à propos de la «cruche»[29], qu'est-ce que le pain en tant que «chose» (par opposition à l'«objet»)? quelle en est l'essence, le «Wesen»?, il est clair que l'on ne peut réduire celle-ci à sa consistance physico-chimique. Il est en effet essentiel au pain d'être partagé; et cela, non pas d'abord au plan scientifique de sa valeur d'usage (la quantité de calories qu'il fournit pour la subsistance), mais d'abord au plan *symbolique*: le «pain», qu'il faut prendre ici, tout comme le *lehem* de la Bible hébraïque, le «donne-nous notre pain quotidien» du Notre Père, ou le «gagner son pain» du proverbe français, comme le représentant symbolique de toute nourriture (et même plus largement de tout ce dont l'être humain a besoin pour pouvoir subsister), est, par essence même, un aliment socialement institué. Il est fait pour la convivialité. Il lui est essentiel d'être partagé avec autrui en un repas. Si, pour de multiples raisons, il ne l'est pas toujours, il n'en conserve pas moins en lui-même cette destination qui fait que manger, pour le sujet humain, n'est pas réductible à un acte utilitaire. C'est pourquoi, le pain, le pain-repas, est médiation d'entre-tien de parole autant que de vie biologique. Il est nourriture du désir (ou du «cœur») autant que du corps. Dans la problématique heideggérienne du «Quadriparti», on remarque donc qu'il ne «retient» le «ciel» (le soleil, la pluie...) et la «terre» (le sol où le froment a germé, grandi et mûri) qu'en vue de les partager avec les autres «mortels» dans une «offre» qui leur permet de «s'entre-tenir». Mais il arrive aussi que le pain soit présenté à Dieu comme la plus haute parole de reconnaissance de l'homme: recon-

---

29. M. HEIDEGGER, *Essais et Conférences*, Paris, Gallimard, 1958, p. 202-205.

naissance *de* Dieu comme celui qui fait don du pain et, à travers lui, de l'existence elle-même; reconnaissance *envers* Dieu. Pensons ici aux offrandes rituelles ou aux sacrifices de communion que connaissent la grande majorité des religions. Comme la «cruche» de Heidegger, le pain ne manifeste jamais aussi bien son être de pain que dans cet acte d'oblation religieuse où, fruit de la nature (terre et ciel) et fruit de l'histoire (le travail des hommes), il est reconnu comme don gracieux de Dieu et où, en le partageant comme tel (i.e. comme don gracieux de Dieu), les hommes s'en nourrissent. Il n'y a pas plus pain que ce pain-là. En partageant ce pain «essentiel» et en s'en nourrissant, ils entre-tiennent leur rapport filial avec leur Dieu et ils s'entre-tiennent mutuellement comme sujets croyants dans une communion fraternelle fondée sur la communion de tous avec leur Dieu. C'est bien là, en tout cas, que le pain réalise pleinement son essence de pain.

La réflexion précédente ne constitue évidemment qu'une approche du mystère de la présence eucharistique. Il y a en effet un *abîme* entre l'affirmation selon laquelle le pain n'est jamais autant pain que dans l'acte religieux où on le reconnaît comme un don gracieux de Dieu et l'affirmation de la foi chrétienne selon laquelle ce pain est l'autodonation gracieuse de Dieu même en Christ. Cependant, pour n'être qu'une approche, la réflexion proposée ne manque pas d'intérêt. Le maintien d'une distance entre la confession de foi et l'aboutissement de la méditation phénoménologique ne serait-elle pas en effet la condition pour que le pain eucharistique ne devienne pas idole?

3.3. L'idole et l'icône

En effet, la doctrine catholique insiste sur le fait que la présence du Christ dans l'eucharistie se donne dans la médiation d'un *sacramentum* qui a une triple caractéristique de matérialité, d'extériorité et de précédence. Parce qu'elle advient dans la matérialité sensible du pain et du vin et qu'elle se donne comme extérieure aux croyants, comme face à eux et comme antérieure à l'usage qu'ils en font dans la communion, cette présence constitue une sorte de butée sur laquelle vient s'évanouir la tentation de réduire le mystère de Dieu ou de Jésus-Christ à ce que les chrétiens disent, pensent ou expérimentent de lui. Elle joue ainsi, dans sa matérialité sensible même, comme la plus haute figure de l'interdit d'idolâtrie qui leur est fait; elle inscrit devant eux l'altérité absolue de Dieu et l'impossibilité de toute mainmise sur lui.

S'il en est ainsi, on est en plein paradoxe. D'un côté, en effet, parmi les propositions de la foi, l'affirmation de la présence du Christ dans l'eucharistie est sans doute celle qui est la plus menacée de dérive idolâtrique, voire fétichiste; et cela, en raison de la triple caractéristique du *sacramentum* mentionné plus haut. Or, d'un autre côté, et pour les mêmes raisons de matérialité, d'extériorité et de précédence, auxquelles on pourrait ajouter le caractère non figuratif du pain et du vin, nous disons ici qu'on peut la comprendre au contraire comme la plus haute figure symbolique de l'interdit d'idolâtrie. Rappelons, sur ce point, que l'idolâtrie réside dans la réduction de Dieu aux conditions de l'expérience que l'on dit avoir faite de lui. Le corps eucharistique du Christ, en sa matérialité et extériorité, figure bien, dans cette perspective, le barrage le plus résistant à cette réduction idolâtrique: le mystère du Christ et de l'Évangile résiste aux multiples tentatives imaginaires de le réduire à ce qui est dit ou expérimenté de lui. Dès lors, un geste comme l'inclination ou la génuflexion devant le pain consacré ne serait-il pas porteur d'une intentionnalité qui rejoindrait la «fonction méta» précédemment évoquée, mais exprimée cette fois-ci par mode d'attitude, et non pas simplement de discours, et d'attitude confessante. N'aurions-nous pas là l'expression symbolique de ce «toujours plus grand» ou plutôt de ce «toujours plus autre» que la tradition apophatique a tenté d'exprimer sur le plan théorique en affectant ses affirmations sur Dieu d'un exposant négatif de suréminence? On est alors conduit à penser que, loin de relever du statut de l'idole, l'eucharistie relève de celui de l'icône, étant entendu que cette dernière vise à préserver l'altérité de ce qu'elle cherche pourtant à donner à «voir». On n'oubliera cependant pas que si la distinction entre idole et icône est claire sur le plan théorique, elle est beaucoup moins tranchée dans les faits. Un peu comme dans la distinction entre «religion» et «magie», on a affaire concrètement plus à une polarité qu'à une frontière franche: toute représentation «iconique» peut fonctionner comme idole, de même que tout comportement «religieux» peut dériver vers une conduite «magique». Par conséquent, contrairement au soupçon fort idéologique qui porte à ne percevoir d'idolâtrie que chez «les autres» (le catholique avec son eucharistie, le protestant avec sa Bible, l'orthodoxe avec son culte des images saintes, etc.), on rappelle ici qu'il n'y a, en fait, qu'un pas entre l'idole à l'icône. Ce pas n'en franchit pas moins un abîme. Voilà pourquoi, sans réduire la théologie de l'eucharistie à la théologie de l'icône, puisque le rapport entre le signifiant et le signifié n'est pas du tout le même dans les deux cas[30], on peut reconnaître à la

---

30. Rappelons à ce sujet que jamais les défenseurs des icônes, lors de la rude querelle iconoclaste du 8° siècle en Orient, n'ont voulu assimiler l'eucharistie à une icône. Ceci, pour deux raisons. La première est que les iconoclastes s'appuyaient sur l'anaphore de S. Basile qui, dans l'anamnèse, appelle le pain et le vin *antitypes* du corps et du sang du Christ, pour soutenir que la seule «icône» que nous ayons le droit de vénérer est l'eucharistie. La seconde est que si les icônes sanctifient ceux qui les vénèrent, selon la tradition orientale, c'est seulement en raison de leur participation relationnelle à l'hypostase du Christ, comme le précisent S. Jean Damascène et S. Théodore Studite; l'eucharistie, elle, sanctifie, parce qu'elle *est* le corps même du Seigneur *in sacramento*. (Cf. Christophe

présence eucharistique un statut d'icône par différence avec le statut de l'idole. On se garde ainsi théoriquement de toute emprise imaginaire sur la présence du Christ.

3.4. Une présence par mode d'Ouvert

a. La présence comme venue

L'altérité que préserve l'icône est en outre inséparable du concept de «présence». Celui-ci en effet n'est pas d'ordre cosmologique, mais anthropologique, et l'on sait depuis longtemps qu'il désigne autre chose que la simple factualité des étants subsistants qui s'étendent sous nos yeux ici et maintenant dans cette salle: l'*adesse* d'une présence est d'un autre ordre que le simple *esse* d'une chose brute. Rien ne nous est plus présent que l'autre en son altérité même, donc du fait qu'il nous échappe et que d'ailleurs, puisque le sujet est «brèche», qu'il s'échappe à lui-même: c'est toujours «comme un autre» que chacun s'appréhende «soi-même»[31]. Comme concept, la présence est donc constitutivement barrée du trait de l'«absence». Cela ne veut pas dire seulement que le rapport présence / absence serait comme celui, dialectique, de recto à verso. Une telle représentation est insuffisante: elle n'empêche aucunement d'imaginer la présence sur le mode «plein» d'une transparence saturante ou d'un donné sans faille. Dire qu'il n'est de présence que barrée par l'absence c'est précisément refuser la représentation d'une telle saturation. Cela, bien entendu, ne vient pas affaiblir la réalité de ladite présence, mais vient la qualifier pour ce qu'elle est: présence *humaine*. Dès lors, la présence ne peut être qu'avènement; en son essence même, elle est «venue». Qui dit «présence» dit donc «venue-en-présence».

b. La fraction du pain

À cette première ouverture vient s'ajouter une seconde en ce qui concerne la présence du Christ dans le pain et le vin de l'eucharistie. Cette seconde ouverture porte précisément sur la préposition «dans» qui vient d'être employée. Les scolastiques avaient appris d'Aristote qu'il est de multiples manières pour un étant quelconque d'être «dans» un lieu et ceux du XIII° siècle avaient critiqué à cet égard l'image trop matérielle de Hugues de Saint-Victor qui comparait les sacrements à des «vases» contenant un remède. Par ailleurs, Thomas parmi d'autres avait rappelé que le corps glorieux du Christ dans l'eucharistie ne peut être localisé

Von Schönborn, *L'icône du Christ. Fondements théologiques élaborés entre le 1er et le 2° concile de Nicée*, Fribourg/Suisse, Éd. universitaires, 1976). C'est donc seulement dans le cadre de sa différence avec l'«idole» que la catégorie d'«icône» est pertinente pour notre propos.

31. On aura reconnu le titre de l'ouvrage de P. RICŒUR, *Soi-même comme un autre*, Paris, Seuil, 1990.

puisque la localisation est elle-même accidentelle. Il n'en demeure pas moins que la critique conceptuelle des représentations est toujours à reprendre, probablement parce que ces dernières sont liées au désir, en l'occurrence le désir de «voir» avec tout ce que peut avoir de captateur ce voir quand il s'agit de l'hostie consacrée. De ce point de vue, on a vu combien les théories préscolastiques de la présence eucharistique étaient grevées par l'immédiateté de ce voir. Aujourd'hui encore d'ailleurs, l'exposition du saint sacrement pour l'adoration dans un ostensoir rayonnant n'est-elle pas soupçonnable de jouer sur ce registre fort ambigu? Je ne veux pas dire que la pratique de l'adoration du Christ dans l'eucharistie, même si elle ne s'est développée que dans l'Église latine et à partir du Moyen Âge, ne serait pas théologiquement légitime quand elle est vécue, ainsi que l'a rappelé Vatican II, dans le sillage de l'action eucharistique, avec ses grandes dimensions de manducation de la Parole de Dieu, d'action de grâce, d'offrande, de supplication... Je veux simplement rappeler que dans le domaine des pratiques rituelles les signifiants ou les figures symboliques sont plus déterminants que les signifiés idéels.

Le rite de la fraction du pain est de première importance à cet égard, en ce qu'il manifeste que si la présence du Christ est bien inscrite dans le pain et le vin, elle n'y est pas circonscrite. La tradition biblique y insiste d'ailleurs: Dieu est bien présent au milieu de son peuple; plus précisément, il est présent dans son Temple, dans le Saint des Saints, sur le propitiatoire qui recouvrait l'arche d'alliance. Or ce propitiatoire constituait un espace délimité par deux Kheroubim aux ailes jointes («toi qui sièges entre les Kheroubim»), c'est-à-dire un espace ouvert. Du point de vue phénoménologique, cette ouverture manifeste que Dieu n'est pas assignable à résidence. On se souvient à ce sujet de la force avec laquelle le prophète Ezéchiel fustige le peuple d'Israël qui, comme les idolâtres, croit pouvoir manipuler son Dieu: la gloire de Dieu va quitter le Temple de Jérusalem pour aller rejoindre les exilés en Babylonie (Ez 11). La présence du Christ dans l'eucharistie ne peut évidemment pas davantage, et en raison du concept de présence, et en raison de son caractère eschatologique et pneumatique, être enclose dans un étant intra-mondain. Pourtant, il est facile de se laisser prendre à des représentations fantasmatiques en ce domaine: le sujet croyant se laisse alors psychiquement leurrer par cette instance du psychisme qu'il est convenu d'appeler avec Lacan l'«imaginaire» et qui s'acharne à vouloir atteindre l'obscur Objet du désir. Ce leurre est lié au matériau symbolique lui-même de l'eucharistie: le pain en effet est une réalité compacte et close, où il est facile d'assigner imaginairement le Christ à demeure; en outre, sa manducation et son assimilation dans la communion mettent inévitablement en mouvement des fantasmes oraux d'agressivité destructrice et d'assimilation amoureuse, donc de domination et de possession.

Contre ces risques de régression, il est important de rappeler ce qui a été dégagé de la réflexion précédente: le pain ne déploie jamais aussi bien son essence de pain que dans l'acte de sa présentation à Dieu en hommage et de son partage en présence de Dieu avec autrui; c'est là qu'il advient à sa vérité essentielle. Dans cette perspective, le geste de fraction du pain est un rite fondamental de la messe. Il l'est pour des raisons de tradition d'abord, comme le montrent les récits de la Cène et les propos de Luc et de Paul; mais il l'est plus originairement encore pour la raison qu'on vient de dire. Par la fraction, un vide est creusé dans le pain. Non pas un simple vide physique, certes, mais un vide symbolique, puisqu'il s'agit d'un partage, c'est-à-dire d'un vide «pour», dont l'intentionnalité est la communion avec autrui. Pas plus que l'acte de verser le vin, dans la méditation heideggérienne sur la cruche, n'est assimilable à un utilitaire débit de boisson, puisqu'il est «offre» ou «offrande» à autrui (*schenken*, *Geschenk*), le vide ne peut être ici réduit à une simple nécessité physique. En tant qu'il est fait en présence ou au nom de Dieu et en faveur d'autrui, il manifeste en effet l'essence même du pain.

Bien sûr, ici encore, le discours proprement théologique, c'est-à-dire confessant, va immédiatement mettre en avant sa différence. D'abord, ce qui est rompu ne l'est pas seulement en présence et au nom de Dieu, puisque, pour la foi chrétienne, le pain est devenu le Christ lui-même en tant porteur de la vie divine même. Ensuite, et consécutivement, la communion créée par la participation sacramentelle au Christ est bien plus qu'une simple convivialité. «Un seul pain, un seul corps»: la formule paulinienne (1 Co 10,16) requiert d'être comprise en un sens fort. Nous voulons dire qu'il faut ici faire rendre à la métaphore du corps la force que lui donne la fonction «méta» qui la «porte au delà» de la simple image.

Dès lors, le *sacramentum* fondamental de la présence du Christ dans l'eucharistie est bien le pain, mais en tant que rompu (ou destiné à l'être); le pain donc, mais dans son être-essentiel de pain, c'est-à-dire non pas en tant que chose close et compacte, mais en tant que réalité-pour-le-partage. Le vide-pour-autrui de la fraction apparaît ainsi comme la grande figure sacramentelle de la présence du Christ: c'est de ce vide que celle-ci surgit en quelque sorte. Ce vide, comme vide-pour-autrui, produit au milieu des croyants la figure même de la kénose du Christ «se vidant» de lui-même (Ph 2,7) pour renouer l'alliance de Dieu avec et entre les hommes. La présence eucharistique du Christ n'est donc jamais déliable du rapport à autrui comme membre effectif ou potentiel de son corps. Cela ressort avec une force particulière, comme annoncé plus haut, de la séquence rituelle formée par la fraction du pain dans son rapport avec le geste de paix qui la précède immédiatement et la démarche de communion qui la suit. Chacun de ces trois rites revêt une double dimension de rapport au Christ ressuscité lui-même et de rapport entre les participants.

Le premier geste, celui de la paix, est centré d'abord sur la seconde dimension: on s'y reçoit les uns les autres comme frères; mais on le fait «dans la charité du Christ». Le troisième, celui de la communion, est centré au contraire sur la première dimension: c'est bien le Christ ressuscité (et non les frères ou l'Église) qu'on y reçoit, mais on ne peut le faire en vérité sans s'être reçus préalablement comme frères. Quant au geste central, celui de la fraction, il exprime les deux dimensions précédentes au même niveau: d'une part, ce qui est partagé, c'est le corps même du Christ ressuscité; mais ce corps eucharistique du Christ Tête est inséparable, quoique distinct, de son corps ecclésial édifié par le partage du même pain. On en a dit précédemment la raison théologique: c'est le corps personnel du Christ qui advient dans l'eucharistie, et non pas le corps-Église; mais c'est le corps personnel du Christ *en acte de vivification de son corps ecclésial par l'Esprit-Saint.*

Dans le sillage de la problématique qui vient d'être développée, la meilleure manière de penser le mystère de la présence eucharistique dans l'actuelle modernité est, semble-t-il, de faire écho à la théologie augustinienne du *Christus totus*, en ce qu'elle énonce la vérité (ici, la *res* de l'eucharistie) sous mode métaphorique sans la réduire pour autant à une simple «image». On connaît à ce propos la célèbre formule d'Augustin à propos du corps eucharistique: «soyez ce que vous voyez et recevez ce que vous êtes». La vérité qui s'y énonce est irréductible à une simple métaphore littéraire tout en étant inséparable de la forme métaphorique qui la médiatise et qui, précisément, la «porte au-delà» de toute représentation. L'eucharistie est la figure symbolique ou sacramentelle qui dit à la fois l'impossibilité de confondre le Corps du Christ ressuscité et son corps ecclésial (on ne symbolise que des différences) et l'impossibilité de les séparer. Elle est la réalisation de ce que l'auteur de la lettre aux Ephésiens, au terme d'une superbe méditation, appelle le *mega mystèrion* (v. 32), à savoir l'indissoluble alliance du Christ et de l'Église.

Institut Catholique de Paris Louis-Marie CHAUVET
21 Rue d'Assas
F-75270 Paris

DO WE STILL NEED THE SACRAMENTS?

Sacraments have always been of great importance in the concrete life of the Catholic Church. But at the same time there always have been questions about the link between faith and the celebration of the sacraments.[1] Today once more this link is under discussion.

1. Pastoral Care and Sacraments

For the past few decades sacramental practice has been going through a crisis. Together with the profound cultural changes, the sacramental practice has also undergone some changes. One of the important elements in these radical shifts was the fact that there was no longer a link between the religious identity and the prescribed religious practice. The personal experience of the believer finds it hard to identify itself with the sacramental services of the Church. The tension between the fixed liturgical pattern and spiritual life just seems too high.[2]

And so one must acknowledge that when it comes to pastoral care the link between faith and the sacraments is profoundly questioned, to the extent that in actual practice one can start doubting the necessity of the sacraments. According to Chauvet there exists, in the sacramental celebration a strong objective and structural tension between the 'rational' logic and the 'emotional' logic of the spiritual life.[3] The sacraments seem to be a growing stumbling block or obstacle for a fresh and liberating practice of faith.[4] This evolution in pastoral care does raise a few questions. Why do we have this opposition against the *ritual* celebration of *faith*? Are the sacraments essential for the church community? In short, does the Church still need the sacraments?

Chauvet, and other theologians with him, points to a common denominator causing much opposition: the actual resistance against each

---

1. F. Deniau, "Proposer la foi dans la pastorale sacramentelle," in *La Maison Dieu* 216 (1998) 21. Cf. L.-M. Chauvet, "Pratique sacramentelle et expérience chrétienne," in *Christus* 171 (1996) 275.
2. Cf. Chauvet, "Pratique sacramentelle," 275.
3. *Ibid.*
4. Cf. L.-M. Chauvet, *Les sacrements, parole de Dieu au risque du corps* (Paris, 1993) 130.

form of mediation.⁵ But the sacraments of the Church are just that, i.e. symbolic forms of mediation. Chauvet puts it as follows: "Therefore one can see that the liturgy has no other fundamental aim than to establish a living communication between the believers and God. This communication however is *never direct*: it goes by means of our body; moreover it takes 'place' in our 'corporality'."⁶

The importance of mediation and of corporality was long neglected but today it deserves special attention. One can ask oneself where all this resistance and distrust against the mediating and interpreting authorities comes from.? After all, the acceptance of mediation is substantial in the forming of an identity, in the psychological sphere as well as in a social or religious context.⁷

In this paper it is my aim to find an answer to the above-mentioned pastoral problem based on L.-M. Chauvet's thinking. He makes a plea for reconciliation with the mediation structures within the Church. In doing so he points out that faith, the Church and the sacraments are inextricably bound.

2. The Meaning of Mediation

Chauvet argues that "the fact that the Christian identity is never dissociated from the sacraments (especially at the initiation) means that faith, even in its most spiritual aspects, can only exist by means of the body, or even a society, a longing, a tradition, a history, an institution, etc. The most 'spiritual' always takes 'place' in the most 'corporal'."⁸ To fully fathom the importance of this proposition, we need to examine the meaning of "mediation" as found in the work of Chauvet.

2.1. Philosophical Backgrounds

To fully grasp the meaning of mediation, this Parisian theologian starts by showing us a new way of thinking. For a long time the aspect of mediation was prone to a very one-sided interpretation in philosophy and theology. This issue is deeply rooted in the western mentality. It does not solely apply to the sacraments, but the sacraments do clearly reveal the problem. In fact, this is one of the presuppositions of the western way of

---

5. K. Depoortere, "Sacramenten vieren (I), Waar het leven icoon wordt," in *Collationes* 24 (1994) 366.
6. Chauvet, "Pratique sacramentelle," 280.
7. Depoortere, "Sacramenten vieren (I)," 366.
8. Chauvet, *Les sacrements. Parole de Dieu au risque du corps*, 4. Cf. L.-M. Chauvet, "L'avenir du sacramentel," in *Recherches de science religieuse* 75 (1987) 245; L.-M. Chauvet, *Symbol and Sacrament. A Sacramental Reinterpretation of Christian Existence* (Collegeville, MN, 1995) 146.

thinking.[9] Seen against the metaphysical background of the 'onto-theology', the philosophers and theologians attempted "at explaining the totality of being."[10] They sought the tangible basis of reality. They were well aware of the distance between thought and reality but they tried to bridge or even wipe out this distance.[11] This way of thinking was also applied to theology, in which God was perceived as the Highest Being or as foundation of all things.

In this philosophical and theological tradition, the forms of mediation were considered as purely accidental. Mediation was nearly automatically branded as something pejorative. The presuppositions of the onto-theology typically depict language, history or corporality as mere accidental or instrumental components of life.[12] They are even perceived as obstacles standing in the way of pure thought, human dialogue and the realisation of existence.[13] For example, language is depicted as a means of translating thoughts. But to translate is to betray.[14] And a dualistic pattern remains. For the time being the human ideal must settle for this limited and transitory 'structure'.[15]

In this classical, metaphysical line of thought of the onto-theology, God, grace and therefore also the sacraments were conceived in terms of causality and a productionistic scheme of representation was used.[16] It

---

9. Chauvet writes: "The Scholastics were *unable to think otherwise*; they were prevented from doing so by the onto-theological presuppositions which structured their entire culture." Chauvet, *Symbol and Sacrament*, 8.

10. Chauvet, *Symbol and Sacrament*, 8. Thus the theology is described which in its thought goes in search of an ontological ground or a foundation of being. (*Ibid.*, 26-29). While looking for a foundation for the 'impermanence' in reality, being was postulated as ultimate ground

11. Chauvet continues by saying that there is a difference between thinking this distance and basing thought on this distance. Chauvet, *Symbol and Sacrament*, 8-9.

12. *Ibid.*, 34.

13. In this metaphysical tradition, man faces reality in the relationship of a subject towards an object. (Descartes played an important role in this. Cf. Chauvet, *Symbol and Sacrament*, 35) This dichotomy prevents from seeing man in connection with his language, his history or his body. To which Chauvet protests: "Metaphysics thus reveals itself, according to its most characteristic tendency, as the logic of its own knowledge, forgetting, in the words of Maurice Merleau-Ponty, that 'every relationship with being is simultaneously to take and to be taken',..., in short, that humans never utter their judgements from a distant height and with sovereign neutrality, but rather start with a concrete language in which a universe is already structured into a 'world', that is, from a place that is socially arranged and culturally organised." Chauvet, *Symbol and Sacrament*, 36.

14. Chauvet, *Symbol and Sacrament*, 33.

15. "For the decision to describe either the body or language as an instrument presupposes an anterior existence, at least of the logical order, of humanity in relation to its 'tools'; it presupposes an ideal human essence that, since its fall and exile, has been thus imprisoned – 'body-sign (*soma-sema*) – in the empire of the sensible." Chauvet, *Symbol and Sacrament*, 34.

16. Chauvet, *Symbol and Sacrament*, 21-22.

may be an 'analogous' way of thinking but it still is a utilitarian pattern of thought.[17] Grace on the other hand does not belong to the utilitarian level; grace is not tangible or calculable. Grace wishes to be infinite and isn't material or monetary. In the onto-theological mode of thought grace is presented as something that can nearly be touched by hands and sacramental mediation is perceived as a tangible *remedium*.

2.2. Changed Relations

After taking leave of this metaphysics, the new pattern of thought must be developed. To approve of mediation and to accept distance means abandoning the desire to control, objectify and calculate things.[18] This change in thinking however does not result from an opposition against this metaphysics.[19] It is in fact a change of scope, a different attitude in which the forms of mediation are accepted in a positive way.[20] This change is an ongoing and never-ending transition. To accept mediation of language and corporality is a process. Chauvet puts it as follows: "As a discourse that takes into consideration the human characteristic of being-body – its enfleshed signifiers, its 'living words' ('*logoi embioi*') – analytic discourse knits together concrete corporality with philosophical questioning of humans as always *unterwegs*, always 'on the way' toward the word that goes ahead of them."[21]

This transition is not easy. Man no longer holds the position of possessor towards reality. The distance in the relations between man and reality is no longer a negative element needing to be erased, but it is where mediation takes place. The secret longing for total transparency, linked to a way of thinking without this mediation of language, body or history, is no longer a means of finding reality. The distinctness of this symbolical order clarifies that language and corporality are by no means accidental aspects of our condition. Material things are more than mere *res extensa*.

The other attitude consists more of an openness towards the gift of existence and grace bestowed on us. This truth of being comes to us through everyday things. It is the gift of all that exists appearing "wher-

---

17. *Ibid.*, 28.
18. *Ibid.*, 28 and 61-62.
19. One must not forget that the onto-theological presuppositions were a part of the culture. Therefore it is not easy to go beyond this metaphysics. Moreover, Chauvet agrees with Heidegger that this metaphysics will never disappear. (It would therefore be wrong to place all the sins of Sodom on this classical metaphysics Cf. Chauvet, *Symbol and Sacrament*, 48.) Chauvet notes: "The critical thrust for Christian theology does not consist in the apophatic purification of our concepts in order to express God but rather in the use that we make of these concepts, that is, in the *attitudes,* idolatrous or not, they elicit from it." Chauvet, *Symbol and Sacrament*, 42-43.
20. *Ibid.*, 48.
21. *Ibid.*, 81-82.

ever an attitude of listening to the gift of the presence and a sense of human poverty and mortality are simultaneously born and reborn in humans."[22] Thus man discovers the gratuity of existence. "The human mode of the appropriation of Being as play and grace is through the disappropriation.[23]

2.3. The Symbolic Order

In this new train of thought, L.-M. Chauvet finds the words to describe the mediation structure or the symbolic order, i.e. the entirety of culture, language and symbols (signifiers) of which every human being is a part. He calls it the *'corporality' ('corporéité')* of our existence. Here we use *corpus*, body in the broader sense. Our body is more than mere flesh. Culture, history, space and time are also a part of it:

Our world
We live in a world which is always filled with meaning. This world is already inhabited and rich in symbolic references. They determine our culture, our notion of time and space and our history. This symbolic order is "the mediation through which subjects build themselves while building the real into a 'world', their familiar 'world' where they can live."[24]

Our language
Language and the body are not instruments or attributes one possesses but they form the environment or the mediation in which humans as subjects come to be.[25] Following Heidegger[26], Chauvet sets great store by language.[27] Humans are born into language and that language determines our world: "There is no thing where the word is lacking."[28] Language is an essential part of our being in the reality : "Thus, language does not arise to translate after the fact a human experience that preceded it; it is *constitutive* of any truly *human* experience, that is to say, significant experience."[29] Language builds our identity. "The original difference out of which every subject arises is thus no longer understood, with resentment, as an obstacle – inevitable perhaps

---

22. Chauvet, *Symbol and Sacrament*, 60.
23. *Ibid*, 61.
24. *Ibid.*, 86.
25. "Like the body, language is not an instrument but a mediation; it is in language that humans as subjects come to be. Humans do not pre-exist language; they are formed in its womb. They do not posses it like an 'attribute', even if of the utmost importance; they are possessed by it." Chauvet, *Symbol and Sacrament*, 87.
26. Chauvet, *Symbol and Sacrament*, 47.
27. *Ibid.*, 88.
28. *Ibid.*, 88. And he continues: "There is no human reality, however interior or intimate, except by expressing it through the mediation of language or quasi-language that gives it a body." Chauvet, *Symbol and Sacrament*, 90.
29. Chauvet, *Symbol and Sacrament*, 87.

but still relatively reducible, - to the truth but as the *very place where truth is brought about*."[30]

Our body
Distance and mediation go hand in hand. We can also experience this in our corporality. Just like language, our body mediates in our expression. Once again it must be stressed that the body is not an instrument: "Humans do not ex-sist except as corporality whose concrete place is always their *own bodies*."[31] Our body is a living anamnesis of a threefold body. The body is like a memory: its presence brings about this world, this culture, this community.[32] Using the words of D. Dubarle, Chauvet goes even further: "The living body is indeed, in the expression of D. Dubarle, 'the arch-symbol of the whole symbolic order'."[33]

Thus symbolic no longer means 'detached from reality' or as Chauvet puts it: "Far, then, from being opposed to the 'real', as the reigning logic of signs would have it *the symbol touches the most real aspect of ourselves and our world*."[34] The symbolic union is in the centre of reality but does not erase the differences. The bond which comes into being, is a pact between two different persons or things. By acknowledging the difference and by acknowledging the mediation, a mutual acknowledgement of the union comes about.

3. Faith Is Sacramental

Do we still need the sacraments? This question was the starting-point. This question resulted from a reflection on the situations in pastoral care. The sore spot lay in the aversion towards the sacraments because forms of mediation are hardly accepted. Chauvet however brings in the possibility of reassessing the Christian symbolic order. And in this we will discover the inner link between faith and the sacraments in a whole new way.

Through the mediation of the church community, the Christian identity is able to flourish. As a Christian, we always receive grace through mediation. The relationship with God is formed through the contact with the Scriptures, with the sacraments and with the Christian testimony. The church community exists within this threefold mediation structure.

---

30. *Ibid.*, 95. Cf. Fr. MIES, "Présence et absence de Dieu dans la relation interpersonnelle," in *Revue théologique de Louvain* 30 (1999) 32-58.
31. Chauvet, *Symbol and Sacrament*, 146.
32. Cf. *ibid.*, 150-151.
33. *Ibid.*, 151.
34. *Ibid.*, 123.

Chauvet bases his argumentation for the build-up of the ecclesiastical symbolical order on an analysis of certain New Testament passages.[35] He pays special attention to the Lucan story on the journey to Emmaus (Luke 24) in which two important elements come forward. Firstly, the disciples are invited to become reconciled with the absence of the historical Jesus.[36] And secondly, the disciples are urged to faithfully recognise and acknowledge the Lord through Scripture, the sacraments and the testimony of the church community.[37]

Acceptance of this ecclesiastical symbolical order presupposes a certain attitude, i.e. to give up the longing to touch Jesus himself. Or in other words: our Lord's Easter clearly shows us that we must accept his absence just as we must accept his presence in the community of the faithful.[38] By accepting the Church as a sacrament, we acknowledge the Lord's empty place: "Faith as such finds its beginning in renouncing the directness of seeing/knowing and in accepting the mediation of the Church."[39]

Within this threefold structure, the eyes of faith are opened, as shown in the analysis of the story of Emmaus. That is why entering into faith is "to learn to consent, without resentment, to the corporality of the faith."[40] The corporality of faith, in the Church and in the sacraments, indicates the sacramentality of the entire faith. Thus Chauvet states: "Therefore it is clear that, if the liturgy has no other fundamental purpose than to establish a living communication between the faithful and God, this communication will never be direct: it happens through the body; moreover it takes place in our 'corporality'. This is the result of the incarnation."[41]

In this way the believer is always confronted with a specific symbolical order. This 'corporal' mediation structure is necessary to build up the religious identity. The role of the sacraments in this symbolical order must now be clarified even further.

---

35. Chauvet examines what he calls *'trois textes matriciels'*: The story of Emmaus in the Gospel of St. Luke (Lk 24:13-35), the baptism of the Ethiopian eunuch (Acts 8:26-40) and the pericope on the conversion of Paul (Acts 9:1-20). Chauvet, *Symbol and Sacrament*, 162-166.
36. Chauvet, *Symbol and Sacrament*, 177-178.
37. *Ibid.*, 167-170.
38. *Ibid.*, 163; cf. 83.
39. Chauvet, *Les sacrements. Parole de Dieu au risque du corps*, 43. Cf. Chauvet, *Symbol and Sacrament*, 177-178.
40. Chauvet, *Symbol and Sacrament*, 153.
41. Chauvet, "Pratique sacramentelle et expérience chrétienne," 280.

4. The Specific Role of the Sacraments

In this discourse, as we could read up till now, the question still remains why exactly we need sacraments in order to celebrate our faith. After all, the sacramentality of faith shows us that grace is not exclusively linked to sacraments. Gods gift of grace manifests itself in our whole life. So we come back to the same question: are sacraments necessary for a Christian? The further application of the symbolic line of thought will clarify how the sacraments occupy a special position in the symbolic order of the Church.

While referring to K. Rahner, Chauvet states: "Under such conditions the originality of the sacraments comes only from *the Church* which radically involves itself and puts into play its whole identity."[42] Chauvet agrees with Rahner but at the same time he goes further. He expresses in a clearer way the own modality of the *sacramentum* and the originality of the absolute character of the Church's involvement in the sacraments.[43]

The difference between Scripture and ethics on the one hand and the sacraments on the other hand does not lie in the intentions of the Church or of the believers but in the anthropological modality with which the Church confirms its identity.[44] The rituals are symbolic expressions belonging to the highest level of man's active symbols. It is precisely in the celebration of the sacraments that faith is taken in and nurtured within the corporal symbolic order. The mediation structure of faith can be de-

---

42. Chauvet, *Symbol and Sacrament*, 322. Cf. K. Rahner, *Wort und Eucharistie*, in *Schriften zur Theologie*, Band IV (Einsiedeln, 1960) 329.

43. Rahner only summarily deals with the symbolic dimension of the sacraments. He perceives the symbol mainly as a sign of identity. A quote from his description of the symbol (K. Rahner, *Zur Theologie des Symbols* in *Schriften zur Theologie*, Band IV, Einsiedeln, 1964, 285) will illustrate this: "Durch 'Ausdruck' kommt das Seiende zu sich selbst, soweit es überhaupt zu zich selbst kommt. Der Ausdruck, also das 'Symbol',..., ist die Weise der Selbsterkenntnis, der Selbstfindung überhaupt."

Rahner mostly deals with the radical nature of the sacramental effectivity on a purely ecclesiological basis. In his article on sacramental effectivity. (K. Rahner, *Wort und Eucharistie*, 313-355.) He writes: "Die höchste Wesensverwirklichung des wirksamen Wortes Gottes als Gegenwärtigung der Heilstat Gottes um radikalen Engagement der Kirche (d.h. als deren eigene, volle Aktualisation) bei entscheidenden Heilssituationen des einzelnen ist das Sakrament und nur es." *Wort und Eucharistie*, p. 329. As the article progresses, the ecclesiological dimension gets more attention. "Es ist das Wort Christi im Munde der Kirche, das ex opere operato Gnade bewirkt." *Wort und Eucharistie*, p. 336. And regarding the Eucharist: "Die Eucharistie ist das Wort der Kirche schlechthin." *Wort und Eucharistie*, p. 349. Chauvet's description shows a better balance between the ecclesiological and the christological dimension of the sacraments.

44. Chauvet, *Symbol and Sacrament*, 374.

scribed by means of the threefold corporality which is characteristic for existence:[45]

Heaven and earth[46]
The liturgy contains many simple objects which portray our existence, our 'being-in-the-world'.[47] These material elements express on the one hand the 'autochthony' or the cosmic condition of man and on the other hand the bond with the Creator and his gift of grace.[48]

History and tradition
The historic body is in fact the *traditio* of faith. The Christian tradition has its very own perception of history. Throughout history the Christian tradition has upheld the memory of the Lord. In faith history also has a symbolic expression. This memory of a personal history is the very essence of the Christian meetings. "The memory of the presence anticipates the presence to come in the actuality of a presence veiled under the symbol of Christ's Easter."[49] Everyone can 'incorporate' his own history in the history of Christ.

The Christian community
The social context is the third dimension of the 'corporality of the Christian'. As a symbolic order the Church leads to community. She gives the members of her community an identity and at the same time she builds a relationship. By acknowledging the Church, Christians can recognise each other as members of a community.

Now Chauvet can say: "The concrete affirmation of the world and of the body as the place of God is not verified just in the sacraments [...]. But, it is indeed in them that this affirmation finds its *primordial symbolic expression*."[50] The sacraments are situated on the point where everything (the Scriptures, the *symbolum*, the Christian expression, the personal experience, the concrete testimony) converges. All these elements form as it were the keystone of the whole Christian identity and also of the functioning of this symbolic order.

---

45. Or as Chauvet puts it: "For, being ritualistic activities, they [the sacraments] stage human corporality as such through its numerous expressive possibilities: postures; gestures; voice either speaking or singing, beseeching or rejoicing. And in this way, they 'epiphanize' the threefold body – social, historical, and cosmic – which dwells in the believing subject: the Church-as-body (...); the body of this Church's history and tradition (...); and finally the body of the universe as creation." Chauvet, *Symbol and Sacrament*, 491.

46. This is also known as the chthonic dimension (*cqwn* means: earth, ground or land).

47. "Well before we become aware of these elements or declare what we intend to do with them, they convey to us intimations of our indissoluble marriage to the earth, our original existential condition of 'being-in-the-world'." Chauvet, *Symbol and Sacrament*, 356.

48. Chauvet, *Symbol and Sacrament*, 152.

49. J. Moingt, *Le tracé d'une absence. Les sacrements font notre histoire*, 298.

50. Chauvet, *Symbol and Sacrament*, 537.

The memory, which the Church received from the Lord, is an own symbolic liturgy. As already mentioned above, to talk of symbolism means attaching extreme importance to the presence of the other, to an attitude of '*dépossession*', of expectance and willingness to listen to the other.

The Church's involvement is an active whole which she herself *received* from Jesus Christ, received as an action of her Lord.[51] This is true for the whole Church, but also for each member of this community: "In agreeing to submit oneself to the sacramental gesture of the Church, one no longer avails oneself of one's own theological ideas, as incisive as they might be, or of one's own religious feelings, as sincere as they might be, or of one's own ethical accomplishments, as generous as they might be. All this certainly causes us to act, but it is not what is at work in the sacramental rite. Here the self is put at the disposal of the Other whom it can let act in the Church's mediation."[52]

The sacraments offer the opportunity of a transition to receptivity, to an attitude of '*dépossession*'. Thus, the sacraments constitute a dynamic moment. This transition is a moment which the believer must continually recapture. With the sacraments, we are always on our way, passing through. At this point of the passage, the believer is touched by the sacramental *'event'*. This motion of the sacraments as a symbolic whole is active here as highest uniting power. The threefold corporality and the identity structure of the Christian are converged into a whole. In this convergence the Church opens in an absolute way to communication with God and to His gift of grace.[53]

---

51. "We must add this important specification, this pragmatic whole is 'received' by the Church as coming from Jesus Christ, as an action of its Lord, an action over which it confesses to have no power. It is in this way we understand the 'absolute' character of the involvement of the Church which, according to K. Rahner, marks the difference between the sacraments and other ecclesial mediations of the communication of God." Chauvet, *Symbol and Sacrament*, 374. Elsewhere Chauvet talks of this receptive attitude in a slightly different wording: [The Church] can only be the Church to the extent that she realises that she depends on Jesus... She cannot proclaim Jesus as Christ and Saviour without she herself being affected at present by what she proclaims in the past. The Church only has an identity because she constantly receives it from Him." Chauvet, *Les sacrements. Parole de Dieu au risque du corps*, 150.

52. Chauvet, *Symbol and Sacrament*, 375.

53. This uniting power of the sacraments can be seen in biblical terms as celebrations of the convenant. The uniting power of the Church's symbolic order shows the structure of the convenant: "Passing through them [the sacraments] is part of the unique structure of the convenant." Chauvet, *Les sacrements. Parole de Dieu au risque du corps*, 162.

5. Conclusion: Back to Pastoral Care

5.1. Not without the Sacraments

The concrete pastoral situations sometimes can lead to doubt the necessity of the sacraments. The description of the sacramentality of faith however goes against this. So one can safely state that for a Christian to agree to mediation means agreeing to the sacraments. If faith is detached from the sacraments, there is a danger of losing a constituent element of identity. These facts form an appeal towards the practice. In practice, for example, the link with the Eucharist must always be maintained.[54] In absence of the Eucharist, this lack must not be erased.

5.2. The Sacraments as a Stumbling Block

Despite the attempts of reconciliation, the sacraments still encounter resistance. Symbolic thinking also offers an answer to this point. The tension existing between the objective fact and the subjective perception, between institute and experience, can be accepted as characteristic for the faith.[55] Wanting to erase the tension or the distance created by the symbolic mediation, would lead to polarising and reducing positions. In this context Chauvet clearly states: "In their significant materiality, the sacraments thus constitute an *unavoidable stumbling block* which forms a barrier to every imaginary claim to a direct connection, individual and interior, with Christ or to a gnostic–like, illuminist contact with him."[56] The expectation of an immediate benefit from the sacraments is situated on that magical or individualistic level which inevitably leads to disappointment.

5.3. Liturgy and Experience: Polarisation or Balance?

Without wanting to lean towards gnostic or ideologically laden theology, the pastoral practice is often marked by the waves of the objectivistic and subjectivistic tendencies. To compensate for the loss of a conscious faith, some stress the need for more religious knowledge and for acceptance of

---

54. The last few decades this has become quite evident for theologians. A well-known study by H. de Lubac can serve to illustrate this. H. de Lubac, *Corpus Mysticum L'Eucharistie et l'Église au Moyen Age* (Theologie, 3; Paris, 1949²). H. de Lubac: "Il serait donc, semble-t-il, d'un grand intérêt, disons même qu'il est d'une actualité pressante, en l'état présent de ce qui reste de la 'chrétienté', de revenir, pour nous y retremper, aux origines sacramentelles du 'corps mystique'. Ce sera revenir aux sources mystiques de l'Église. L'Église et l'Eucharistie se font, chaque jour, l'une par l'autre: l'idée de l'Église et l'idée de l'Eucharistie doivent pareillement se promouvoir et s'approfondir l'une par l'autre." de Lubac, *Corpus Mysticum*, 292-293.
55. Chauvet, *Symbol and Sacrament*, 374.
56. *Ibid.*, 153.

the objective rite. But here there is the risk of a certain rigorism, a hard position with a dogmatic discourse.[57] Ritualism is never far off.[58]

As well as the trap of ritualism, there is also the risk of the sacraments merely being used as binding agent for a social group. The danger exists of always having to conduct the service according to one's own subjective criteria.[59] Chauvet expresses the difficulty as follows: "The conversation, which the receiver would like to perceive as a 'dialogue' and beyond 'power', risks becoming no more than a more or less perverted theatralisation: this 'dialogue' could unconsciously aim at neutralising the frightening fortuities of the communication; and the power, which was relinquished by the right hand is slyly regained by the left hand."[60]

5.4. Conclusion

We can conclude that both the objectivistic (or 'conservative') and the subjectivistic (or 'progressive') tendencies are influenced by categories of thought which surprisingly resemble one another. They are two very different attempts to erase any kind of distance. Both tendencies display the same striving for control. Neither one of them adequately acknowledges the mediation structure of the Church. Therefore many perceive the sacraments as opaque elements of the Christian faith. The danger of the sacraments being further marginalised remains. Once again, it is necessary to get to know Chauvet's new line of thought. His plea for reconciliation with the Church's symbolical order leads us to rediscover a treasure of Christian life: the sacraments of the Church.

Heilige Geestcollege   Luk DE VOLDER
Naamsestraat 40
3000 Leuven

---

57. Chauvet, *Les sacrements. Parole de Dieu au risque du corps*, 209.
58. Chauvet, *Symbol and Sacrament*, 332; 343.
59. *Ibid.*, 417. Cf. A critical review by M. Scouarnec: "In the reaction against the ritual formalism, the wish is often uttered to simplify to the extreme and to banish every ceremonial aspect: decoration of the space, the clothing, prayer formulas, the order of the ritual actions. To heal the Liturgy of its heaviness, of its rigidity, of its timelessness, of its 'strangeness' with regard to the culture of a certain environment, an allopathic treatment was opted for. To provide the Liturgy with some energy, to liven it up and pep it up a little, inspiration was found in slightly similar but nevertheless strange practices: meetings, happenings, spectacles and popular feasts." M. Scouarnec, "Liturgie et évangélisation. Des clivages surmontés," in *La Maison Dieu* 216 (1998) 65. His criticism continues for a while. He wants to stand up for a liturgy which is not burdened by these secondary elements. He doesn't deny the necessity of passing on knowledge and explaining the symbols but the right place to do so is outside the liturgy, in sacramental catechisation. Cf. Scouarnec, "Liturgie et évangélisation," 71.
60. Chauvet, *Les sacrements. Parole de Dieu au risque du corps*, 209.

FROM SACRAMENTALITY TO SACRAMENTS AND VICE-VERSA

Here is a snapshot of sacramental life as reported by a parish priest[1]:

In 1980 I baptised Christine. After the rite, I asked the parents for their marriage certificate. In the record I wrote: "Christine, daughter of John and Mary," and, "Baptised in Saint Paul's Church on June 15."

After the baptism of Sven in 1984, I asked his parents for their marriage certificate. While handing it over the mother whispered that they were not married in the church.

In 1988, there was no marriage certificate and no marriage. Jean's parents cohabited.

1992 seemed promising. Convinced Christians, a married couple and teachers in a catholic school. After I asked for the name of the child, they answered, "Lute." "Oh, such a beautiful name," I responded naively, "and short for Lutgard, the Flemish saint". A bit embarrassed, they replied: "No... not the saint... the musical instrument". They hoped that their girl would be joyful and lyrical.

In 1996 I sheepishly asked the parents, "What name do you give your child"? The father barked: "Our boy will not have a name. He should decide for himself rather than bearing a name that has been imposed".

After these different experiences, I came to this realisation: "I have baptised these children and with serious damage to my sacramentology, I might add. I have also seen how these parents love their children and go through fire and water for them as God's fiery Spirit goes through the waters of Baptism for them as well."

This story is not shared in order to provoke a debate on the priest's pastoral decision to baptise some or all of these children. Instead, by carefully reading, a broader concept of sacramentality erupts from this story.[2]

---

1. S. TUYLS, "Het heeft genen naam," in *Pastoralia*, September 1999, 9-10.
2. See among many other authors, dealing with the topic from very different perspectives: A. SCHMEMANN, *Sacraments and Orthodoxy* (New York: Herder and Herder, 1965); J. SEGUNDO, *The Sacraments Today* (Maryknoll: Orbis Books, 1974); G. GRESHAKE, *Gott in allen Dingen finden. Schöpfung und Gotteserfahrung* (Freiburg: Herder, 1986); L. BOFF, *Sacraments of Life: Life of the Sacraments* (Washington: The Pastoral Press, 1987); P. DE CLERCK, "La sacramentalité et les sept sacrements," in *Recherches*

While this reflection lacks some nuance, it is nevertheless meant to clarify certain and appreciable sacramental, ecclesiological and ministerial shifts that result from a broadening sacramentality. Lastly, it is hoped that this can stimulate further discussion given some pastoral applications.

1. Utilisation of the Greek-Latin twin concept mysterion-sacramentum reverses almost all tensions in modern sacramental theology[3]

On the one hand, Saint Paul's *mysterion* designates God's hidden plan to save all persons, a plan determined from the beginning and kept secret until it was revealed fully in Christ (1 Cor 2,7-10; Rom 16,25-26; Col 1,26-27; 2,3; 4,3; Eph 1,9-10; 3,3-12; 1 Tim 3,16; Eph 5,32 as the verse refers to marriage). According to the first Greek patristic authors, that eternal plan of salvation continues to be realised after Christ's ascension through the Spirit in the community of the faithful. It becomes tangible and visible in the mysteries that are lived. Origen, in particular, made the distinction between *Mysterion* – understood as the threefold manifestation of the Word in Christ's incarnation, in the Church and in the Scriptures – and the plural *mysteria* – understood as Baptism, Eucharist and other Christian rituals. The distinction situates the second meaning singularly against the background of the first. Thus, God's permanent but elusive activity through the Spirit and in the world is expressed through an active participation, not an 'administration,' which is typically scholastic.

On the other hand, there is the Latin word *sacramentum*, used to translate the Greek *mysterion*. *Sacramentum*, however, stems from a different context, with a double meaning. The first is more juridical describing a pledge of sorts. In certain circumstances, a deposit or guarantee is left with the religious authorities to underline the seriousness of the forthcoming procedures at a trial. Secondly, *sacramentum* is also a mili-

---

de science religieuse 75 (1987) 211-218; G. De SCHRIJVER, "Experiencing the Sacramental Character of Existence: Transitions from Premodernity to Modernity, Postmodernity, and the Rediscovery of the Cosmos," in *Questions Liturgiques-Liturgical Questions* 75 (1994) 12-27; A. VAN EIJK, "Pleidooi voor een ruimer sacramentsbegrip," in *De lengte en de breedte, de hoogte en de diepte. Peilingen in de theologie van de sacramenten*, ed. A. H. C. VAN EIJK and H. W. M. RIKHOF (Zoetermeer: Meinema, 1996) 105-131; K. W. IRWIN, "Sacramentality and the Theology of Creation: A Recovered Paradigm for Sacramental Theology," in *Louvain Studies* 23 (1998)159-179.

3. A very good *status quaestionis* can be found in T. M. POOVATHANIKUNNEL, *The Sacraments: the Mystery Revealed. An Enquiry into the Meaning of Mysterion and Realsymbol for a Revelatory Concept of Sacramental Mysteries*, Doctoral Dissertation, K.U. Leuven, 1996, xcvii+465 p.; C. ROCCHETTA, *Sacramentaria Fondamentale: Dal 'mysterion' al 'sacramentum'* (Bologna: Dehoniane, 1989); A. H. C. VAN EIJK, "The Church: Mystery, Sacrament, Sign, Instrument, Symbolic Reality," in *Bijdragen. Tijdschrift voor Filosofie en Theologie* 50 (1989) 178-202.

tary term describing an oath of loyalty. This would include gestures, such as a soldier placing his hand on a banner and confirming his readiness to serve. Common to both meanings is the idea of guaranteed engagement (*sacrement-serment*), realised procedurally through a number of sensible acts. Starting from this Latin root, Tertullian forged the more ritualistic meaning of *sacramentum* as visible signs of involvement that are guaranteed by God, and in so doing a process of narrowing *mysterion* to *sacramenta* has started.[4] This is furthered in St. Ambrose's *De Mysteriis* where the Greek term is assumed into the Latin translation. While *mysterium* points to the inner reality of the sacraments, *sacramentum* denotes the outer celebration in the first place, while presuming the inner reality.

The privilege given to the external, ritual aspects of the mysteries – and consequently the restriction of meaning – has continued in the scholastic *signum-causa* theory. At that moment the polysemy of the New Testament's *mysterion* is narrowed to sacramental 'remedies,' 'channels' or 'containers' of grace. At the same time and despite this, the broader appreciation of *sacramentum,* grounded in the true sense of *mysterion,* never disappears entirely from ecclesial vocabulary. The Church was called, "*sacramentum* of salvation for the world" in the *Missale Romanum* of Pius V,[5] and even in the writings of Saints Thomas, Augustine and Cyprian.

This sketch is offered to trace the essential complementarity of *mysterion* and *sacramentum*, emphasising respectively the invisible and the visible part of God's hidden plan of salvation for the whole world, and the mysterious participation of God's people in this plan. In the final analysis, these twin terms should not be separated. The *mysteria* or *sacramenta* are the actualisations of the salvific *mysterion*, which is 'already' and 'not yet.'

2. The great majority of documents from the Roman Catholic Magisterium holds the narrow and limited definition of a sacrament

Emphasised is an official ritual with certain precise gestures guaranteed by the Church and presided over by an empowered minister who is usually ordained. Sacramentals and other pious exercises are mentioned only in passing.

Vatican II prudently retrieved the broader use of the term sacrament as traced from the writings of Dom Odo Casel, Romano Guardini and

---

4. Cf. D. MICHAÉLIDÈS, *Sacramentum chez Tertullien* (Paris: Editions Augustiniennes, 1970).
5. *Oratio* after the 5th reading of the Liturgy of Holy Saturday.

Otto Semmelroth.[6] In *Lumen Gentium* Vatican II called the Church "*veluti sacramentum seu signum et instrumentum...*" and at the end of the same document, "*universale salutis sacramentum.*"[7]

Following Vatican II and in celebration of it, the *Catechism of the Catholic Church* (1994) uses the term 'sacrament' in this broader context. Take n 1111: "Christ's work in the liturgy is sacramental: because his mystery is made present there by the power of his Holy Spirit; because his Body, which is the Church, is like a sacrament (sign and instrument) in which the Holy Spirit dispenses the mystery of salvation." However, this pales next to the use of the word in its proper sense as reserved for one of the seven rituals. The summarising definition in n 1131 clearly testifies: "The sacraments are efficacious signs of grace, instituted by Christ and entrusted to the Church, by which divine life is dispensed to us. The visible rites by which the sacraments are celebrated signify and make present the graces proper to each sacrament. They bear fruit in those who receive them with the required dispositions." At the very end of the section on the sacraments, the *Catechism* deals with "other liturgical celebrations, such as sacramentals and Christian funerals." Further, n 1677 states that, "Sacramentals are sacred signs instituted by the Church. They prepare [us] to receive the fruit of the sacraments and sanctify different circumstances of life."

In the previous sections to the aforementioned definition, sacramentals are clearly separated from sacraments. As stated in n 1670: "Sacramentals do not confer the grace of the Holy Spirit in the way the sacraments do, but by the Church's prayer they prepare us to receive grace and dispose us to co-operate with it." In sum, sacramentals are distinct preparations for the sacraments, not essential to them.

---

6. O. SEMMELROTH, *Die Kirche als Ursakrament* (Frankfurt: Knecht, 1953); For further details see also K. RAHNER, *The Church and the Sacraments* (New York: Herder and Herder, 1963); M. SCHMAUS, *The Church as Sacrament* (Dogma, 5; New York: Sheed and Ward, 1975); H. VORGRIMLER, *Sacramental Theology* (Collegeville: The Liturgical Press, 1979).

7. *Lumen Gentium*, resp. n. 1 and n . 48; parallel expressions in *Lumen Gentium*, n . 8, 9, 59; *Sacrosanctum Concilium*, n. 5 (The Church as sacrament is born *e latere Christi*), 26; *Gaudium et Spes*, n 42 and 45.

3. Overall, the "official" reflection on sacrament(s) does not take into account some major shifts that have taken place on the level of sacramentology, ecclesiology and ministerial theology. These shifts upset the neat distinctions between the sacramental, sacraments and sacramentals

3.1. On the level of sacramentology, theologians are realizing the consequences of a renewed anthropology, based on the symbolic and the intersubjective

The symbolic has replaced the scholastic metaphysical approach characterised as onto-theological and employing the *causa-signum* theory. The main characteristics of today's holistic and integrating approach can be summarised as follows.[8]

Prior to the twentieth century, theology and philosophy started from the enlightened subject/object dichotomy. Knowledge was an interaction between an autonomous subject and a *vorliegend* object (*ob-jectum*). In the twentieth century, Edmund Husserl was one of the most authoritative philosophers to contest this centuries-old conviction. He stated that *Voraussetzungslosigkeit* was impossible. Knowledge without prejudice does not exist; it is participation from within. *Connaître* is *co-naître*. One is always already implied. Read with Husserl is his French colleague Gabriel Marcel, who distinguished a 'problem' from a 'mystery', noting that the former is containable and objectifiable. As such, a problem is placed before the subject for analysis and ultimate resolution. In the final analysis, the object is solved, and disappears. A mystery, however, is not objectifiable and it does not disappear. Persons are a part of it as it embraces and encompasses a subject. Thus, persons cannot solve a mystery without being solved, cannot grasp anything without being grasped. Understanding or awareness does not come from without; it comes from within. With the words of the German philosopher Martin Heidegger, the passage is made from distant calculating thinking to implied commemorative thinking, not once and for all, but again and again.

The implications are ripe for a harvest in theology. Recall the words of Jesus himself: "Do this in memory of me." To commemorate means to remember and memorialise God always already commemorating the human community. At each moment of human life, God's creative memory sanctifies. He transforms personal as well as communal history in a memorial that is a living testimony to Him. To commemorate is to present. With this evolution in twentieth century thought, the former '*claire et*

---

8. Cf. L.-M. CHAUVET, *Symbol and Sacrament. A Sacramental Reinterpretation of Christian Existence* (Collegeville: The Liturgical Press, 1995); French original: *Symbole et sacrement. Une relecture sacramentelle de l'existence chrétienne* (Paris: Cerf, 1987).

distincte' separation between subject and object has been overcome, *causa* and *signum* as separable entities is undermined.

Because of this, the onto-theological character of sacramentology is abandoned. Onto-theology reduces *Sein* to *Seiendes*, Being to Entity. *Ho Theos* is reduced to *To Theon*, and God is grasped merely as the 'understandable' Supreme Being, the Unmoved Mover, the Ultimate Reason or the rootless Root. A more respectful and engaging approach can replace this narrow – even overly productionistic – one. It is an approach permeated by the otherness of God so that an encounter with a different God results.[9] So not to mislead, this shift is not necessarily facilitating a pleasant encounter. In fact, it can be somewhat disconcerting as the images of a sympathetic or suffering God illustrate. Still, for the shift to occur, conversion is imperative. The turn must be made from the God of the philosophers to the God of Abraham, Isaac and Jacob, from a disinterested God to the God of the Covenant, the *sym-bolon*, the encounter and the relationship. Not surprisingly and in the company of Blaise Pascal, the shift brings us much closer to the covenant dimension of the ancient *mysterion*.

There is a third move in sacramentology. In the symbolic field the relationship between the signifier and the signified is characterised by a play between presence and absence, appearing and disappearing. A visible *signifiant* renders 'present' an invisible *signifié*. Conversely, the hidden significance is necessarily deciphered in and through the appearing signifier. Thus, the Word is deciphered in the Scriptures and he economy of salvation must be deciphered in the mixed human economy that is a mingling of good and bad, salvation and doom. Such interplays highlight symbol as 'already' and 'not yet.' 'Already,' the Word is revealed in the Scriptures. And, the scriptures draw us into an ongoing encounter with the Word for the eschaton is 'not yet.' This is the tension between inchoative and eschatological fulfilment. Accordingly, one day, God will be all things in everybody (1 Cor 15,28; Col 3,11). The Spirit of Jesus Christ will have permeated everything and all will be transparent or iconic. At the same time, the permeation by the Spirit does not take away the essence of persons or things. On the contrary, the more people are permeated by the Spirit, the more they become transparent and thereby themselves. François-Xavier Durrwell applies this permeation by the Spirit to the Eucharist, trying to re-think onto-theological interpretations of transubstantiation.[10] In the Eucharistic celebration the Spirit permeates bread and wine bringing them to their fulfilment, their eschatological

---

9. Cf. K. DEPOORTERE, *A Different God. A Christian View on Suffering* (Leuven/Chicago: Peeters/Eerdmans, 1995).

10. F.-X. DURRWELL, *L'eucharistie, présence du Christ* (Paris: Éditions Ouvrières, 1971). A remarkable booklet!

fullness. The heart of bread and wine is realised. Bread and wine as the Body and Blood of Christ reach their full significance. Not to encourage neologisms, but permeated bread organically becomes 'bread-er' and 'bread-est,' wine becomes 'wine-er' and 'wine-est.' Both are so that humans become 'human-er' and 'human-est,' the Church, then, 'Church-er' and 'Church-est.'

Such a view on the *epiclesis*, the permeation of the Spirit, means a radical anthropological re-evaluation of the entirety of Christian existence. The most spiritual takes place in the most corporeal; the theological is unveiled in the anthropological. As Chauvet puts it, "The anthropological is the place of every possible theological."[11] Sacramentality becomes again characteristic of Christian existence as such, and not merely through a series of structuring rituals.

3.2. Connected to the three-pronged shift in sacramentology comes an erupting ecclesiological turn concerning the whole of Christian identity

For all too long Christian identity and the practice of faith was gauged by mass attendance. Even today, this is the case as the stacks of statistical reports indicate. Christian identity, however, is far richer as put forward in the age-old triadic schema of believing (kerugma), celebrating (leitourgia), and loving (ethics - diakonia).

According to Vatican II, liturgy – more specifically the Eucharist – is the source and summit of Christian life. In reference to this, Chauvet uses the image of a keystone in the vault of a ceiling to emphasize that liturgy as source and summit is never distanced from the other aspects of Christian identity. Liturgy, as a keystone, keeps the arches of a ceiling vault together and is equally dependent on these arches: without the pressure of the arches the keystone collapses. Thus, there is a necessary interdependency between the arches of belief and ethics in relation to their keystone, the liturgy. Moreover, they protect each other against sliding into the extremities of literalism, fundamentalism and sectarian fanaticism.

Through this rediscovery of the fullness of Christian identity, liturgy and the expanses of life are bound together and with far reaching implications.

Secondly, belief, celebration and ethics in their inter-connectedness form a triangle of meaning. However, this triangle, if it is Christian, must be encompassed by a circle representing the community of the faithful. To be clear, this is not to suggest that the Church is the place where

---

11. L.-M. CHAUVET, "L'avenir du sacramentel," in *Recherches de science religieuse* 75 (1987) 241-266, p. 245; *Symbol and Sacrament*, p. 152; *Les sacrements. Parole de Dieu au risque du corps* (Paris: Éditions Ouvrières, 1993) 81.

Christian identification 'happens' randomly. The Church always already mediates persons becoming Christian. While there is salvation outside the Church for people who are not Christian, there is no other way for Christians: the Church-community functions as a mediator.

On a last ecclesiological point, greater dimensionality must be given to this encircled triangle of meaning. So not to flatten Christian identity into a static form, it must be appreciated organically. By way of encompassment, then, what is a circle is in fact a spiral. Christian identity is a progressing or propelling identification in belief, worship and ethics mediated by the Christian community. It varies from person to person, from one culture to another, even period to period. Pax Christi and Taizé are equally important and valuable points of entry into the spiralic triangle of meaning and identity. Furthermore, some Christians will develop their 'diakonal-pole' more than the 'creedal-pole'; others will do the exact opposite. What results is not an impoverishment, but a creative and organic tension that is a journey of diversity in unity. The first Christians understood this pathway of identity and called themselves, "men and women belonging to the Way"(Acts 9,2). Appreciating that Christians today belong to the same 'Way' means that identity is always already unfolding. In this vein, there are numerous persons who do not attend weekly mass, but choose to be identified as Christian.[12] In their view, Christian identity is not exclusively defined by the praxis of the sacraments. Sacramentality in its ebb and flow seems to be larger than sacramental praxis.

3.3. Having touched shifts in sacramentology and ecclesiology, a third shift is taking place in applied ministerial theology with immediate implications for a praxis of sacramentality

Today in the Roman Catholic Church, ministry is in the plural, whether accepted or not. The gulf between ordained and lay ministries is lessening, at least in practice and a fusion is taking place. As a result, pastoral work by lay people is no longer reducible to a preparation for the reception of sacraments at best or of no consequence to them at worst. By way of example, laity who minister to and accompany the sick and dying are essential to the experience of healing. They are "strengthening the brothers and sisters in faith," (Luke 22,32) which is based on the baptismal priesthood. Such ministerial activity, on their part, can be called rightly a liturgy of the Word for the sacrament of the sick. That means, integral to it. Ministry can no longer be qualified as the work of ordained persons. In fact, ordained ministry is at the service of the baptismal priesthood. The very first task of the ordained minister is to edify the faithful through the

---

12. J. KERKHOFS, *Dieu en Europe (Pro Mundi Vita. Dossiers Europe- Amérique du Nord 2.37)* (Brussels, 1987).

Word in order that all become aware of their pastoral vocation (*Presbyterorum ordinis* 4).

These ministerial reflections are a further evolution of what Vatican II promulgated on the People of God as subject of liturgy. With reference to *Sacrosanctum Concilium* n 26, the *Catechism of the Catholic Church* affirms: "It is the whole community, the Body of Christ united with its Head, that celebrates" (n 1140) and: "In the celebration of the sacraments it is thus the whole assembly that is *leitourgos*, each according to his function, but in 'unity of the Spirit' who acts in all." (n 1144)

4. There are still further implications to the aforementioned shifts. By bringing these together, an enhanced concept of sacramentality results

In the first place, a (re-) valorisation of *sacramentalia* as humus or a potting soil is essential. As soil, here is where a process of sacramentalization germinates and develops. Therefore, *sacramentalia* should not be considered distinct preparations for sacraments.

Secondly, such a revaluation of sacramentals breaks up the monopoly of ordained ministers as 'administers' of the sacraments. Justice is done to the baptismal priesthood and a broader concept of ministry flourishes, fully respecting the contribution of every Christian as a 'presentification' of God. The sacramentality of ministry in its diverse expressions comes on the scene.

Next, a plea in favour of broadening the appreciation of sacramentals includes a valorisation of the sacrament as dynamic. There are three conditions for such an experience of dynamic sacramental density. First, God must be named more readily. Secondly, a person must symbolise his/her faith more explicitly. Thirdly, this necessarily involves a community. The *Rite of Christian Initiation for Adults* is a precious guide. The sacramental process begins with a period of inquiry, followed by a free choice to enter the Order of Catechumens from where the elect who choose initiation come. These then follow the way to the summit of full sacramental initiation in Baptism, Confirmation and Eucharist; a summit which is at the same time the beginning of a further sacramentalization of Christian existence. In this manner sacraments cease to be punctual events. Instead of rituals which separate a before from an after, sacraments are ongoing processes in the bosom of a broadening sacramentality.

At the end of this continuum of sacramentality appear the sacraments *sensu stricto*. Here, sacramental rituals are like seals put at the end of the all-encompassing *mysterion* charter. Sacraments as seals have three dimensions. They authenticate, perfect (*per-ficere*) and send forth.

In the first place, sacramental seals authenticate the previous practice of faith. In the anointing of the sick, for example, all action done by doctors, nurses, relatives and friends is acknowledged as authenticating. God is working incognito where persons dwell together in charity. Even the most seemingly insignificant gesture has an undeniably eternal value. This acknowledgement is, yes, an official guarantee given by the minister as a representative of the community of the faithful and speaking *in persona Christi*. The hidden significance of the multi-faceted care for the sick is revealed and sealed. Thus, illuminated is the revelatory dimension of the sacraments.

In the second place, every sacramental seal includes a public and official *epiclesis*, a calling upon the Spirit, a performative word that effects what it affirms. The Spirit of Christ completes, perfects, and brings all things to fullness by abiding in the human reality. As explained already, the abiding of the Spirit does not destroy the human; no, it expands and enhances the human ever closer to fullest humanity. As fulfilling, human gestures are progressively transformed into icons of grace. Human history becomes the history of salvation through the performative word of a minister inviting the Spirit to transform the human till God will be all things in everyone. This movement is expressed well in a word play in Dutch. 'Voltooien' means to complete, and 'tot volle tooi brengen' means to bring to full decoration, ornamentation or adornment. As alluded to by the play on words, sacraments are operative and effective.

Seals put at the end of a charter authenticate, perfect, and thirdly, send forth. Every sacramental seal entails a mission. The explicit encounter with God is missionary. The experience of grace in the broadened appreciation of sacraments is an imperative to 'go'. Sacramental anointing calls a person to 'go' and be an anointing and not just to others that are sick, but to care givers such as doctors, nurses, relatives or friends. Through mission, sacraments demonstrate a symbolic function. More sectors of life are integrated and humans are bound together a new. Sacraments are symbolic seals on the way to a further sacramentalization of Christian existence.

5. There are concrete ramifications to what has been said thus far. If liturgical and sacramental celebrations are spread over a broader trajectory an overall sacramentality will burst forth

Take baptism… from the first liturgical prayer offered during pregnancy to entering the live-giving waters, from calling upon God at the birth of a son or daughter to clothing the child in white, these actions and gestures mission us towards the sacramentalization of life.

Take the Anointing of the Sick... From caring for the sick with implicit religious motives, to a first 'Our Father' prayed together, from the sick person who is skiddish about anointing to wanting all her care givers present at the anointing, all that was prior to the seal is essential. This liturgy of care givers intensifies the sacramental experience. All involved were presentifications shaping a Word liturgy that climaxes in the reception of the oil for the sick.[13]

Reconciliation is also a process of sacramentalization. God is already sacramentally at work from the psychological process of renouncing vengeance to accepting the ramifications of one's action, from a prayer for forgiveness to forging new behaviour. By harnessing all these dimensions together, a greater appreciation of conversion and penance will emerge, affording a deepening self-awareness and development. In turn, the sacramental celebration will be placed on the continuum of life, not as a disruption in the midst of the expansive everyday.

Regarding marriage,[14] the instantaneous character of the sacramental celebration could be broadened. Marriage is ongoing, from a first encounter to the announcement that the couple is engaged into the very day when intentions are stated and consent is exchanged. Authenticating the whole of the relationship as marital liturgy could equally give greater impetus to mission, to 'go' and become more and more an icon of God's creative love in each other, in the midst of a community, and for the world. There are also the sticky points, such as cohabitation before marriage or without a desire to marry. Is every living together outside of marriage indistinctively a 'state of sin'? Or, by applying categories from Paul Ricoeur, should there be an acknowledgement of the attainable optimum (*l'optimum réalisable*) in given circumstances, without compromising the Christian maximum (*l'absolu souhaitable*)?[15] The denial of any sacramentality to this achievable optimum needs to be reconsidered. And, positively speaking, can some sacramentality be attributed to a second relationship when one is the victim of abandonment in a previous marriage? These complexities surrounding marriage require further exploration.

---

13. K. DEPOORTERE, "Recent Developments in the Anointing of the Sick," in *Concilium* 278 (1998/5) 89-100.

14. J. C. K. GOH, "Christian Marriage as a Realsymbol: Towards a Performative Understanding of the Sacrament," in *Questions Liturgiques - Studies in Liturgy* 76 (1995) 254-264; H. DENIS (ed.), *Le mariage, un sacrement pour les croyants?* (Paris: Cerf, 1990) 174-207.

15. P. RICŒUR, "Sens et fonction d'une communauté ecclésiale," in *Cahiers du Centre Protestant de Recherche et de Rencontres du Nord* 26 (1968) 15-37, p. 26.

Conclusion

Remember the parish priest who baptised all the children, from Christine to the nameless one. I guess, after all, that I do want to reflect for a moment on his pastoral choice to baptise all those babies. From a broadened sacramentality of life, I would not have refused categorically baptism to any of the children, remembering the *mè-koluein*-argument from theology classes at the seminary. I would have tried to baptise each of them - while journeying with their parents - step by step, slowly progressing in a combined movement of human respect, friendship and insertion in a small community. This movement would also include talks, catechesis, symbols and unedited rituals, which I would call sacramental. The hope is to bring all of them, at their own rhythms of life, to the fullness of the sacramental sealing.

    Heilige Geestcollege   Kristiaan DEPOORTERE
    Naamsestraat 40
    B-3000 Leuven

LOUIS-MARIE CHAUVET'S THEOLOGY OF SACRAMENT AND ECUMENICAL THEOLOGY:

CONNECTIONS IN TERMS OF AN ECUMENICAL HERMENEUTICS OF UNITY BASED ON A KOINONIA ECCLESIOLOGY

Introduction

This paper entertains possible connections between Louis-Marie Chauvet's theology of sacrament, as this unfolds in *Symbol and Sacrament: A Sacramental Reinterpretation of Christian Existence*,[1] and ecumenical theology. My discussion is framed within the context of a koinonia ecclesiology and the recent developments in ecumenical hermeneutics. Like any discussion of ecclesiology, research which examines the concept of '*koinonia*'[2] as expressive of understanding the church and its unity naturally touches upon sacramentology. In recent years, in fact, the relationship of church and sacraments draws renewed ecumenical attention. This is due to multilateral study on sacraments and ministry, on the relationship of church and world, and on the emergence of a renewed hermeneutics of unity.[3] Each of these is founded upon an understanding of the

---

1. Louis-Marie Chauvet, *Symbol and Sacrament: A Sacramental Reinterpretation of Christian Existence* (Collegeville, MN: A Pueblo Book/Liturgical Press, 1995) is the English translation of the French Original: *Symbole et Sacrement: Une relecture de l'existence chrétienne* (Paris: Éditions du Cerf, 1987). This paper refers to the English translation, hereafter cited as Chauvet, *Symbol and Sacrament*. Citations from the book will be selective.

2. This biblical term is multivalent. In ecumenical theology it is most commonly translated as "communion" and "fellowship" and, to a lesser extent, as "community" and "participation." To render its richness, it is frequently used in transliterated form, "koinonia."

3. Ecumenical methodology is essentially that of dialogue, which takes place in bilateral and multilateral settings. At the Fifth World Conference on Faith and Order in 1993, added to this fundamental dialogical method was the notion of ecumenical contextual theology. Taking place in a definite ecumenical context, dialogue is both deductive and inductive. It draws on the wider ecumenical context for the narrow focus of topic-specific discussion; and it draws from that specificity for a more general reception. See Thomas F. Best and Günther Gaßmann (eds.), *On the Way to Fuller Koinonia: Santiago de Compostela 1993: Official Report of the Fifth World Conference on Faith and Order* (Faith and Order Paper, 166; Geneva: World Council of Churches, 1994). This report is one of various texts which account for the parallel that follows. Ecumenical hermeneutics is

church as communion, an essential component of which is sharing sacramental life.[4] Ecumenical convergence on sacraments is grounded upon the metaphysical, foundational language, concepts and principles of the classical theology of mainline churches. In the postmodern context, this has been called into question.

Noting the ecumenical impasse, that convergence on sacraments has yet to bring the churches to their common celebration, this paper proposes that Chauvet's project invites widening ecumenical language, not only to poise the inter-ecclesial middle but also to transcend confessional extremes. This I interpret as a sort of overarching *coincidentia oppositorum* of the givenness and the creativity of sacrament which seems to characterise Chauvet's thinking. Perhaps this notion might serve as a hermeneutical tool in the reconfiguration of an ecumenical understanding that will advance a convergence which fosters consensus.

My presentation is structured in two main parts. Part I highlights pertinent features of Chauvet's thinking. Part II entertains possible implications of Chauvet's proposal for ecumenism. A few personal remarks form a conclusion.

1. Features of Chauvet's Thinking

An attracting feature of Louis-Marie Chauvet's thinking is his interdisciplinary approach. As he attempts a linguistic defeat of the onto-theological structure of sacraments, based on the foundations of metaphysics, Chauvet employs diverse fields – philosophy, anthropology, linguistics, psychoanalysis, exegesis, ethics, liturgical history, christology, ecclesiology – to present his thesis. Each is a tool used in his retrieval of symbolisation, by which sacraments may be seen as mediations in language. The argument in *Symbol and Sacrament* is divided into four parts, which may be paraphrased as follows: 1) making the shift from metaphysics to symbolisation; 2) proposing the sacramental within the symbolic network of ecclesial faith; 3) positing sacraments as ecclesial, symbolising acts of Christian identity; and 4) viewing sacramental discourse in terms of trinitarian christology. Evident throughout is the author's penchant for cultural and pastoral considerations. Coupled with his wide referential, this makes for an appealing style which draws a broad audience

---

essentially that of unity. In the post-Santiago ecumenical context, this has been described in terms of understanding the church as koinonia. See Commission on Faith & Order, *Faith and Order in Moshi: The 1996 Commission Meeting* (Faith and Order Paper, 177; Geneva: World Council of Churches, 1998); hereafter cited as *Moshi*.

4. The other three components are common confession of the apostolic faith, recognised and reconciled ministry and common witness in the service of church and world.

– so much so that a reader is impelled to consider looking at anything via his methodology.

Part One of *Symbol and Sacrament* presents Chauvet's critique of metaphysics and its use of causality in discourse on the sacraments. With his ultimate focus on sacraments as mediations of grace within a symbolic order, Chauvet relies on the philosophy of Martin Heidegger to plea for a departure from the classical notion of causality. In short, his thesis states that causality cheapens the personal graciousness of God and the gratuitous nature of his grace mediated in the celebration of the sacraments. Causality makes language instrumental and productionist.[5] This results in an objectification of grace, which devalues the relationality of God and human in sacraments, and in a manipulation of language, which fixes on right thinking at the expense of symbolic thinking regarding the presence of God to the church in Christ via the Spirit. In its place, Chauvet aims to retrieve the symbolic.[6] He proposes a rethinking of language and ritual by which the church is understood as a community of grace and interpretation.[7] Such rethinking calls the ecclesial community to see itself as inheritors, not merely users, of a language system which serves its symbolic order. At the heart of Chauvet's thought here is the language of the cross,[8] the expression *par excellence* of divine self-giving. As the argument unfolds in the subsequent sections of the book, gift and divine self-giving[9] emerges as central to Chauvet's symbolic scheme explaining sacraments.

Having so grounded his thesis philosophically, our author attends to ecclesiology and foundations of the sacramental in Part Two. Given their scriptural warrant, sacraments are situated within the church, which is the structural identity of Christianity and the symbolic order that gives the sacramental system its coherence.[10] Christian identity is given a tripartite structure of scripture, sacrament and ethics.[11] The structure has a trinitarian foundation, and each of its components has a corollary character which describes its function. The threefold elements may be delineated as follows:

---

5. Chauvet, *Symbol and Sacrament*, 7.
6. See Chauvet, *Symbol and Sacrament*, 84-155 for the author's foundational reference to this notion and how it will be developed throughout the book.
7. Chauvet, *Symbol and Sacrament*, 185-187.
8. *Ibid.*, 69.
9. The initial discussion of gift in terms of symbolic exchange is in Chauvet, *Symbol and Sacrament*, 99-109. Sacrament as gift is then developed on pages 459-548. The climax of the divine self-giving is discussed in terms of God's effacement on pages 490-509.
10. See Chauvet, *Symbol and Sacrament*,159-60.
11. See the diagrams on pages 172 and 278 and their accompanying narratives in Chauvet, *Symbol and Sacrament*.

Scripture	sacrament	ethics
gift	reception	return-gift
recognition	cognition	praxis
sign:	symbol:	practice:
conceiving a world	celebrating a world	acting in a world

Sacrament is the point of passage from the gift/grace received in the scriptural word to the gift/grace accepted in ethical *agape*.[12] Scripture is the written language describing the originating event which establishes meaning in the symbolic order.[13] Ethics is the agapeic mission which verifies the event taking place in sacramental celebration.[14] Among the three, a dynamic of past, present and future fosters the renewal essential for the continual becoming of the church to take place.

The Third Part of *Symbol and Sacrament* is a reflection upon the sacraments in terms of rituality and institution. Ritual is understood as symbolic and practical. As such, ritual/rite is the mode by which sacraments are expressed.[15] Institution is understood as human and dynamic, not juridical. As such, sacraments are both instituted and instituting mediations.[16] Chauvet presents various dialectics throughout this discussion. He addresses the tensions between the old and the new, with the attempt of the Second Vatican Council to surmount the impasse[17] of objectivity (i.e., sacraments viewed as channels of grace, instruments of healing, remedies for sin) and subjectivity (i.e., sacraments viewed as human acts, downplaying their mediatory role and the otherness and transcendence of God). Also examined is the author's play between the presence/absence of Christ in the eucharist[18] and his notion of the always/already in sacramental celebration.[19] Regarding efficacy and grace, the causal *ex opere operato,* which sees sacraments as instruments which render grace, is juxtaposed with performative relationality, which sees sacraments as events which live in grace.[20] Throughout, an overarching *coincidentia oppositorum* seems to be the givenness of sacraments on one side and their creativity on the other.

---

12. Chauvet, *Symbol and Sacrament*, 281-282.
13. *Ibid.*, 213-216.
14. *Ibid.*, 277-279.
15. *Ibid.*, 324, 319.
16. See the opening pages of Chapter Ten, 377-382, and Chapter Eleven, 409-413, in Chauvet, *Symbol and Sacrament*.
17. For the discussion of the impasse and the Middle Way of Vatican II, see Chauvet, *Symbol and Sacrament*, 410-424.
18. Chauvet, *Symbol and Sacrament*, 404-408.
19. *Ibid.*, 379, 423.
20. *Ibid.*, 410; see also Part Four, 531-538.

In Part Four Chauvet draws the connection between his sacramental theology and his trinitarian christology. The section builds on the ecclesiological foundation of sacraments constructed earlier in the book and forms a mélange of philosophical, anthropological and theological language now readily associated with the author. Chauvet's attention here is fixed on the paschal Christ, the crucified-resurrected, whose memorial is celebrated in sacrament. Stressed is the trinitarian dimension of gift. God is given a body in the incarnation of the Word, Jesus, by the power of the Spirit. As the "surplus value of the death and resurrection of Christ,"[21] the church celebrates sacraments as symbolic figures of the self-giving, the self-effacement, of God. This takes place in creation, in the body of person, church and history, and it tends towards redemption, "...for us and for our salvation...," as the Roman rite proclaims. The liturgical act is thus always and already the Pasch of Christ, the Pentecost of the Spirit and the eschatological fulfillment of the Father. Ritual manifests and actualises the divine presence/absence as Other, as the revelation of the invisible God in the visible symbolic mediation. By otherness God makes possible communication. As Other, the Holy One draws near; by withdrawal God comes close. Hence, here too a sense of sacrament as mediations reflecting a *coincidentia oppositorum* is apparent.

Given his holistic approach, Chauvet offers both a critique and a synthesis. It is a proposal of new thinking by critique of the old which offers a synthesis of both old and new in light of current trends in liturgical theory and practise. In a sense, his study bridges classical metaphysical thinking and contemporary contextual thinking, leaving the argument open ended for reception in diverse theological disciplines and pastoral settings.

2. Implications of Chauvet's Proposal for Ecumenism

In broad strokes, then, the following sketches the possible import of Chauvet's thinking on ecumenical theology as the churches converge upon an ecclesiology of communion. I begin by making connections of Chauvet and a general ecumenical portraiture of sacraments. I end with a more narrow tracing of "communion" in *Symbol and Sacrament* as this connects with heightened ecumenical interest in the links between sacrament and ethics in a koinonia ecclesiology.

Louis-Marie Chauvet's defeat of onto-theological structures of sacraments is a welcomed challenge as the ecumenical enterprise confronts the

---

21. Taken from personal notes, this is an expression of Georges De Schrijver, used during a lecture on "Fundamental Theological Reflection: Discussion of Chauvet Part IV" given at the Katholieke Universiteit Leuven, Belgium, 02 March 1999.

question. Welcomed, because, appreciably, Chauvet focuses on the two dominical sacraments, baptism and eucharist, from the perspective of the giftedness of God's grace. Ecumenical consideration of Christian sacraments limits itself to baptism and eucharist, which are viewed as gift and call of God's promise. Thus, Chauvet's method and hermeneutics have the potential of meeting a certain openness from ecumenical partners of the Roman Catholic Church. Challenge, because his philosophical matrix for sacramentology is likely to encounter considerable resistance from a more rooted ecumenical tradition. His linguistic defeat of the classical thinking underlying Christian sacramentology overturns ecumenical discourse and convergence on sacraments, whose articulation thus far relies on classical Protestant and Roman Catholic theological and philosophical language. The gamuts within and between the two traditions are quite wide. This breadth is complicated by the fact that, on both sides, denominational extremes tend to linger longer in sacramental/liturgical expression than in other theological disciplines approached ecumenically. Catholic extremes range from possessing a Baroque flair of rich symbolism to augmenting a medieval mode of instrumental thinking; Protestant extremes from preserving an apostolic spirit of pristine *leitourgia* to stripping *Gottesdienst* of its symbolic competence. Thus, if taking seriously, Chauvet's handling of metaphysics to surpass its limitation might be the hermeneutical tool by which ecumenical language broadens, not only to poise the inter-ecclesial middle of least common denominator interchurch agreement, but also to transcend confessional extremes of denominational retrenchment. In a hermeneutics of unity based on the koinonia concept, being church means that Christianity remains confessional as it becomes ecumenical. Because sacramental unity is at the heart of this koinonia, the churches must get beyond the *cul-de-sac* that baptismal unity has yet realised one eucharistic fellowship. Perhaps Chauvet's *coincidentia oppositorum* of the instrumental and the symbolic has the capacity to help us beyond the present impasse.

The issue has already drawn the attention of those engaged in ecumenism. Dutch Reformed theologian, Martien Brinkman, refers to the much needed balance in ecumenical dialogue between the Protestant and Catholic to offset denominational differences. Brinkman recognises Chauvet among those who provide "a balance between the causative and significative function of the sacraments":[22]

> Such a balance is found by authors like Otto Hermann Pesch, Edward Schillebeeckx, Karl Rahner and Louis-Marie Chauvet in their emphasis on the interwovenness of the two, often denominationally separated axioms of

---

22. Martien Brinkman, "Towards a Common Understanding of the Sacraments," *Louvain Studies* 23 (1998) 43; hereafter cited as Brinkman, "Sacraments."

the classic doctrine of the sacraments, namely, the axiom that the sacraments not only instrumentally effect what they signify (*efficiunt quod figurant*) – the main Roman Catholic approach – but that they also signify what they effect (*figurant quod efficiunt*) – the main Protestant approach.[23]

The balance called for here might enable ecumenical dialogue on sacraments to deal more creatively with its inevitable dual focus, namely, that discussion of sacraments necessitates discussion of ministry. The focus becomes blurred by seemingly opposing perspectives. High liturgical churches, i.e., the Roman Catholic and the Orthodox churches, stress the role of the minister as *in persona Christi*, while non-liturgical churches, i.e., churches of the Classical and Radical Reformation, emphasis the role as *in nomine ecclesiae*. Tensions mount, of course, when the ministry question concentrates on presidency at the eucharistic liturgy. It seems that, by employing Chauvet's language of mediation and network for the sacraments and the symbolic order in which they are situated, this 'either/or' tension might be poised to a par of 'both-and'.[24] The liturgy, he says, "is within a... language whose unity seems assured, ...[establishing] a new relation of place between the community and God."[25] A "communion [of the members] is at work in the act of ritual language."[26] The priest "acts as the bearer of the 'symbolic capital' of the ecclesial assembly."[27] Might this be the resolve of the *coincidentia oppositorum* concerning the 'church' and 'who' does 'what' in its 'name' during worship?

Likewise, studies also indicate an ecumenical proclivity for a shift from instrumental to symbolic thinking and for a more acceptable meta-language in which the churches might together articulate common thinking.[28] This is most notable in the multilateral work done on baptism, eucharist and ministry[29] and an ongoing process this initiated. Asking churches to recognise in each other the "faith of the church throughout

---

23. Brinkman, "Sacraments," 43.
24. See Chauvet, *Symbol and Sacrament*, 471-4.
25. *Ibid.*, 429.
26. *Ibid.*, 429.
27. *Ibid.*, 429.
28. The French ecumenist George H. Tavard calls for an ecumenical meta-language in "The Bilateral Dialogues: Searching for Language," *One in Christ* 16:1/2 (1980) 19-30. When read in light of Chauvet's overturning of foundational language, Tavard's proposal deserves further attention as the concern for a new ecumenical methodology nd hermeneutics grows.
29. This study culminated in the document, *Baptism, Eucharist and Ministry* (Faith and Order Paper, 111; Commission on Faith and Order, Geneva: World Council of Churches, 1982), which received various process reports, including a six-volume set of responses from particular churches and confessions. Hereafter, this document is cited as *BEM* and its study as BEM.

the ages,"[30] the study's document, *Baptism, Eucharist and Ministry*, sought to retrieve and employ language of scripture and tradition which was neither polemical nor denominational.[31] This opened new perspectives for multilateral reflection on ecclesiology, at the heart of which is understanding the church as koinonia. In this context, confessionality is viewed in terms of a hermeneutics of unity which raises "the possibility of complementarity" among different, but not divided, confessions and denominational contexts.[32] As "interpretive community,"[33] each confession claims its proper place in the koinonia. So perceived, each is viewed in terms of the 'gift' it offers to the fellowship and not by what it must 'give up' in order to participate in the fellowship. Operative here is a feature of the method initiated in BEM:

> ...those who interpret the Christian tradition differently should attempt to understand each other on the presumption that each has a "right intention of faith."[34]

Does this not sound like Chauvet language?

Future study in this area would be well served by the ecclesial grounding Chauvet gives to Christian faith and sacraments and to his crafting of language and ritual which perceive the church as a community of grace and interpretation. Chauvet speaks of the ecclesial community as inheritor of a language system at the service of its symbolic order, whose meaning is given and received in the language of the cross.[35] Ecumenical discourse refers to the koinonia as "partakers of the promise,"[36] whose covenant with God is sealed in the cross of Jesus. What the ecumenical can appropriate from Chauvet here is the place given to the pneumatological and the eschatological dimensions, which Orthodox and Pentecostals sense are too often understated by their western and mainline partners. Our author quotes Hans Urs von Balthasar's conviction that "It is only as the action of the Trinitarian God that the scandal of the cross can be endured by the believer."[37] The only way the christological di-

---

30. See *BEM*, x. Grounding this phrase is the compatibility of the faith as received from the apostles with its ongoing contextual expression in different times and places.

31. See the preface of *BEM*, vii-x, especially ix-x.

32. "Towards a Hermeneutics for a Growing Koinonia" I 24 in *Moshi*, 270.

33. "Towards a Hermeneutics for a Growing Koinonia" I 18 in *Moshi*, 269.

33. "Towards a Hermeneutics for a Growing Koinonia" I 24 in *Moshi*, 270, quoting *BEM* M52.

35. Chauvet, *Symbol and Sacrament*, 69.

36. One source in which this ecumenical expression relates closely to issues of worship is *Partakers of the Promise; Biblical Visions of Koinonia*, ed. Thomas F. Best (Geneva: United Bible Societies, 1993).

37. Chauvet, *Symbol and Sacrament*, 532, quoting Balthasar's "Le mystère pascal," *Mysterium salutis*, volume 12 (Paris: Cerf, 1972) 133, and *Pâques: Le mystère* (Paris: Cerf, 1981) 133.

mension is theologically acceptable, says Chauvet, is if "balanced by a second, pneumatological dimension."[38] Preserving the difference in the trinity, he says, makes possible "the communion" among the Father, the Son and the Spirit, as it also "makes possible God's communication with humankind."[39]

While these rather general points impact the question of a koinonia ecclesiology, the more specific references to the concept of communion in Chauvet[40] bear even more upon the topic of current ecumenical concern of linking ecclesiology with ethics. I focus on two points: a parallel of Chauvet's sacramental proposal in koinonia studies and the idea of relationship in Chauvet and in koinonia ecclesiology. The two are not unrelated in either Chauvet or ecumenical theology.

First, the parallel. Perhaps the most explicit illustration relating Chauvet's thinking to the ecumenical ecclesiology of koinonia is his tripartite structure of scripture, sacrament and ethics.[41] A parallel may be drawn by ecumenical reference to 'faith, life and witness', the three components for the realisation of full koinonia.[42] The ecumenical structure may be delineated as follows:

---

38. Chauvet, *Symbol and Sacrament*, 509.
39. *Ibid.*, 513.
40. Although no *koinon*-term *per se* appears in the index of Chauvet, *Symbol and Sacrament*, the terms "koinonia" and "communion" appear *passim* throughout the book. Cited here are selected pages with references which hold ecumenical interest:

165, koinonia as community in Acts 2:42-47; 4:32-35: the sharing of material goods as an expression of koinonia; reference is ethical;

166, koinonia as sign of the realisation of the messianic community in Acts 2:45; 4:35; reference is eschatological;

170, communion and diakonia: ethical witness of the communion between brothers and sisters lived as the expression of Christ's service for humankind; reference is christological >ecclesiological;

170, Lk 24:1-35: the renewed communion of the post-Easter disciples; reference is ecclesiological;

256, koinonia as community in Heb 13:15-16: charity, sharing, sacrifices; reference is liturgical/cultic;

381, mediations of the church's communion with God; reference is sacramental, grace;

409, essence of the church us its communion with the Father through Christ in the Spirit; reference is sacramental, ecclesiological, trinitarian;

438, believer's communion with Christ in his death and resurrection; reference is baptismal unity.

513, communion of Father, the Son and the Spirit makes possible God's communication with humankind.

41. See above, 3.
42. The sources which discuss this idea are many. Already cited, *Santiago* is one document which details the notion of "koinonia in faith, life and witness" in detail.

gospel   *faith* received in the word
gift   ecclesial *life* celebrated in sacraments (baptism and eucharist)
call   *witness* in justice, peace and creation

One wonders whether liturgical theology is informing ecumenical here or vice versa. Or, better still, is this mutual informing, a hoped-for result of ecumenical dialogue. For example, Chauvet's sacramental theology gives a primary role to scripture, as does ecumenical ecclesiology, as it grounds its understanding of the church in the biblical notion of koinonia. Likewise, ethics shares a certain priority in both schemas. For Chauvet, it is the return of gift; for ecumenism, it is response to call. Ecumenists will be attracted to this connection for many reasons. A fundamental one is that the two topics, scripture and morals, often emerge as ecumenical 'neuralgic points'. In other words, the ecumenical jury is still out on the relationship of scripture and tradition, and evidence of baptismal-eucharistic ethics remains ecumenically circumstantial. Furthermore, from their scriptural warrant, in theory, sacrament, especially eucharist, is the locus of unity. In practise, sacraments are the focus of disunity. Hence, such an interplay frees the denominational edge off both scripture and morals, and it opens the sacramental question beyond concerns for the unity of the church to matters touching upon the renewal of the whole of humanity. After all, the heart of the matter is not the liturgy alone, but the "liturgy after the liturgy."

Second, relation. At the core of Chauvet's proposition is the understanding of sacraments as symbolic media of relationship. The heart of a koinonia is its relationality, which embraces many dimensions: trinitarian, directional/ecclesial (vertical: God with human; and horizontal: human with human), sacramental, soteriological/ eschatological. Central to both perceptions is the idea that in relationship one discovers not only the other but also oneself. Sacrament is conduit for this relationality, as is church. Due to the theological nexus of church and sacrament in the ecclesiology of communion, this idea has resulted in new ecumenical approaches to the relationship of the two. That is, questions are now raised whether the ecumenical focus ought to fix on the ecclesiological consequences of sacramentology or on the sacramental consequences of ecclesiology. Such a question leads to another: in what way do the sacraments make the church, and in what way does the church make the sacraments. While it is beyond our scope here to answer the question, I venture to say that perspectives of scholars like Chauvet invite thinking sacrament and church in ways yet ecumenically entertained. For instance, I would suggest playing a language game on church and sacraments as *coincidentia oppositorum*. In order to discern the tenets of a common ecclesiology inclusive of both sacramental, liturgical, credal and non-sacramental, non-liturgical, non-credal churches, such examination must be incorporated into ecumenical theology.

Conclusion

Ecumenical engagement assumes a continual re-telling of the Christian story and re-interpreting Christian tradition. Efforts to write an ecumenical history and attempts to craft an ecumenical hermeneutics mark the field since its inception. This is essential for Christian identity to be always and everywhere *ecclesia semper reformanda*. Credence to new developments in sacramental and liturgical theology, such as those of Louis-Marie Chauvet, serve this process.

Those engaged in the work of Christian unity are not looking for a symbolic language or a symbolic ecclesiological order which fosters ecumenical syncretism in Christian sacraments. They are looking to live life as sacrament in the sense that their baptismal koinonia shall be realised in the koinonia of one eucharistic fellowship, in recognised and reconciled ministry, and in mission. In light of an ecumenical reading of *Symbol and Sacrament*, the question becomes: (how) could ecumenical convergences, particularly but not solely those on sacramentality, be reconfigured in light of Louis-Marie Chauvet's method? For me, his language of "coincidence of opposites" is an attractive point of departure. It emerges as he crafts a specific meta-language in order to transcend the philosophical and theological framework that marked sacramentology since the Middle Ages. The current, 'middle age' of the ecumenical movement, *mutatis mutandis*, is marked by a parallel reduction in a theological reflection grounded in the foundational thinking of confessionality and denominational contextuality. Efforts to construct a language for an ecumenical ecclesiology of communion is an attempt to break out of this. If the classical axiom, *lex orandi lex credendi*, does indeed confirm that worship is our *prima theologia*, then its embodiment in renewed language is not only valid but imperative for the church to become the symbolic order it is – so that its unity may be visibly manifest in common faith, life and witness.

Graymoor Institute
475 Riverside Dr.
10115 New York

Lorelei F. FUCHS

CHAUVET AND PICKSTOCK: TWO COMPATIBLE VISIONS?

Both Louis-Marie Chauvet's *Symbole et Sacrement: Une relecture sacramentelle de l'existence chrétienne*[1] and Catherine Pickstock's *After Writing: On the Liturgical Consummation of Philosophy*[2] exemplify a turn to liturgy or doxology for the purposes of pursuing what might be considered a postmodern agenda. For example, they both put forward a critique of the sovereign subject, affirm a notion of the subject as always in process, and emphasize the apophatic tradition of theology. These similar motifs suggest that placing their works in dialogue may yield worthwhile results.

Pickstock's argument is representative of a classical Christian vision in that she advocates the restoration of a Christian philosophy. In her work, she draws a firm line between pre-modern and modern philosophy on the grounds that the former is open to transcendence, indeed possesses a liturgical dimension, while the latter is not and now announces its own demise in so-called "postmodern" philosophy. After rescuing Plato from Derrida's reading and critique, she turns to the medieval liturgy and a theology of the Eucharist in order to overcome the nihilism and necrophilia presumably inherent in modernity *and* postmodernity. Nevertheless, one finds in *After Writing* many of the common themes and concepts prevalent in postmodern discourse. For example, Pickstock speaks of deferral, supplementation, temporality and linguisticality, but situates these in the context of a Christian metaphysics of participation where God is seen as an inexhaustible and overflowing plenitude of Being. By appealing to a Divine plenitude, Pickstock attempts to affirm the postmodern critique of modernity and its celebration of play without accepting its alleged resignation towards arbitrariness, nothingness and death.

Influenced by Heidegger, psychoanalytic thought, and elements of structuralism, Chauvet's work is more representative of what is commonly characterized as postmodern. In the realm of sacramental theol-

---

1. L-M. Chauvet, *Symbole et Sacrement: Un relecture sacramentelle de l'existence chrétienne* (Paris: Cerf, 1987). Published in English as *Symbol and Sacrament: A Sacramental Reinterpretation of Christian Existence* (Collegeville MN: Liturgical Press, 1995).

2. C. Pickstock, *After Writing: On the Liturgical Consummation of Philosophy* (Oxford: Blackwell Publishers, 1998).

ogy, his concern is to expose an idolatrous attitude he links to the onto-theological paradigm of Western metaphysics. As a result, Chauvet is especially critical whenever liturgical practice and/or sacramental theology emphasize causality and presence. More specifically, he argues that Thomas Aquinas' sacramental theology is dominated by a "metaphor of production" that necessarily compromises the Otherness of God as well as the graciousness and gratuitousness of grace.[3] Partly for these reasons, he advocates a turn to corporeality and the symbolic order in order to overcome a metaphysics of presence and the accompanying desire to circumvent embodiment and mediation.

Chauvet's argument is at least partly grounded in the Continental thought that Pickstock has so thoroughly criticized. This raises the question of the compatibility of their work and the fruitfulness of any dialogue between the two. While there are some similarities found in the work of these two authors, we will in the following make note of a few fundamental differences in their approaches and offer some critique. The essay is organized around three sets of questions that should focus our attention on the practical implications for shaping Christian liturgy today. The first set concerns the pedagogy of the liturgy. How does the kind of liturgy Chauvet and Pickstock aspire to convey what each wants the faithful to experience and learn? A second constellation of questions concerns how we think about the relationship between the Church and the World. In the context of the debate over postmodernity, this has very much to do with how we evaluate the collapse of Christendom and the emergence of the secular with the advent of modernity. Does the world outside Christendom have any legitimacy? Why do our authors either accept or reject the autonomy of the world? In the final set of questions, we will turn away from "what their theology says" and consider how it is likely to be understood, if at all, and put into practice. How exactly would one implement the visions of liturgy to which each author aspires? What kinds of social practices and cultural attitudes are their visions likely to inspire and/or legitimize? Are there specific dangers or risks inherent in their projects?

The Pedagogy of the Liturgy

Influenced by John Milbank,[4] Pickstock essentially finds nothing redeeming in modernity and therefore seeks to overcome all its aspects.

---

3. See, for example, Chapter One "Critique des présupposés onto-théologiques de la sacramentaire classique", in Chauvet, *Symbole et Sacrement*, 13-50.

4. J. Milbank, *Theology and Social Theory: Beyond Secular Reason* (Oxford: Blackwell Publishers, 1990).

The postmodern situation fares no better in her eyes because it merely perpetuates the establishment of a secular world devoid of spiritual depth and transcendent meaning. It is impossible here to examine the multiple errors and heresies of modernity and postmodernity that she identifies. Instead we shall consider one critique directed towards the modern exposition of the subject. This is less controversial and in fact something held in common between Pickstock and Chauvet. It also represents Pickstock at her best.

Pickstock effectively demonstrates that the modern subject is ultimately disembodied and naively thought to be totally self-present. Many contemporary philosophers have similarly criticized this modern subject. For example, they argue that total self-presence is impossible because the subject is thoroughly constituted by language. There is no vantage point outside of language from which the subject can reflect upon itself. Moreover, no signifier can exhaustively disclose the nature or identity of the subject. For this reason, poststructuralists like Derrida argue that deferral and supplementation constitute the subject.

Pickstock understands this insight to be fraught with difficulties primarily because it posits a fundamental lack of being or abyss at the heart of human existence. From her perspective, this betrays the incipient nihilism of modernity and postmodernity that the theologian must speak against. As an alternative, she suggests that we turn back to the premodern. In the medieval Roman Rite, with its transubstantiation of the bread and wine, the insights of postmodernity can be substantiated without the nihilism of the abyss. For example, the medieval liturgy with its multiplicity of genres and frequency of repetition show that the liturgical subject is always constituted by deferral and supplementation.[5] However, she argues that this deferral and supplementation is distinct from that which constitutes the deconstructed or linguistic self of poststructuralist thinkers. Her argument rests on the theological presupposition that our subjectivity is received as a gift from a donating God thought of in terms of an excessive and overflowing plenitude of Being.[6] Furthermore, she in her own way confirms the postmodern view of the subject as always in process.[7] In the framework of her thought our identity is always *in media res* because it is constituted by our approach to God, which is first initiated by God's movement towards us.[8] Theoretically and minimally, the function of the Christian liturgy is to foster and express this never-ending

---

5. See, for example, Chapter Four "I will go unto the Alter of God: The Impossible Liturgy", in Pickstock, *After Writing*, 169-219.
6. *Ibid.*, 178. See also 170, 177, 192, 196, 198, 212, 214.
7. Pickstock, *After Writing*, 181-184, 208-216.
8. *Ibid.*, 180-183, 185.

journey. Who we are, like the liturgy itself, is always an "expectant work".[9]

Pickstock also makes more ambitious claims concerning the function of the liturgy. Quoting Michel Serres, she claims that "the definition, aim and purpose of ecclesiastical liturgy is to imitate the gestures, dances, music, song, words and actions of angels, in the presence of God,".[10] Ultimately, this has the effect of bringing us to "reside within the Trinity."[11] This is accomplished through our being "figured as angels" which implies that "we become one with their worldlessness and unfallenness, and are displaced from the earthly congregation to a position where we can momentarily participate in the economy of salvation."[12] She would object to this being characterized as being world denying or having a negative regard towards embodiment on the grounds that Christian liturgy in the end turns us "back to the world so as to confer upon it peace and good will".[13]

There are a few similarities in Chauvet's work. For example, he also evokes the theme of the self as always on the way.[14] His argument, however, is more indebted to Heidegger, the linguistic turn and the perspective of the human sciences than to a particular kind of metaphysical theology of creation and renewal. Our subjectivity is received as gift in Chauvet's thought because a process of symbolic exchange constitutes the self. This exchange involves a configuration of bodies, e.g., an individual somatic body, a cosmic body, a social body, and a historical body as well as the body of the Risen One. Theoretically, this configuration takes place in the liturgical and sacramental acts that inform the Christian subject.

In contrast to Pickstock, Chauvet also brings a hermeneutics of suspicion to the analysis of liturgical acts. This is probably due to his own perspective which is rooted in an anthropological and phenomenological approach, rather than a theological theory of Trinitarian relations. Above all, it is his appreciation of psychoanalytic thought that forces him to be keenly aware of the fragile character of sacraments.[15] Sacraments can become understood as direct channels or instruments that render and guarantee God's full presence or blessing for us. When they do so, they function in an idolatrous manner. But despite this ever-present tempta-

---

9. *Ibid.*, 186, 193-195.
10. M. Serres, *Angels: A Modern Myth* (Paris: Flammarion, 1993) 94. Cited in C. Pickstock, 209.
11. Pickstock, *After Writing*, 251.
12. *Ibid.*, 209.
13. *Ibid.*
14. Chauvet, *Symbole et Sacrement*, 58-59.
15. L-M. Chauvet, "The Liturgy in its Symbolic Space", in *Liturgy and the Body*, ed. J. Bowden and L-M. Chauvet (Maryknoll NY: Orbis Books, 1995) 34.

tion, Chauvet argues that liturgy and sacraments properly understood should counteract a "necrotic temptation" or a metaphysical desire for full unmediated presence of the Divine.[16] From his perspective, entering into the Christian liturgy should be a "consent to mediation" by which the worshipper in a state of "mourning" over the loss of an imaginary self-presence and idolatrous identification with God, awakens to the "presence of the absence" of the Risen Lord.[17] Liturgy then should create a "transitional space" (Winnicott)[18] wherein we maintain the right distance from God.[19]

This emphasis on distance stands in contrast to Pickstock's notion of "residing within the Trinity" which presupposes a kind of 'angelification' by way of mimesis in Christian liturgy. Ultimately, the metaphors employed by Pickstock (e.g., being "figured as angels" and turning *back* to the world) work against her intentions to hold corporeality and embodiment in positive regard. Chauvet, on the other hand, consistently argues that "the most 'spiritual' happens through the most 'corporeal'."[20] Remaining true to this principle, Chauvet concludes, "the corporeality constitutive of human beings is the place of God."[21] From his perspective, to be figured as angels and shed our worldliness could be construed as only drawing us further from a God who takes on body in this world. As we shall see, these different emphases have major implications for our second question.

The Legitimacy of a World outside Christendom

At the end of *Symbol and Sacrament*, Chauvet briefly engages in a reflection on creation.[22] This reflection on creation is vitally important for any discussion of sacramental presence because there is an intrinsic relationship between the sacramentality of creation and God's presence in the sacraments of the Christian community. Chauvet argues that two schemes have dominated Christian thought about creation.[23] Of course, each of these influence how we think about the efficacious presence of God in sacramental events. An artisanal view of creation emphasizes the free and

---

16. Chauvet, *Symbole et Sacrement*, 179-182.
17. *Ibid.*, 182-184.
18. D. W. Winnicott, *Playing and Reality* (London: Tavistock, 1971).
19. Chauvet, "The Liturgy in its Symbolic Space," 34-36.
20. "Le plus 'spirituel' advient dans le plus 'corporel'." Chauvet, *Symbole et Sacrement*, 153.
21. "La corporéité qu'est l'homme est le lieu de Dieu." *Ibid.*, 541.
22. *Ibid.*, 559-566.
23. Chauvet, *Symbole et sacrement*, 559.

deliberate character of God's act of creation.[24] The disadvantage of this perspective is that it can lead to Deism. In such a framework, any event of God's efficacious presence would have to be regarded in an extrinsic manner as a miracle that suspends the laws of nature. The other view of creation conforms to a biological scheme often attached to a model of Divine emanation.[25] The weakness of this perspective is that creation can appear to be driven by necessity.[26] Although Christian theologians who have articulated this idea maintain the free nature of God's act of creation, a certain conflict between God's freedom, emanation, and participation metaphysics remains unresolved. Furthermore, it will be shown that this onto-theological argument prohibits any positive affirmation of the autonomy of the human world.

Chauvet seeks to offer an alternative account of creation. He argues that God's creative act is best understood in terms of the symbolic order because God creates through the Word.[27] Metaphysical schemes of causality and participation are therefore judged to be inadequate for understanding creation. As an alternative to a metaphysical theology, Chauvet embraces a biblically based historical theology. In the Hebrew Scriptures, the Genesis account of creation begins with the word, *Bereshit*, best translated as 'in *a* beginning'.[28] Chauvet, citing the work of André Neher,[29] draws the conclusion that the Genesis text is not primarily concerned with giving a metaphysical account of how the cosmos came into being, but rather how history or time itself has arisen.[30] Indeed, Yahweh is primarily made known, not through creation, but rather through Divine intervention in history. "The divine word," says Chauvet, " is before all else the *creator of history*, and each new word of God makes a new event-advent arise."[31]

This Hebraic account of time stands in contrast to a cyclical view of time ruled by the eternal return of the Same. Yahweh as the "creator of history" breaks the chains of fate constitutive of cyclical time and opens up a history full of new horizons. Furthermore, the entire account of creation itself can be read as a breaking open or "act of differentiation" of the primordial chaos.[32] By establishing difference, God continually cre-

---

24. *Ibid.*, 559.
25. *Ibid.*
26. *Ibid.*, 560.
27. *Ibid.*
28. *Ibid.*, 236.
29. A. Neher, "Vision du temps et de l'historie dans la culture juive," in *Les cultures et le temps; Études préparées pour l'Unesco* (Paris: Presses de l'Unesco, 1975) 171-174.
30. Chauvet, *Symbole et Sacrement*, 236.
31. "La parole divine est avant tout creatice d'histoire, et chaque nouvelle parole de Dieu fait surgir un nouvel événement/avénement." *Ibid.*, 236.
32. Chauvet, *Symbole et sacrement*, 561.

ates/donates a place for play.[33] This place, rendered as *"free space"* in the English translation of Chauvet's work,[34] must be understood as gift. It is *gratuitous*, therefore necessitated by nothing and *gracious*, excessive beyond measure or reason.[35] Moreover, the creation of this free space entails a certain risk. Human beings are called to engage their own creativity for the purposes of making a world, or rather worlds, for themselves.[36] Clearly then God's gift to us in creation is not a ready-made and foreordained world, but rather a possible world or as Chauvet says elsewhere a "historical perhaps".[37] As a consequence, human beings must assume responsibility for creating a just world. Indeed, the world that humanity creates is good only insofar as it keeps covenant with God.

The worlds created and sustained by humanity do not lose their fundamental character of gift and they always remain a "possible sacramental place".[38] However, we lose sight of this when we deny Divine transcendence either by a spatialization or sacralization of our world. Pickstock astutely describes the nature of a completely spatialized world as characterized by the absence of Divine transcendence.[39] Perhaps one can argue that spatialization is the error of modernity to the extent that modernity gave rise to scientism in some circles. A sacralization of the world on the other hand is characterized by the full presence of the Divine. This can be established either through a romanticized view of history that conflates eschatology and teleology or by a belief in an oracle, object, rite, or institution that serves as an exclusive gateway to and vehicle for the full presence of the Divine. Perhaps one might say that this was a common error of pre-modernity.

Insofar as Pickstock combines a metaphysics of participation with a kind of Trinitarian emanation of God, she can be located in the biological scheme of creation identified by Chauvet. She stands against the modern view of nature as the "given" and refuses to separate ontology from theology.[40] From her perspective, creation is the gift given continually by God. In other words, all things that exist, exist insofar as they participate in God's donating and overflowing Being.

Three things immediately present themselves as problems in Pickstock's vision of creation. First, Pickstock's confessed allegiance to the apophatic tradition is threatened by the fact that she appears to know a lot

---

33. *Ibid.*, 561-562.
34. Chauvet, *Symbol and Sacrament*, 550.
35. Chauvet, *Symbole et Sacrement*, 113.
36. *Ibid.*, 561.
37. "Peut-être historique." *Ibid.*, 236.
38. *Ibid.*, 565.
39. Pickstock, *After Writing*, 49.
40. *Ibid.*, 162-164.

about God's nature. This in fact is the danger of every metaphysical theology. Chauvet, on the contrary, argues that there cannot possibly be a scientific answer to the question, "why is there something rather than nothing?"[41] Pickstock, while certainly not providing a scientific answer, does have an answer to this question founded on knowledge of God's very nature as Being. Secondly, history has shown that her type of metaphysical theology can give rise to a kind of romantic mythology and ecclesiology, which in today's context would pressure one to indiscriminately demonize not only the de-mythologization tendency of modernity, but also the very advent of a world outside Christendom. Lastly, God's freedom as well as human freedom is necessarily compromised in Pickstock's metaphysics. Indeed, human autonomy appears to only have negative implications in her work.

Turning to Chauvet, we see a willingness to grant a certain level of autonomy to the human world. The affirmation of human freedom is deemed important to him because only then can we come to fully appreciate our responsibility in history. To be sure, both Pickstock and Chauvet reject any notion of total self-sufficiency by their insistence that creation be understood as gift. The problem however with Pickstock's biological scheme of creation based on a model of emanation is that it allows no sense of autonomy for a human world. Indeed, Pickstock leaves one with the impression that human beings, like angels, are created solely to praise God. Chauvet's work, on the other hand, may allow us to affirm a degree of autonomy *and* our existence as gift. This has important consequences for the third question regarding the reception of their ideas.

Implementing their Visions

Implementing either Pickstock's or Chauvet's vision of the liturgy is a difficult challenge. It is doubtful that any more than a handful of people has experienced the liturgy as either Pickstock or Chauvet have described it. Few have sung with the angels and few have mourned consciously over the loss of an imaginary self-presence. The psychoanalytic themes, to take one aspect of Chauvet's work, make it difficult to implement Chauvet's vision of liturgy. These themes may have a communicative and symbolic power in the "psychoanalytic culture" of France, but it has been my experience that blank stares are produced in North American audiences who are introduced to concepts such as the "test of 'melancholy'."[42] It would seem that the faithful would have to undergo a particular kind of psychoanalysis in order to awake to this dimension of

---

41. Chauvet, *Symbole et sacrement*, 562.
42. "L'épreuve de la 'mélancolie'," in Chauvet, *Symbole et sacrement*, 83.

Christian liturgy. Then one may wonder about the risk of Eucharist becoming merely a "transitional object" akin to a pacifier that helps us accept the presence of the absence of Jesus Christ.

The implementation of Pickstock's vision raises greater concerns however if we think about shaping liturgy today and in the century to come. One might be led to believe that we need only bring back the medieval Roman Rite. However, Pickstock recognizes that there is no way of simply going back. Today, we live in a culture that resists traditional religious ritual and is dominated by the instrumental values of the market place. Indeed, Western culture has much to learn, perhaps re-learn, before sacred liturgy can once again saturate the public realm. Nevertheless, as a step in this re-learning process, Pickstock urges a return to Plato, whose dialogues she believes can serve as a stepping stone towards a new sacred *polis*. Yet the effectiveness and even relevance of this return is doubtful. Contemporary Christianity increasingly stands apart from the Greek world of Plato and this is a separation not just by historical distance, but also cultural difference when we consider the growing number of Christians in the non-western world.

Pickstock's preference for the pre-modern also needs to be critically examined. First, is her portrait of the past historically accurate and free from idealization? Secondly, one must entertain the possibility that the implementation of her vision would resurrect the dangerous imperialism and intolerance of medieval Christendom. In regards to this first concern, and with respect to the liturgy, Pickstock's devoted admiration of the medieval liturgy seems to conflict with Chauvet's insistence that religious ritual is subject to constant evangelization.[43] Indeed, Pickstock has indicated elsewhere that the message of liturgy should be regarded as "immutable, so it is a necessary corollary that its rites be couched in a non-mystifying fixed form, and be transmitted relatively unchanged through time."[44] One must bear this in mind when considering her critical stance towards the liturgical reforms of Vatican II. They, she says were "not radical enough."[45] Her argument is essentially that Vatican II capitulated to modernity. Perhaps, but we must acknowledge that Pickstock's privileging of the medieval rite, a rite located in a particular time and place and interpreted by her in distinct way, is very questionable. Ultimately, does this not suggest that an a/historical and a/cultural view of the liturgy is operative in Pickstock's thought?

---

43. Chauvet, "The Liturgy in its Symbolic Space," 34.
44. C. Pickstock, "Liturgy and Language: The Sacred Polis", in *Liturgy in Dialogue: Essays in Memory of Ronald Jasper*, ed. P. Bradshaw and B. Spinks (Collegeville MN: Liturgical Press, 1993) 126.
45. Pickstock, *After Writing*, 171.

As for the second concern, the historical narrative that Pickstock weaves maintains that Christianity lost its way in the middle to late medieval period giving birth to the monstrosity of modernity and postmodernity. Thus today, she calls for the creation of a new "sacred *polis*" that at least functions in the same way as her idealized liturgical city of early medieval Christendom. However, by appealing to one moment of history and holding it up as the golden age Pickstock, at best, runs the risk of ignoring the diversity of Christian traditions and, at worst, comes close to portraying their differences as errant. In the end, Pickstock's idealization of Christendom puts her vision at risk for being appropriated as another foundation for totalitarianism wherein positive regard for the other is made difficult. "Radical Orthodoxy" could turn into another powerful "logic of the same" yielding yet another debased "sacred *polis*" especially at the expense of the non-Christian.

Conclusion

There are no doubt some divisive issues between the liturgical theologies that Pickstock and Chauvet are developing. It would be all too easy to draw the battle lines along the lines of conservatism and progressivism. But instead of arguing for one against the other, I propose that together Pickstock's critique of the linguistic turn as it has developed in poststructuralist thought and Chauvet's qualified appropriation of structuralist and psychoanalytic thought are both valuable for contemporary thought concerning liturgy and the sacraments. Both perspectives have their merits and can challenge each other. However, in order for a beneficial exchange to be realized, Pickstock's polemical stance against nearly every Continental thinker born after the thirteenth century needs to be reexamined.

What is most disturbing is that often Pickstock's anti-modern stance is equivalent to anti-Protestantism. Does not all Reform theology, including the Anglican tradition, come after the thirteenth century? Her theology indeed exhibits an anti-catholicity that may in fact elicit some unwanted consequences. For example, at the end of *After Writing*, Pickstock asks why Christianity instead of Platonism?[46] She comes close to suggesting that Christianity is better than Platonism. Medieval Monastic Christianity, at the very least for Pickstock, is the consummation of Plato's thought. Following this manner of thinking might some of her readers be encouraged to narrowly see the New Testament as the consummation of the Old Testament or the Reformation as the fall of Christianity?

---

46. Pickstock, *After Writing*, 270.

Going into the twenty-first century, Christian communities must be open to the possibility of positive answers to questions such as why Thomas, why Scotus, why Luther, why Calvin, indeed why Judaism, why Islam, why Hindism, why a multitude of other paths of faiths new and old. What in fact may help us give a positive answer to these questions is the kind affirmation of difference that Chauvet's theology appears ready to encourage. To speak of the world as a "possible sacramental place", as Chauvet does,[47] also implies that the sacraments of Christian communities are possibly a sacramental place. First, this indicates a need to develop a critical eye for discerning God's presence in the Christian community and second, it prepares us to expect to find God's presence outside the confines of Christianity. Perhaps then we can look at the emergence of the secular in modernity, not in exclusively negative terms as the road to atheism, but as the creation of a place for the recognition of difference. Christianity can then be understood as one "way of life" orientated towards God. By moving in this direction, Christianity is faithful to its apophatic tradition and affirms its belief in a 'Bigger' God. A God too big for any single body of sacred scriptures to contain, a God too big for any one religious institution to reveal, and maybe even a God too big for any single life to reveal.

Graduate Theological Union Glenn P. AMBROSE
2400 Ridge Road
Berkeley, California 94709-1212

---

47. Chauvet, *Symbole et Sacrement*, 565.

'GIFT-EXCHANGE' IN SACRAMENTOLOGY
A CRITICAL ASSESSMENT FROM THE PERSPECTIVE OF PIERRE BOURDIEU

Anthropological and sociological research is one in saying that 'gift-exchanges' pervade the whole of traditional societies. Contemporary theology then appropriates this anthropological data into their discourses to provide a metaphor to the human-divine relations.[1] In sacramentology, it is Chauvet who makes 'gift-exchange' a central framework to his project towards a fundamental sacramental theology in the postmodern context.[2] This article aims to engage him in critical dialogue from the perspective of Bourdieu's analysis of 'gift-exchange'. It is our contention that Chauvet's neglect of the latter's perspective leads to some contradictions within his whole theological enterprise as it also betrays his social location in the field of contemporary production of theological thought. We also suggest that the direction provided by Bourdieu can complement Chauvet's project by helping us enunciate 'sacramentality' from the perspective of the growing number of the 'excluded' within the global capital economy.

1. The Gift in Chauvet's Sacramental Structure

To provide an anthropological framework to the *'admirabile commercium'* between God and humanity which we call 'grace', Chauvet's proposal for a sacramental theology in the context of postmodernity privileges the concept of *gift-exchange* worked out in anthropological research.

---

1. See, among others, J.L. Marion, *L'Idole et la distance* (Paris, 1977); Id., *Dieu sans l'être: Hors-texte* (Paris, [1982]1991), translated as *God Without Being* (Chicago, 1991); Id., *Prolégomènes à la charité* (Paris, 1986); J. Milbank, "Can a Gift be Given? Prolegomena to a Future Trinitarian Metaphysic," in *Modern Theology* 11 (1995) 119-161; D. Powers, *Sacrament: The Language of God's Giving* (New York, 1999).

2. L.-M. Chauvet, *Symbole et Sacrement: Une relecture sacramentelle de l'existence chrétienne* (Paris, 1987); Translated as *Symbol and Sacrament: A Sacramental Reinterpretation of Christian Existence*, trans. Madigan and Beaumont (Collegeville MN, [1987] 1995); Id., *Les sacrements. Parole de Dieu au risque du corps* (Paris, 1993). For an earlier seminal work, see Id., *Du symbolique au symbole. Essai sur les sacrements* (Paris, 1979).

He hereby makes use of the classical work of Marcel Mauss, *Essai sur le don*,[3] but in view of its application to contemporary society, he also complements it with insights from more contemporary authors like Barthes, Benveniste and Baudrillard.[4] The process of symbolic exchange, as exemplified in the gift – basically in the schemes of Mauss – provides Chauvet with a model with which to understand how subjects interrelate in the sphere of gratuitousness beyond the calculable "order of [*economic or utilitarian*] value."

There are three basic features in Mauss's work which Chauvet incorporates into his project.[5] He states that gift-exchange: (1) is a *total social fact*, that is, these exchanges involve all aspects (food, women, precious metals, etc.) on all levels of society; (2) that it is an exchange of the *symbolic order*, as opposed to the order of utility and market value and; (3) that it involves one in a whole structure of *obligatory generosity*. The first assertion maintains that gift-exchange pervades the whole of society and does so in all archaic societies. Mauss' project was an extensive examination of the processes of exchanges in the so-called archaic societies from the potlatch and *kula* in Native America, Alaska, Oceania and Australia to the law systems of ancient Hindu, Roman, Germanic and Indo-European societies. With the second assertion, Chauvet wants to emphasise that there is a way of exchange in societies that has 'nothing to do with business', one which is ruled by *super-abundance* and *graciousness* – a different level of relationships where subjects find their authentic human identities in "the relationship of alliance, friendship, affection, recognition, gratitude that it [the gift] creates or recreates between partners."[6] This leads us to his third assertion: that these 'free' exchanges which are also mandatory permit us "to live as subjects and structures all our relations in what they contain of the authentically human."[7]

Mauss' account of the phenomenon of exchange is transformed by Chauvet to the level of a *structural model* in the manner of Lévi-Strauss' *cycle of reciprocity*. Following the model of Delzant, Chauvet suggests a

---

3. M. Mauss, "Essai sur le don," in *L'année sociologique*, 2e série, vol. 1 (1923-24), 30-186; Reprinted in M. Mauss, *Sociologie et anthropologie*, intro. C. Lévi-Strauss, (Paris, 1950) 143-279.

4. R. Barthes, *Le système de la mode* (Paris, 1967); E. Benveniste, *Le vocabulaire des institutions indo-europénnes*, vol. 1, *Économie, parenté, société* (Paris, 1969); J. Baudrillard, *Pour une critique de l'economie politique du signe* (Paris, 1972).

5. Chauvet, *Symbol and Sacrament*, 100-102.

6. *Ibid.*, 107.

7. *Ibid.*, 103.

structure which would function as a schema for understanding Christian sacramental identity.[8]

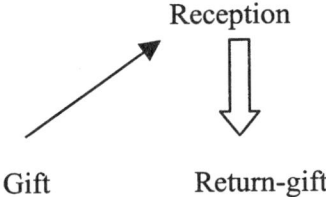

While 'market exchange' shows a double movement (X ⇔ Y), 'symbolic exchange' consists of a triple movement. Chauvet places importance on the intervening moment between gift and counter-gift: the time that is needed for the 'reception' of the gift as gift and not as anything else.[9]

In a next step, Chauvet consistently applies this framework to Christian realities. The structure of Christian identity is understood within this model: Scripture is seen as Gift; Sacrament as Reception, and Ethics as Return-gift.[10] Everything in life is seen then as a gratuitous gift that needs to be celebrated and be given back as return-gift through ethical praxis. Chauvet proceeds to justify his framework by re-reading key scriptural narratives and church tradition.[11] It is this foundational triple structure which serves as a springboard towards his main framework of the whole Christian sacramental structure as shown in the following diagram.[12]

---

8. *Ibid.*, 267. See A. Delzant, *La communication de Dieu, par-delà utile et inutile. Essai théologique sur l'ordre symbolique* (Paris, 1978).

9. Id., *Les sacrements*, 137.

10. Id., *Symbol and Sacrament*, 172. Chauvet's 1979 book already employed this same framework. See Id., *Du symbolique au symbole*, 96. But Delzant's earlier work already employed the framework *(kérygme-appartenance-éthique)* which is also based on the anthropological structure of *'don–réception–contre-don'*. See Delzant, *La communication de Dieu*, 156.

11. For instance, his hermeneutics of the Emmaus experience and other resurrection accounts reveals that these stories also display a threefold plan: an initiative of the Risen One (gift), recognition in faith (reception) and sending on mission (return-gift). Chauvet, *Symbol and Sacrament*, 161-170; *Du symbolique au symbole*, 82-97. For the triple structure of Jewish identity, see Chauvet's analysis of Deut 26:1-11 in *Symbol and Sacrament*, 283-286; Id., *Les Sacrements*, 163-166. For the same structure present in the texts of the Eucharistic Prayer II, see Id., *Symbol and Sacrament*, 268-277; *Les Sacrements*, 145-163.

12. Id., *Symbol and Sacrament*, 278.

2. RECEPTION
a) Sacrament

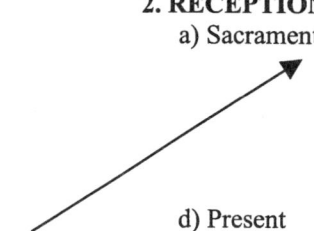
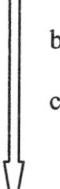

b) Sacramental body of Christ
c) Reception under the mode of oblation and thanksgiving

d) Present

1. GIFT
a) Scripture
b) Historical & glorious body of Christ
c) Gift from God: giving grace
   + already now
   + in the Kingdom
d) Past

3. RETURN-GIFT
a) Ethics (agape)
b) Ecclesial body of Christ
c) Return-gift of living-in-grace between brothers & sisters

d) Eschatological future
   + already
   + not yet

The basic questions this article seeks to answer are: How warranted is Chauvet's use of this anthropological data? What implications does this have for his theologising in general and for sacramental theology in particular? We suggest that Pierre Bourdieu can help us critically assess this anthropological-theological inquiry.

2. Pierre Bourdieu on 'Gift-Exchange'

2.1. Pierre Bourdieu: Beyond Mauss and Lévi-Strauss

Bourdieu locates his own position beyond what he calls the *subjectivist* school and *objectivist* thinking in anthropological thought. Mauss' exercise in positivist research is read by Bourdieu as one of the representatives of the former while Lévi-Strauss' structuralist analysis of the *cycle of reciprocity* belongs to the latter. Subjectivist thinking accepts the truth of primary experience of the social world with unquestioning apprehension. Bourdieu criticises this as not self-reflexive enough. For him, the first task of any social analysis is to establish an epistemological break with common sense and everyday representations by analysing statistical regularities with the purpose of uncovering the underlying principles of human practice. Lévi-Strauss, for his part, in fact accuses Mauss of situating himself in the level of a 'phenomenology' of gift-exchange[13] which

---

13. Lévi-Strauss, "Introduction à l'ouvre de Marcel Mauss", xxxv. For the same assessment, see P. Bourdieu, *The Logic of Practice*, trans. R. Nice (Stanford, CA [1980] 1990) 98.

naively embraces 'native' experience and the native theory of that experience, that is, "primary knowledge whose tacitly assumed presuppositions give the social world its self-evident, natural character."[14]

This critique on Mauss serves to bring out the direction of Lévi-Strauss' structuralist project: to announce a break from subjectivist knowledge and to search for some underlying principle behind social phenomena. In the case of gift-exchange, this means a search for the 'automatic laws' of the *cycle of reciprocity*[15] – the unconscious principle behind the obligation to give, to receive and to give back. What structuralist-objectivist knowledge seeks to establish is the limits of primary experience by looking into its conditions of possibility – conditions which phenomenological analysis neglects. Subjectivism and objectivism, therefore, give two contrasting perspectives on the reality of gift-exchange: the *gift as experienced* and the *gift seen from the outside*.

For Bourdieu, however, there is a need to overcome this impasse. He proposes a 'second epistemological break' – a break from 'objectivist' knowledge so as to allow us to also grasp its own limits. He criticises the structuralist anthropology of Lévi-Strauss of reducing human practice to mere execution of atemporal and theoretical models. He argues that even if objective structures exert influence, social agents also exercise *practical mastery* of those structures. Though Bourdieu considers structuralist-objectivist knowledge 'an inevitable moment in scientific thought', he proposes to bring it back to its feet again by integrating the truth of practical experience – that which he calls the *logic of practice*. In polemics with structuralism, Bourdieu emphasises that there is something in practice which the objective gaze fails to grasp. The objectivist position fostered by the discourse of 'models', 'rules' and 'structures' enhances a decidedly detached perspective similar to "that of God the Father watching social actors like puppets controlled by strings of structure"[16] or that of a "virtuoso with a perfect command of his 'art of living' [who] can play on all the resources inherent in the ambiguities and uncertainties of behaviour and situation in order to produce the actions appropriate to each case."[17] This emphasis on practice does not at all signal a simplistic return to 'phenomenological' subjectivism. Bourdieu's 'theory of practice' intends "to make possible a science of *dialectical* relations between the objective structures to which the objectivist mode of knowledge gives access and the structured dispositions within which those structures are

---

14. Bourdieu, *Outline of a Theory of Practice* (Cambridge, 1977) 3.
15. Lévi-Strauss, "Introduction à l'ouvre de Marcel Mauss," xxxvi.
16. Bourdieu, *In Other Words: Essays Towards a Reflexive Sociology*, trans. Adamson (Cambridge, 1990) 9.
17. Bourdieu, *Outline of a Theory of Practice*, 8.

actualised and which tend to reproduce them."[18] Bourdieu, therefore, aims to go beyond the impasse of the oppositions – subjectivism/objectivism, structures/agency, culture/society – in contemporary sociological-anthropological research. Just as structuralism inquires into the conditions of possibility of 'phenomenological' knowledge, the theory of practice explores the limits of structuralism by bringing into the analysis the truth of practice, the *practical sense*, or what he calls the 'feel (*sens*) for the game'. We will concretise this further in Bourdieu's discussion of 'the work of time' in gift-exchange.

2.2. Deferred and Different: Temporal Structure of Gift-Exchange

The structuralist emphasis on 'models' and 'schemas' such as the automatic laws of the *cycles of reciprocity*, or in Chauvet's diagram, the 'gift/reception/return-gift' structure, only exists in the "absolute gaze of the omniscient, omnipresent spectator, who, thanks to his knowledge of the social mechanics, is able to be present at the different stages of the 'cycle'."[19] Bourdieu argues that in practice, a gift may remain unreciprocated as when one encounters an ungrateful person or may be rejected as a gesture to express insult. In other words, there are instances in practice where a gift obtains no 'reception' nor 'return-gift'. Bourdieu remarks that any analysis of gift-exchange must allow for a possible interruption of the so-called 'cycle of reciprocity' because each initial act of giving can always be "liable to fall flat and so, for a lack of response, to be stripped retrospectively of its intentional meaning."[20]

What Bourdieu wants to emphasise is that there is more truth to gift-exchange beyond what the objectivist model bears out. From an 'outside' perspective, the structuralist schema telescopes, as it were, into one synchronised instance and renders timeless what, in fact, is a lived experience characterised by uncertainty. Synchronisation, therefore, produces a reversibility effect to the otherwise irreversible strategies an agent enacts in actual practice. From an objectivist view, it can now be taken for granted that every 'gift' obligates a 'return-gift' and a 'return-gift' automatically presupposes an earlier 'gift' – a reversible timeless structure indeed. For Bourdieu, however, this timeless structure misses the whole truth of gift-giving. "The simple possibility that things might proceed otherwise than is laid down by the 'mechanical laws' of the cycles of reciprocity," he claims, "is sufficient to change the whole experience of practice and, by the same token, its logic."[21] Uncertainty in fact reigns

---

18. Bourdieu, *Outline of a Theory of Practice*, 3. [Emphasis his]
19. Bourdieu, *The Logic of Practice*, 98.
20. *Ibid.*, 105.
21. *Ibid.*, 99.

until the whole sequence is completed. Crucial to this assertion is the factor of 'time': "to reintroduce uncertainty is to reintroduce time, with its rhythm, its orientation and its irreversibility, substituting the dialectic of *strategies* for the *mechanics of the mode*."[22]

Time – a neglected dimension of structuralist thought – is crucial to all gift-exchanges. Bourdieu points out that in every society, the return-gift must be *deferred*. To avoid insulting the giver, that is, to 'recognise' the gift, the recipient has to give back something different and, most crucially, only after a considerable interval of time. To give back something 'too soon', and thus "to reveal too overtly one's desire to pay off services rendered or gifts received, to be quits, is to denounce the initial gift retrospectively as motivated by the intention of obliging one."[23] Thus, the time-interval between gift and return-gift is crucial in order to conceal from the agents what otherwise is the objective truth of their practice. What in fact is called with the euphemism 'gift exchange' conceals the exercise of power that underlies it. For "[u]ntil he has given in return, the receiver is *'obliged'*, expected to show his gratitude towards his benefactor, or, at least, to have regard for him…"[24] Not to insult the giver by withholding the return-gift for a while also means that the recipient recognises the giver's exercise of power over oneself. By agreeing to play this social game of 'gift exchange', s/he in fact contributes to the mystification of the situation and the legitimation of power.[25] The *time-interval* between gift and return-gift is therefore crucial as "an instrument of denial which allows a subjective truth and a quite opposite objective truth to co-exist, in both individual experience and common judgement."[26] In other words, 'the work of time', to use Bourdieu's own phrase, is to transpose what otherwise are 'interested' and power-laden exchanges into 'generous' *cycles of reciprocity*.

Beyond the need to *defer*, the gift also needs to be *different* (i.e., not an exact equivalent, as is done in barter, lending or the market). Bourdieu tells of a mason who asked for 200 francs in addition to his daily wage in lieu of not participating in a *closing ritual meal*. The final meal at the end of a house-building project serves to ritualise and seal the alliance made

---

22. Bourdieu, *The Logic of Practice* [Emphasis mine]
23. *Ibid.*, 105.
24. Bourdieu, *Outline of a Theory of Practice*, 6.
25. Symbolic power does not only refer to the act of domination exerted from above but also presupposes a kind of *complicity* on the part of those subjected to it. "Dominated individuals are not passive bodies to which symbolic power is applied, as it were, like a scalpel to a corpse. Rather, symbolic power requires, as a condition of its success, that those subjected to it believe in the legitimacy of power and the legitimacy of those who wield it." Cf. John Thompson, "Introduction," in Bourdieu, *Language and Symbolic Power*, trans. Raymond and Adamson (Cambridge, MA, 1991) 23.
26. Bourdieu, *The Logic of Practice*, 107.

and, according to Bourdieu, is "intended to transmute an interested transaction retrospectively into a generous exchange."[27] By placing a price-equivalent to what otherwise was 'generous' relationship, the mason caused shock to the community for exposing "the best-kept and worst-kept secret (one that everyone must keep), and breaking the law of silence which guarantees the complicity of collective bad-faith in the good-faith economy."[28]

Thus, for a gift then to be so 'recognised' (*reconnaissance*), it has to be 'misrecognised' (*méconnaisance*) for what it really is. What Chauvet calls 'obligatory generosity' is, in Bourdieu's analysis, less of a gesture of 'generosity' than an 'obligation' – in fact an exercise of power and domination. It is only through such an analysis of the *temporal structure* of gift-exchange in the manner of Bourdieu, that one can confront this so-called commonly shared belief but also socially repressed truth and collective denial – something which a timeless structuralist model is incapable of doing.

2.3. Symbolic Violence and Symbolic Capital

In archaic societies where there are few institutions to give objective form to relations of power, violence can only be maintained through interpersonal relations. This is done either through debts or gifts; the former being an overt violence (physical or economic), the latter a form of symbolic violence, censored and euphemised. When overt violence (e.g., usury, forced labour, etc.) is not socially acceptable, invisible violence (in its 'gentler' forms – confidence, obligation, personal loyalty, hospitality, gifts, gratitude, piety) serves as the most economical mode of domination.[29] In Bourdieu's view, gifts present themselves as

> operations of social alchemy which may be observed whenever direct application of overt physical or economic violence is negatively sanctioned, and which tend to bring about the transmutation of economic capital into symbolic capital. Wastage of money, energy, time, and ingenuity is the very essence of the social alchemy through which an interested relationship is transmuted into a disinterested, gratuitous relationship, overt domination into misrecognized, 'socially recognized' domination, in other words, *legitimate authority*.[30]

In order to keep someone under one's 'gentle' domination, one needs to shell out not only economic capital but also 'personal' resources such as time, care, attention. A landowner may consider the tenant part of his

---

27. Id., *Outline of the Theory of Practice*, 173.
28. *Ibid.*
29. *Ibid.*, 192.
30. *Ibid.*

own household, place him/her in charge of 'personal' transactions, arrange and spend for his/her children's marriage, shower her/him with gifts on every important occasion, etc. – all these to keep his/her loyalty but also to conceal the otherwise asymmetrical relationship. Yet power and violence are hidden under the mantle of these enchanted relationships. Symbolic violence where affective bonds are woven into the economic is in fact the most economical mode of domination.[31] This only shows that the division between the economic and non-economic gets to be quite blurred. What for Chauvet were transactions of a different order (i.e., symbolic) are for Bourdieu only different modes of the same domination – economic, political and cultural. Symbolic capital, "a transformed and thereby *disguised* form of physical 'economic' capital, produces its proper effect inasmuch, and only inasmuch, as it conceals the fact that it originates in 'material' forms of capital which are also in the last analysis, the source of its effects."[32] For material and economic power can be exercised most effectively when its interested character goes misrecognised. And 'gift-exchange' is one of the social microdynamics which helps in this concealment and legitimation. For as Bourdieu concludes: "Gift exchange is the paradigm of all the operations through which symbolic alchemy produces the reality-denying reality that the collective consciousness aims at a collectively produced, sustained and maintained misrecognition of the 'objective' truth."[33]

3. Gifts, Symbols and Sacraments: Critical Perspectives

Reading Mauss and Lévi-Strauss: Comments on Chauvet's Use of His Sources

Chauvet's use of Mauss serves to bring out the idea that there are exchanges in society which lie beyond the order of utilitarian value. Mauss and Durkheim were in polemics with English utilitarianism as they

---

31. *Ibid.*, 190-191.
32. *Ibid.*, 183. [Emphasis his]
33. Bourdieu, *The Logic of Practice*, 110. In this article, we focus mainly on the role of gift-exchange in the process of legitimation of economic power in archaic societies. This is to respond to Chauvet's use of Mauss' research in the same context. However, it is also good to emphasise here that Bourdieu also finds the same concealment happening in contemporary society. The philanthropic and charitable activities of big companies, the funding of public media by private business, the flourishing of the non-profit sector and the so-called humanitarian aids to developing countries or to continents in crisis all lead to the conversion of economic to symbolic capital and are intended to secure legitimation of the dominant groups. In the process, therefore, we also indirectly respond to Chauvet's use of Baudrillard and others in order to argue for the similar nature of 'gifts' in contemporary societies. See Bourdieu, "The Economy of Symbolic Goods," in Id., *Practical Reason: On the Theory of Action* (Cambridge, 1998) 92.

sought to prove that society gels, as it did in archaic communities, even without modern market mechanism. The phenomenon of gift-exchange, therefore, provided Mauss with an explanation for social cohesion without resorting to market exchange. Yet it also echoes Adam Smith's 'invisible hand'. For like the market, it also furnishes individuals with incentives for collaborating in the politico-economic exchanges of archaic societies. This parallelism, not contrast, between 'gift-exchange' and 'market exchange' is quite revealing of the real meaning of the former: that 'gift-giving' in fact is quite 'interested' and power-laden. Though Chauvet acknowledges this by asserting that generosity is in fact obligatory, he refuses to admit that these differing notions of 'interests' involve the exercise of social power embedded in uneven social relations. For him, gift-exchange belongs to a different order – the symbolic – the privileged domain of human authenticity.

It is precisely the core of Bourdieu's research to prove the opposite. His concept of 'symbolic capital' shows that the border between economic and non-economic spheres of existence becomes non-distinguishable. Chauvet's assertion that the gift is "without doubt what, among our institutions, best resists the imperialism of [economic] value"[34] is not only an understatement but is also a sign of his neglect of the current debate. From Bourdieu's perspective, Chauvet is guilty of 'economism', that is, of a restricted definition of economic interest. This abstraction of the 'cultural' from the 'economic' is a product of an ideological move by an 'interested' group (e.g., writers or artists, in our case, anthropologists and theologians, all *cultural producers*) who want to assert an autonomous position – the autonomy of their own cultural or spiritual practice – in contemporary discourse. For Bourdieu, cultural producers belong to 'the dominated fraction of the dominant class',[35] that is, though finding themselves among the dominant class, their discourse is in fact marginalised by their counterparts in the economic or political field. Thus, the move to detach certain spheres of social life from their material locus of production and isolating them to the realm of the 'symbolic', 'cultural' or 'aesthetic' can only serve to reclaim this groups' autonomy. Though this move appears to be a 'revolutionary' reaction to contemporary economism, it is in fact ambiguous because it also betrays its 'conservative' bourgeois character which ultimately tends to preserve at all cost their own accumulated cultural capital.[36] For while margi-

---

34. Chauvet, *Symbol and Sacrament*, 193.
35. Bourdieu, *In Other Words*, 145.
36. Bourdieu points out that writers and artists and intellectuals in general, "[d]espite their revolt against those they call 'bourgeois', they remain loyal to the bourgeois order, as can be seen in all periods of crisis in which their specific capital and their position in

nalised from the actual workings of the economic field, cultural producers have at the same time the luxury of distancing themselves from bare necessity of material existence. Neglecting the social conditions of the so-called 'pure gaze' or 'disinterested science' denies the uneven power dynamics in these fields. Bourdieu has argued that all actions, material or symbolic, are an exercise of uneven power relations. In such a learned and well-documented work as Chauvet's, not to be able to take account of Bourdieu's perspective on this issue[37] by privileging the 'symbolic', the 'gratuitous' and the 'disinterested' only betrays the author's social location in the field of contemporary cultural production.

Moreover, there is something peculiar in the way Chauvet employs the anthropological data of 'gift-exchange'. He uses Mauss' research on gift-exchange at one point and almost without warning transforms it into a structural schema in the manner of Lévi-Strauss. Though Mauss already made mention of the three obligations – *donner, recevoir, prendre* – we must remember that it was only Lévi-Strauss who read into it the structural model. Mauss had in fact failed to cross the line towards structuralist thinking; his research on 'gift-exchange', though verging towards it, still remained 'phenomenological'. Lévi-Strauss likens Mauss to Moses who, after having led his people to the Promised Land, did not himself step on it to behold its glory.[38] It is this anthropological 'structure' appropriated from these two quite different positions which forms the foundation of Chauvet's theological discourse. This only shows that Chauvet casually adopts a framework without distinguishing the complex debate behind the anthropological data – not to mention his neglect of Bourdieu's significant sociological input.

This observation is crucial because it points to the seeming contradictions in Chauvet's project, one of which is the problem of structuralist 'detemporalisation' as against his emphasis on historicity. Following Heidegger, Chauvet rightly criticises the onto-theological framework as positing an autonomous and detached subject possessing a direct and instrumentalist knowledge of reality. In its stead, he proposes a subject immersed in both language and history whose knowledge of reality can only be mediated by the symbolic.[39] However, when he began describing this subject from the perspective of the believer's Christian identity, he took refuge in structuralist frameworks patterned after Lévi-Strauss' *cy-*

---

the social order are threatened (one need think only of the positions adopted by writers, even the most 'progressive', like Zola, when faced with the Commune)." *Ibid.*

37. Chauvet cited Bourdieu's works 11 times. See Chauvet, *Symbol and Sacrament*, 125-126, 134, 138, 349, 369, 439. But none of these deals with Bourdieu's position on the anthropological data of 'gift-exchange'.

38. Lévi-Ştrauss, "Introduction à l'oeuvre de M. Mauss," xxxvii.

39. Chauvet, *Symbol and Sacrament*, 46-63.

cles of reciprocity. From the 'gift/reception/return-gift' model, he deduces the 'Scripture–Sacrament–Ethics' structure of all Christian identities which, like all structures, also discloses the feature of reversibility, leaving out the (unforeseeable) 'arrow of time'. The omniscient, omnipresent subject is again back on its throne as it begins to observe and oversee from 'outside' the whole process of the Christian coming-to-be, leaving out the sense of uncertainty of Christian existence. We could only ask whether Bourdieu's 'logic of practice' – in the image of a 'player immersed in the game' and having a 'feel' (*sens*) for it[40] – is not a more appropriate framework consistent with Chauvet's critique of the onto-theological project towards a sacramental theology of the 'eschatological in-between time'.[41]

4. Sacramentality, Gift-Exchange and Symbolic Power

The anthropological model of the 'gift' with the corresponding need for its 'reception' is parallel to Chauvet's concept of language which constitutes our being human. Following Heidegger, Chauvet asserts that it is not humans who speak but that they are always-already spoken to by language. We have in fact no direct contact with reality. It is language and the symbolic order which mediates us to the world. This sense of surrender to the 'symbolic' which envelops us invites us to a gracious *'letting be'* in front of reality: an attitude of listening and welcome toward something *ungraspable* by which we are already grasped and *'allowing oneself to be spoken'*, thus renouncing all ambition for mastery.[42]

Thus in Chauvet's project of the fundamental theology of the sacramental, the focus is not so much on individual sacraments as on the basic *sacramentality of the faith*. We have been born into and have been always spoken to by a symbolic-sacramental world – the Church which is the fundamental sacrament. It is only within the context of this fundamental sacramentality that the triple structure of our Christian identity 'Scripture–Sacrament–Ethics' can be properly understood. Catechesis and theology, sacraments and liturgy, morals and Christian praxis are all parts of the fullness of the symbolic world – that *ecclesial institution* which needs 'to be received as grace'.[43] At a certain moment, however, Chauvet himself warns us against how the 'grace' of the institutional Church has already been manipulated all throughout the centuries to legitimise oppressive social orders. Theological research in fact reveals how scriptural in-

---

40. Bourdieu, *The Logic of Practice*, 82.
41. Chauvet, *Symbol and Sacrament*, 546.
42. *Ibid.*, 446.
43. *Ibid.*, 185. [Emphasis mine]

terpretation and theological discourse, sacraments and Christian symbols, as well as ethical practice (e.g., Christian 'charity') were often in complicity with the dominant power. Yet despite these warnings, Chauvet's framework does not allow for a concrete critical component in these matters.[44]

We suggest that Bourdieu's perspectives on language can shed some light on the problem. As we have argued, language is not only a means of communication but also an 'instrument of power'. Linguistic exchanges and their concomitant social relations are not mere 'symbolic' interactions but also "relations of symbolic power in which power relations between speakers or their respective groups are actualised."[45] In other words, language and symbols are social domains where power manifests itself as it betrays the violence in the social structure it also tries to reproduce. As in 'gift-exchange', so it is in language and symbolic discourse. For Bourdieu, the efficacy of words and symbols, the effectiveness of ritual discourse or the 'authority' to speak are in fact arbitrary social constructions.[46] As long as these arbitrary social inventions (which enthrone some and marginalise others) continue to be socially misrecognised, that is, as long as there are convergent social conditions that reproduce the same symbolic violence, language and symbols continue to be potent instruments of power. Chauvet's suggestion "to lose oneself in language," to make oneself "be spoken to" by the symbolic order which already possesses us, to foster an attitude of "letting ourselves be"[47] in front of the ambiguity of language and symbols – without Bourdieu's critical edge[48] – places us in some dangerous position of re-

---

44. See a parallel comment in V. Miller, "An Abyss at the Heart of Mediation: Louis-Marie Chauvet's Fundamental Theology of Sacramentality," *Horizons* 24 (1997) 230-247. While Miller proposes to use Habermas' theory of communicative action as a corrective, our option here is for Bourdieu's theory of practice.

45. Bourdieu, *Language and Symbolic Power*, 37.

46. See *Ibid.*, 1-162.

47. Chauvet mentions the phrase "letting be" several times in his work. Chauvet, *Symbol and Sacrament*, 51, 53, 60, 300, 446.

48. Chauvet's citations of Bourdieu's work mostly come from *Ce que parler veut dire. L'économie des échanges linguistiques*, Paris, 1982. But the way Chauvet reads Bourdieu appears to be in opposition to the latter's whole project. For instance, he cites Bourdieu's work hand in hand with Austin's concept of 'performative language' in order to point out that ritual effectiveness is not found in the words themselves but in the authority invested on the 'speaker' or in the community's common recognition of the rite itself. However, for Bourdieu, speech-act theorists like Austin neglect the consequences of the 'social conditions' in the production of language. Language (e.g., the right to say something, the 'correct' way of speaking and the accepted way of doing rituals) in fact emerge from a set of uneven social relations which have been legitimated (i.e., misrecognised) but which are also themselves areas of constant contestation and struggle. This dimension is absent in Chauvet's reading of Bourdieu. On the contrary, his position even appears to reinforce the very facts which Bourdieu intends to critique. For instance, Chauvet exten-

producing what otherwise does not belong to the realm of liberating grace.

The same danger lurks in Chauvet's interpretation of the anthropological structure 'gift/reception/return-gift'. Central to symbolic exchange is the moment of 'reception'– that intervening time between gift and return-gift – which makes it possible for the gift to be received as a 'gift' and not as anything else. In Chauvet's reading, this distinguishes 'gift-exchange' from 'market exchange' which is a direct transaction (i.e., signified by the double movement) between equivalent values.[49] For Bourdieu as well, the *time-element* between gift and return-gift is necessary in order for something to be recognised as a gift and not as payment of a debt. But in his view, it is precisely this intervening time that allows for the collective 'misrecognition' of the symbolic violence inherent in gift-exchange. In other words, the intervening moment which, for Chauvet elevates the exchange to the level of the symbolic, in fact makes possible the concealment and mystification of the exercise of power and domination.

It is from this perspective that we give our reservation to the paradigm of gift-exchange in order to enunciate the *admirabile commercium* between God and humanity. Though not all gifts are expressions of self-interest and egoistic calculation, neither do they fully proceed from super-abundance, gratuitousness and generosity. They possess in fact the aforementioned *dual truth*. If there is anything to describe the experience of the gift, it is its ambiguity.[50] Any framework, such as Chauvet's, which posits a clear-cut distinction between the economic and the symbolic runs the risk of reading manipulative power into the divine all-gratuitous action, thus turning a blind eye (especially when this divine all-gratuitousness is mediated by such a precarious institution as the church) to the ambiguity inherent in all gift-exchanges.

5. 'Gracious' Existence, Contrast Experience and Sacramentality

In his polemics with onto-theology, Chauvet emphasises the 'presence of the absence'. Against the 'frozen metaphysical presence' of *substantia*,

---

sively quotes Bourdieu's analysis of the 'rites of institution' to explain the symbolic efficacy of the sacrament of baptism (cf. L. Chauvet, *Symbol and Sacrament*, 438-439). But in the overall context of this work by Bourdieu, he intends to argue that 'rites of passage, of 'consecration' or 'institution' also act as 'rites of legitimation' of *arbitrary boundaries*. See Bourdieu, *Language and Symbolic Power*, 117-118.

49. For the crucial consequences this assertion bears for sacramentology, see Chauvet, *Les Sacrements*, 139-143.

50. Bourdieu, "La double vérité du don," in Id., *Méditations pascaliennes*, Paris, 1997, 229-240.

he poses a kind of presence whose very essence is 'essentially marked by the stroke of absence' – a 'trace'.[51] In other words, there is no way for us to 'get hold of' being, for once it begins to be considered as present, it slips away and all there is left for us is just a trace. Echoing Heidegger, Chauvet invites us "to hold ourselves in a mature proximity to [this] absence."[52] This philosophical framework, he carries over to theology in order to emphasise the 'absence of God' in the post-metaphysical setting. He follows Moltmann in speaking about the Crucified God who can only sigh in desperation for his feeling of abandonment. (In the dereliction of Christ, for our salvation, God is – so to speak – abandoned by God). This 'absence of God' discourse serves Chauvet's project by setting the stage for the symbolic mediation of the Church and the sacraments. To respect God's absence, to consent to this loss, we need to accept the Church and its sacramental presence as God's trace. Sacraments then become "symbolic figures *of God's effacement*" always "referring the Church back to *the empty place of its Lord…*"[53]

There is, however, another current in Chauvet's work when seen from his emphasis on the 'gift'. Here, God is more present than absent. In the context of God's creation, life and being itself come to be seen as 'gifts', gratuitous and gracious. "Being is marked with the stamp of the Other. Inasmuch as it is created, the world of entities is posited as a *gift* from the start."[54] From this perspective, the gift which is 'bread' becomes in the sacramental context a symbol of life-sustenance and fellowship of equals sharing in that life. Wine announces the coming of messianic joy. And finally, when life and its ritual enactment are experienced as 'gifts,' ethics then becomes a 'return-gift': a response of thanksgiving to the "graciousness of the whole circuit."[55]

When life is fundamentally a 'gracious' experience, what do we make of God's absence? At this juncture, Chauvet takes refuge in the language of 'excess' of the symbolic order. An effective symbol introduces *something more than life* in that it acts as 'a witness to the vacant place of the Other' – to that which is beyond the immediate data. But here one can object that the discourse of 'excess,' even as it seeks to describe the ungraspable reality, does not at all account for the 'lack,' the 'deficiency', the 'inadequacy' which 'absence' primarily and essentially implies. The talk of the 'more' and the 'beyond' can even become a dangerous ideological ploy to mystify the 'inadequate here and now'.

---

51. Chauvet, *Symbol and Sacrament*, 58.
52. *Ibid.*
53. *Ibid.*, 490, 381. [Emphasis mine]
54. *Ibid.*, 548-549.
55. *Ibid.*, 109.

It is here that Bourdieu's analysis of the gift's *double-truth* becomes necessary. Reading life from such a perspective, we can see that life-experience is not at all that gracious and gratuitous for the majority of peoples in the Two-Thirds World and for an increasing number of the excluded in the so-called 'developed' economies.[56] Opposite to 'gracious' existence is what Schillebeeckx calls 'contrast experience'. In the midst of human suffering and injustice, there we find real absence, the experience of being forsaken by God. It is from this 'experience of loss' that theological reflection on sacraments have to start if theology is to be faithful to its liberating task. What does Eucharist mean when the 'bread' on the altar, instead of symbolising life and fellowship of equals, reminds a jobless father of his hungry children and their empty family table? When millions in mega-cities have to build their shanties over stagnant water contaminated by chemicals from nearby factories which also cause respiratory diseases in their children, what could that old stagnant water in that dark baptistery signify? When creation is seen from this perspective, sacramentology takes a different route. So does ethics. With experiences of contrast as starting point, it could no longer just be a 'return-gift' as response of gratitude to 'graciousness' of creation but rather an act of resistance and liberative praxis – a resilient and indignant human response in the midst of seeming powerlessness.[57]

It appears to us then, that it is this perspective which is more in keeping with Chauvet's emphasis on the 'presence of the absence'. In such situations, the desperate cry of Jesus on the cross being forsaken by his God is not merely an 'object' of theological exegesis but is real and actual, accompanied by tears and sighs of deep anguish and pain. God is really absent and is nowhere in sight. This experience of a 'withdrawing God' in what Gustavo Gutierrez also calls 'the dark night of injustice' rings true to the lives of those from the underside of history – "a journey of an entire people toward its liberation through the desert of structural and organised injustice that surrounds us [where] it is important to persevere in prayer, even if we hardly do more than stammer groans and cries..."[58] It is in these 'contrast experiences' and the 'sacramentality' that they proclaim where we are challenged to discern the 'trace' of a God who has always withdrawn – so that we can also hear that voice

---

56. In the context of the so-called 'developed' economies, see, among others, Bourdieu et. al., *La misère du monde* (Paris, Éditions du Seuil, 1993).

57. For this two opposing ethical approaches, see Schillebeeckx, *Jesus in Our Western Tradition: Mysticism, Ethics and Politics* (London, 1987) 49.

58. Gutierrez, *Drinking from our Own Wells: The Spiritual Journey of a People* (Maryknoll, NY, 1984) 129.

within Elie Wiesel as he stood at the foot of a teenager hanged at Auschwitz:[59]

"Where is your God?"
"Where is he? He is here… He is hung on the cross."

Brusselsestraat 165/ K010   Daniel Franklin PILARIO, c.m.
B-3000 Leuven

---

59. Quoted by Chauvet, *Symbol and Sacrament*, 490.

PART TWO

FACETS OF SACRAMENTALITY

INTRODUCTION

*The heart has reasons of which reason knows nothing;
we know this in countless ways.*

Pensées

In reflecting upon what the meaning of 'sacramental presence' could be in a 'postmodern context', perhaps these oft-quoted words of Blaise Pascal might prove instructive. Though Pascal himself stood at the beginnings of modernity, there can be little doubt that he had a genuine sense of its scope, both in its grandeur as well as its feebleness. Whether demonstrated by mathematical proofs, experiments with a vacuum or developing a calculating machine, his mathematical genius and his scientific/technological prowess were quintessentially "modern." At the same time, as reflected in his *Pensées*, Pascal realized the serious shortcomings, even costs, of this powerful modern reason. As a man of faith, he was well aware of something 'more', something 'else' or 'other', something even disturbing, that could be neither grasped nor touched by such autonomous reason. Indeed, in the depths of human existence there were those "reasons of which reason knows nothing." Not only his *Pensées*, but Pascal's own life have certainly been animated by those reasons of another sort, as difficult as that may have made things.

The core of modernity could well be described as a thorough confidence in the capabilities and self-transparency of human reason. As history has shown, this modern sense of reason presented profound and difficult challenges to the religious sphere, bringing its claims and practices (its words and deeds) "before the tribunal of reason." Insofar as Christianity has understood itself as belief in a transcendent yet present God – the mystery of incarnation – "reason alone" was presented with a paradox it could neither resolve nor accept. As such, theology was presented with a difficult problem. As a *reflective* endeavor, theology would seem to be forced either to adopt this modern reason in speculative idealism – whereby religious faith is taken to be merely inadequately developed/clarified reason and transcendence is ultimately "domesticated" (as might be exemplified by Hegel) or give in to speculative skepticism – whereby religious faith and reason are considered two incompatible and irreconcilable spheres (as might be exemplified by Kant). While clearly a source of advancement for the sciences and technology, the clarity and power of modern reason seemed to have relegated religion to a realm of superstition and rendered its "reasons" mute. Before the tribunal of such reason, what could be a *locus theologicus* that would manifest an incarnate God? Where and how might religion speak its reasons of which reason knows nothing?

While 'postmodern' has become a rather ubiquitous term in recent years, a term aptly bearing a plurality of meanings and spawning rather divergent philosophies and theologies, perhaps the 'postmodern context' might well be described as a profound, even pervading, sense that the tribunal of reason is not final, that there are "reasons of which reason knows nothing," and that it is precisely these "unreasonable" reasons which are of vital importance to us. But again, how to get at such reasons? And give them a place where they may be made manifest and speak to us?

Because modern reason ultimately left no room for anything else, much of the impetus of post-modern thinking has been spent on "undoing" such modern reason. This has taken many shapes in numerous thinkers, opening quite a wide range of possibilities, but this undoing would seem most evident in the rejection of onto-theological metaphysics and the concomitant deconstruction of anything "foundational" or "originary." Instead, radical and unmediated "difference" stands out and refuses to be subsumed. While this surely opens a space for reasons of another sort – providing interesting opportunities for thinking transcendence and grace,[1] as well as appreciating the significance of history and culture[2] – it at the same time brings forth new difficulties. In radicalizing difference, the connection between transcendence and immanence, the very crux of incarnation, risks being overlooked, or even lost. And without incarnation – its paradoxicality included – what would Christianity be?

If there would be no metaphysical grounds as such – no "meta-narratives" or "logo-centric" reasons – for Christian self-understanding, how then are Christians to understand themselves? From where might they "reason"?

In one sense, the answer might seem readily apparent. Do not sacraments in their symbolicity display reasons of another sort, reasons which could never be reduced to reason and its onto-theological metaphysics – in short, "reasons of which reason knows nothing"? Are not sacraments

---

1. Consider, for example, Jean-Luc Marion, especially his discussion of 'distance'/'icon' and 'gift'.
2. Among others, consider for example, Mark C. Taylor and Gianni Vattimo.

themselves an "incarnate" intersection of transcendence and immanence – of spirit and water, of Christ and bread broken, etc.? Still, one must be careful here. Although the sacraments might well be unique *loci* of the presence of God, their incarnational reality is far from simple. While Christians clearly believe that God is present in the sacraments, they would surely not reduce God's presence to the sacrament, creating a sort of 'idol'. Rather, as Louis-Marie Chauvet has shown in his *Sacrament and Symbol*, it is precisely the *symbolic* way in which sacraments work that lays opens a space wherein transcendence and immanence come to touch, "the symbolic place where God becomes enfleshed in our humanity."[3]

As with any symbolic place, this place is neither established nor grounded by reason. Indeed, God is not *held* in the things of the sacrament – which would be an idolization – but is rather *present* in them. This is crucial for sacraments, for they are not simply metaphysical entities which require reasoned/intellectual assent. Instead, like Pascal's "reasons of the heart," the "reasons" of sacraments touch upon and are played out on another dimension, a place from which we truly live. This vital sphere, what might be termed 'existential freedom', is precisely where encounter with 'difference'/'the other' – in this case, God – "*takes place.*" Here, reasons are not simply a matter of acknowledgement/assent, but of grace and whole-hearted response, for these reasons invoke, call upon one's deepest self and demand a life-response. The "place" of sacraments, then, is not to be confused with metaphysical space (though involving it), for this place is a sphere wherein something happens, "takes places," and what happens is of decisive significance in/for one's life.

As such, the "place" of sacraments truly reflects the incarnational, "enfleshed," reality of Christian faith. Because the incarnateness of God is experienced as an "evocative" *presence* (gift/grace) in water, bread, community, etc., sacraments become truly a place of salvation (where salvation "takes place"). Theological reflection which draws upon "the place" of sacraments, keeping the "reasons" of sacraments in view, not only contends with the problems brought forth by modern reason, but also begins to address the concerns and challenges presented by post-modern thinking.

Part two of this volume is devoted to various ways of thinking out the "reasons" of sacraments so that their rightful "place" might come to the fore, both as integral/fundamental to theological reflection and as how they are/might be "enfleshed" in concrete praxis. In this way, the diverse

---

3. *Symbole et Sacrament: Une relecture sacramentelle de l'existence chrétienne* (Paris, Les Éditions du Cerf, 1987) 87.

contributions address the question of the presence of God in a postmodern context by sketching, from various angles, some of the "sacramental contours" of a God incarnate.

In section one, "Discovering the Sacramentality of Sacraments," the contributions seek to bring to light different ways in which the sacramentality of the sacraments addresses concerns brought forward by postmodern thought. Kevin IRWIN does so by pointing out how liturgy is a "privileged focus" from which to describe what we believe, and how what we do in sacraments – "liturgical actio" – needs to be experienced as flowing from and nourishing what we do in daily life. George WORGUL explains how ritual participation brings individuals into its meaning structures and how "root metaphors" therein can more fruitfully express how God is present in sacrament. László LUKÁCS takes communication of symbols as "a matrix for a fresh understanding of the sacramental nature of the history of salvation and the sacraments as real symbols," showing how the "communicative" reality of God, and the concomitant personal commitment this entails, find their pre-eminent place in sacrament. Timothy CRUTCHER likewise reminds us that the "grounds" of faith are "relational." For in language we find underlying "relational vectors" that undergird language and "relational excesses" which always escape words, revealing an impetus for our theologizing which cannot but be ecumenical.

In section two, "Exposing Eucharistic Faces," the contributions each focus upon the Eucharist as taking a central place in the life of faith and how the eucharistic presence of Christ comes to be "given a face" – "enfleshed." First Gino MATTHEEUWS examines the sacramental place and function of the ordained minister as presider, showing how acting *in persona Christi* needs to be rooted in acting *in persona Ecclesiae* so that the presence of Christ retains an absence which calls us to transcendence. Thomas SCIRGHI exposes another eucharistic face, the proclaiming face, by reconsidering how preaching works. Instead of a theoretical, propositional-doctrinal proclamation of words, a new homiletic will "uncover the presence of Christ within the community" in such a way that "meaning happens" and the sacrament is truly "transformative." In his postmodern reading of "Sunday Celebrations in the Absence of a Priest," Jerry FARMER turns the face further by considering what might be termed, and in a fruitful way, "the faceless (non-)Eucharist." While clearly a "directive" (with its "authoritative voice") concerning communal celebrations, in this he finds vital threads of heterogeneity, for even in these celebrations there is a presence of God enfleshed by the very coming together of the assembly. With another shift of perspective, Willem Marie SPEELMAN exposes another eucharistic face by considering the problematic of sacrament through electronic media – i.e. broadcast liturgy where the viewer is not there in the flesh. Though the postmodern context is clearly a media culture, the contribution points out how the sacramental cannot be mediated through ideas or images, but "communicates Him as a tangible presence." From these many faces, the question arises on how sacrament can "take place" in such a way that God's presence comes to be incarnate.

Finally, in section three, "Re-imag(in)ing Sacramental Contours," the various contributions each seek to sketch out some of the contours of how the presence of God does or could comes to be "enfleshed" in sacrament. Eugene MCDOWELL and Meghan FROEHLICH bring an "incarnational grounding of eucharistic discourse" to the fore by examining how it is in and through the Eucharist – the place where humans participate in the relational life of the Trinity – that participants are transformed to become the body of Christ in the world. Next, Dorothy MCDOUGALL draws out the deep ecological contours upon which the incarnational character of sacraments depends, though typically neglected. By so re-imaging the "cosmos as sacrament" we are oriented to an inextricable unity of creation-redemption (ridding us of anthropocentric biases and hegemonic imagery in sacramental theology). Susan ROLL looks again at baptism and seeks to draw out its truly sacramental "enfleshment" by considering "women-identified perspectives." By working from embodied self-understandings, dualistic thinking is replaced with a more "generational" imaging of new life and how nature, for example water, is not to be dominated but a nurturer of our faith. Lastly, Jon PAHL takes specifically water – so integrally part of the Christian tradition – and traces out a way in which this taken for granted "element" can bring forth a vital sense of God's life-giving presence and its call to responsibility.

Katholieke Universiteit Leuven John C. RIES
Faculty of Theology
Leuven, Belgium

SECTION ONE

DISCOVERING THE SACRAMENTALITY OF SACRAMENTS

LITURGICAL ACTIO: SACRAMENTALITY, ESCHATOLOGY AND ECOLOGY

If the academic study and the contemporary pastoral experience of liturgy and sacraments are to resonate with the ever-developing theological enterprise within Catholicism and with the faith life of contemporary believers, they will need to return to some traditional, but often neglected themes, and reappropriate them in new ways.[1] The postmodern context affords sacramental theologians and pastoral ministers both a profound challenge and opportunity to retrieve insights from our whole theological tradition which can serve to stimulate a proper rediscovery of the role that liturgy and sacraments can and should play in the lives of believers of any time and place. Reflection on the liturgy as *actio* can serve both academic and pastoral theologians by grounding inquiry into liturgy and sacraments in the church's *praxis* and by doing so to connect theory about liturgy and its enactment with the life and faith experience of believers at prayer. The traditional axiom *legem credendi lex statuat supplicandi*[2] is the key principle in what follows, a contemporary retrieval of which can and should have enormous implications for the very credibility and desirability of liturgical and sacramental engagement

---

1. By "traditional" here I mean what can be uncovered from retrieving a theological language inspired by the premedieval liturgical rites; this is to be distinguished from "conventional" which I take to mean the theological parameters generally accepted from Trent on.
2. For helpful commentaries on the statement of Prosper of Aquitaine see, among others, K. Federer, *Liturgie und Glaube. Eine theologie-geschichtliche Untersuchung. Paradosis IV. Legem credendi lex statuat supplicandi* (Fribourg: Paulusverlag, 1950).

in our day as well as on an adequate base on which to ground theological reflection on liturgy and sacraments.[3] To return to such principles as liturgy as *actio* and *lex orandi, lex credendi* does not mean repetition of what was done or said in the past; it means true *reappropriation* in order that their core meaning be expressed and developed to suit contemporary needs. When such traditional principles are so regarded, elaborated on and expanded to fit new circumstances, then they avoid the characterization of anachronism (a charge which has not been made illegitimately concerning some aspects of the contemporary revised liturgy).

A study of the liturgical *actio* includes theological reflection on its intrinsic elements – scriptures proclaimed, euchology prayed, symbolic engagement achieved through the use of creation, gestures and the nonverbal.[4] These elements have traditionally been regarded as essential 'sources' for the theology derived from the liturgy. In the context of the present reform of the liturgy, their intrinsic character as dynamic and involving should be emphasized to the extent that, for example, words and symbols and are appreciated as important means to accomplish communal sanctification and salvation because of their inherently dialogical and involving character. In essence we explore the riches of the proclaimed scriptures theologically because what is heard through speech discloses what is actually occurring through speech in the act of liturgical proclamation. Words matter because *through words things happen*. As such, we cannot but appreciate the intrinsically symbolic nature of the liturgy and the multivalent nature of what sacraments "do." We reflect on the theology of the euchology prayed in order to reflect on and experience at liturgy what the church believes, which study is often emphasized given the maxim *lex orandi, lex credendi*. These texts also have a particularly formative character because they reflect the church's world-view, especially its anthropology, wherein the way humans interact and communicate in human life through gestures, signs and symbols is the predicate for symbolic engagement in the liturgy. We appreciate the entire act of liturgy as an experience of communication: of God to us and us to God, speaking and acting in God's name. The present reformed liturgy offers the contemporary church a wealth of theology in what it celebrates liturgically and how the liturgy is enacted. The liturgy is thus understood as a profound anthropological and theological act

---

3. For one example of a survey of contemporary approaches to liturgical and sacramental theology today see, among others, R. Duffy, K. Irwin and D. Power, "Sacramental Theology: A Review of Literature", in *Theological Studies* 55 (1994) 657-706.

4. See my own, *Context and Text: Method in Liturgical Theology* (Collegeville: The Liturgical Press, 1994) Part Two, 85-261.

leading to (theological) reflection and appropriation. In essence the celebration of the present reform of the liturgy offers a privileged *locus* from which to describe what we believe in dynamic ways. This kind of liturgical theological enterprise is crucial, in my opinion, for the sake of the very credibility of the reformed liturgy itself as well as for the theology disclosed in and through it.

Regrettably this kind of theological appreciation of the reformed liturgy and reflection on it can still seem foreign to contemporary believers despite liturgy's centrality in the Christian life. For all too many, liturgy can still be regarded as a cult of fixed forms, as impenetrable because it is derived from arcane sources and as hard to decipher given its terse phrasings and (often regrettably in celebration) its minimalism in human expressiveness and in symbolic engagement. In addition, what often clouds the appropriation of what the liturgy is saying is the theological overlay which people bring to the liturgy and assume is being asserted even though the texts and actions of the liturgy may not be saying that at all. (For example the institution narrative states "this is my body" not "here I am present."[5]) Most challenging of all may well be the fact that worshipers often experience a "disconnect" between what they do at sacraments and what preoccupies them in daily life – rather than seeing sacramental liturgy as a ritual that is meant to structure and give perspective to the whole of the Christian life, both inside and outside the liturgy. Part of the thesis of this contribution is that the liturgy derives from and ritualizes our belief and it offers a faith perspective to issues of contemporary import. The enactment of liturgy – its *actio* – is the pivotal, central root from which to develop an adequate sacramental theology today. The very "aim to be considered above all else" of the conciliar reform of the liturgy, that it foster "full, conscious, and active participation,"[6] need not be understood to refer only to the conduct of the rites. It can (and should) mean reflection on the kind of theology that should be developed about the liturgy, specifically that all liturgical acts are ecclesial acts done in, for and by the whole church. It is our contention that among the many aspects of liturgy there are three pillars of every act of liturgy that can and should be unpacked theologically. Reflection herein can give liturgy its credible place in the lives of Christians today – they are *sacramentality, eschatology* and *ecology*.

---

5. Statement of K. Rahner, "The Presence of Christ in the Sacrament of the Lord's Supper," in *Theological Investigations*, Vol. 4 (New York: Crossroad, 1982) 309.
6. See, *Sacrosanctum concilium* n. 14 and *passim*.

Sacramentality

That the term "sacrament" was broadened at Vatican II (and since) beyond the medieval locus of seven experiences of grace has been a major advance in contemporary theology. That the ground-breaking works of Rahner and Schillebeeckx[7] influenced the conciliar debates expressed in such assertions that the church is "a kind of sacrament"[8] is clear. Contemporary sacramentalists presume such terminology and understandably rely on the admittedly helpful paradigms of Christ and the church as sacraments. However at this point, some thirty years after Vatican II, one can legitimately ask whether this kind of terminology has ultimately been that effective (or even truly adequate) in bridging the gap between what occurs in liturgy and sacraments and what humans are engaged in in the whole of human life. If the attempt to broaden the notion of 'sacrament' was meant to emphasize how the incarnate God is discovered in all of life, one could well reflect today that perhaps the decidedly sacral overtones to terminology surrounding the seven sacraments, especially from the medieval period on, made this term itself less than truly adequate for this purpose. In point of fact this contemporary expanding of the terminology about 'sacrament' reversed what happened when the patristic and early medieval church evolved numerous and varied liturgical and sacramental rites. These rites were themselves based on the theological principle of a broad understanding of sacramentality, which principle grounded how the church eventually came to describe seven of them as 'sacraments'. In this connection it is also at least worth reflecting whether contemporary theology's "turn to the subject" may itself also contribute to an overly anthropomorphic emphasis in liturgical and sacramental theology.

I should like to argue that when the term "sacramentality" is more adequately restored as reflective of one's place in the universe, specifically the intrinsic relatedness of human persons to both the cosmos and to other beings in the world, then liturgy and (the seven) sacraments can be reappropriated as uniquely revelatory of the immanent and transcendent God we believe in – both incarnate (in all that implies) and of drawing us beyond here and now to eternal communion with that same God in eternity.

---

7. See the convenient English translations of E. Schillebeeckx, *Christ the Sacrament of the Encounter with God* (New York: Sheed and Ward, 1963) and K. Rahner, *The Church and the Sacraments*, trans. W. J. O'Hara (New York: Sheed and Ward, 1963).

8. The text of *Lumen gentium* n. 1 reads "cum autem Ecclesia sit in Christo veluti sacramentum seu signum et instrumentum intimae cum Deo unionis totiusque generis humani unitatis..."

Succinctly put, the principle of sacramentality is the notion that all reality

> is potentially or in fact the bearer of God's presence and the instrument of God's saving activity... This principle is rooted in the nature of a sacrament as such, i.e. a visible sign of the invisible presence and activity of God. Together with the principles of mediation (God works through secondary agents to achieve divine ends) and communion (the end of all of God's activity is the union of humanity), the principle of sacramentality constitutes one of the central theological characteristics of Catholicism.[9]

Within this kind of classical Christian worldview, particularly its presumption of our relatedness to the world and all that dwells in it including all other human persons, the cosmic and anthropological rootedness of liturgy and sacraments can be recalled and used to ground theological reflection on a number of things. These include the sacramentality of human life viewed through the prism of the incarnation, and the sacramentality of all things in creation when viewed through the prism of God as creator and as sustainer of the universe.

In other words, from the point of view of articulating an adequate method for a study of the nature of sacraments, what has been missing is what lies behind and undergirds the ritual enactment of sacraments – sacramentality – which notion, when retrieved, roots sacraments in being derived from and having their requisite impact on daily life. In effect one of the problems with post-conciliar language is its highly *sacral* character, which terminology has often replaced the more traditional language that supports its *sacramental* character. From the time of Vatican II on, once the term 'sacrament' came to be applied to a range of things legitimately related to but not really on the same level as the liturgical enactment of sacramental rituals, then the language about sacraments became less precise, not to say too diffuse so as to cause confusion. The endeavor to restore the centrality of Christ and the church as basic elements of any act of liturgy and sacrament (and as pivotal for the whole of the Christian life) is all to the good and to be applauded. However, when Christ and church are called 'sacraments' the notion of *sacramentality* can be severely diminished, if not truly eclipsed, and the more fundamental cosmic and incarnational overtones of sacramentality are diminished if not lost.

This emphasis on Christ and church as sacraments tries to restore the classical understanding that through liturgy and sacraments we experience God here and now as revealer and as transparent in all of life. However, the sacraments themselves, understood as privileged means

---

9. Definition from *The Harper Collins Encyclopedia of Catholicism* (San Francisco: Harper Collins, 1995) 1148.

whereby God's presence and grace are mediated to the believing church, are not to be understood as the unique or exclusive means for this mediation in any way. Rather sacraments serve as regularly repeated ritual reminders of what we believe about God and what the God of Christian revelation discloses about the world and about our role in this graced world.

While what is asserted here is very traditional, it can at least be argued that in fact what occurred in Christianity's second millennium was a progressive eclipsing of this kind of integral vision of God, the incarnation and human life in favor of one that progressively emphasized that and how sacraments 'caused' or 'conferred' grace with the result that these seven channels of grace came to be perceived as almost our only access to the divine. The rigid uniformity of the Tridentine liturgy itself contributed to such an exclusive locus because of its emphasis on the precise performance of the rubrics directing the liturgy. What came to be neglected was the principle of *sacramentality* itself whereby symbols taken from nature or which are the result of human manufacture[10] are themselves to be taken seriously not only for what they cause or confer but also for what they are – goods from this good earth that reflect back on the providence of the God of creation as well as the God of redemption.

One of the contributions which this kind of emphasis on sacramentality can make is that sacramental liturgy can be mined theologically both for what it does and for the way it accomplishes it. This is to say that sacramental liturgy is both a means and an end. It is a key means to the end of experiencing God in the here and now. But the church's particular means to deepen this experience matters a great deal. This is to say that in liturgy all that we do in terms of using the goods of this earth matters theologically because their very use in liturgy makes a theological statement about what we believe the earth to be ("and it was very good" Gen 1,3) and the interdependence of all living things on it. In effect what sacraments do is to articulate in a privileged way the already existing and never ceasing symphony of praise from creation itself. This act of articulation is always the vocation of humans to offer to God. What this requires is an integral vision of the universe and humanity's role in it to appreciate what is expressed through what the (whole of) liturgy actually does and is. In effect the traditional maxim *lex orandi, lex credendi* when combined with the traditional doctrine of sacramentality can be an essential and pivotal locus from which to develop a most adequate liturgical theology of sacraments today, which enterprise would have far reaching theological and spiritual implications. The restoration

---

10. See, for example, *Context and Text,* 130-151.

of sacramentality emphasizes the way what we do in liturgy through symbols and gestures expresses our belief in how and where God is revealed in human life and is expressed how it is through the very material and human means that God accomplishes our sanctification and salvation.

Such a perspective leads to the particular contribution that a liturgically-inspired sacramental theology can make to the contemporary discussion and presentation of what is often termed "creation theology" and "creation spirituality." In effect Catholicism has a great deal to contribute to a creation-based theology and spirituality precisely because of the kind of theology that results from the church's expressed belief in sacramentality and in the church's *lex orandi*. This is to say that some of the perceived overemphases and imbalances in creation theology can be ameliorated or at least addressed by the kind of integral theology about the range of theological topics – not just sacraments – that derives from theology developed with the liturgy as its primary and essential source. This means that any perceived overemphasis toward creation and away from the death and resurrection of Jesus can be set right by a liturgical theology that by its nature and in its ritual expression reflects on creation, the incarnation and the paschal mystery. If in fact all liturgy is intrinsically paschal, the very celebration of liturgy itself reflects how all liturgy is also incarnational, principally through the use of the goods of this earth in its ritual enactment. Similarly any perceived imbalance in creation spirituality toward the earth and nature itself can be ameliorated by liturgical theology because all of creation, humans included, are set in right relationship by the celebration of liturgical rites themselves which by their nature combine the goods of earth with human articulation of praise, thanks and supplication. Christian liturgy holds up the earth, especially its primal elements, and combines them with human speech about God and human speech to proclaim God's revelation. The God we address, revere and invoke in liturgy is the God of creation as well as the God of redemption. One contribution of the liturgy is its integrity, namely *in* and *how* what it says and does ritually with what this has to say about what be believe about God, humanity and all of creation outside of liturgy. The principle *lex orandi, lex credendi* discloses what we believe about sacraments themselves and also about what we believe about the experience of God in human life and in the any synthesis about what we believe about God in Christian theology.

Eschatology

While never absent from Western medieval (and subsequent) sacramental theology, the category of eschatology has experienced an appropriate retrieval in our day. The (over)emphasis placed on presence and sacrifice in the eucharist had its resonance in other sacraments in terms of theological descriptions of what they 'caused' or 'conferred' (to use the oft repeated verbs from Peter Lombard through the Council of Trent[11]). For a variety of reasons the early medievals paved the way for such an emphasis on what sacraments 'do' and 'are' here and now as opposed to the helpful distinctions which patristic authors could offer about what sacraments do here and now and what they anticipate as their fulfilment in the kingdom.[12] Clearly one value of the patristic era was the way its language could countenance important distinctions etymologically, for example between 'original' and 'copy', with 'copy' referring to the full reality of Christ's presence here and now and to eucharistic participation as reflective the 'original' exalted Lord of all creation who died, rose, ascended and who will come again. In comparison subsequent debates about Christ's presence in the eucharist and the (albeit legitimate) theology about presence and sacrifice did not sustain the helpful insights presumed in the patristic statement of the issues. What emerged from the medievals was a sacramental theology that helpfully emphasized how important sacraments were as 'symbolic causes' of sanctification and salvation and as chief channels of grace to us.

In such a conventional schema, eschatology was often restricted to intercessions and other prayers for the deceased. That sacraments were both food for our journey to the kingdom and experiences of the future kingdom here and now were assertions rarely put in parallel or statements on a par with each other. Once again contemporary research into the *lex orandi* of the church's traditional liturgies[13] and the *orandi* of the present reform can serve to redirect emphasis on both what the liturgy is and does, and what it anticipates and longs for. Especially when one considers the range of issues surrounding how one can and should describe the liturgy as the *memoria Christi*, particularly in the way it

---

11. The medieval debates about whether the sacraments 'caused' and/or 'conferred' grace with Lombard asserting that they 'caused' grace and Trent asserting that they 'conferred' grace (DS 1606) are well known. Similarly the debates over how they did so are also well known with the "Dominican school" characterized as insisting on efficient causality and the "Franciscan school" emphasizing dispositive causality (understanding that there is a range of authors and nuances here).

12. Among the more helpful expositions on the eucharist from this perspective, see A. Gerken, *Teologia dell' eucaristia,* trans. B. Mabritto and A. Bressan (Alba: Edizioni Paoline, 1977; German original 1972).

13. See G. Wainwright, *Eucharist and Eschatology* (London: Epworth Press, 1971).

manifests here and now all that Jesus accomplished for our salvation,[14] it is especially pertinent today to recall that sacramental liturgy is always an effective presence and memorial of Christ, which liturgical experience is of the unique, past redemptive events experienced anew here and now, and their fulfilment in the kingdom. Sacramental liturgy is always an experience and expression of "the future present."[15] That eschatology is a fundamental category is as ancient as the cry at the end of liturgies in the early church, *maranatha* to the *sacrum convivium* of Thomas Aquinas to the explicit emphasis much of the contemporary liturgy's *lex orandi*. (For example the explicit eschatological reference in eucharistic prayer four *et, exspectantes ipsius adventum in gloria* helpfully advances the anamnesis of the Roman Canon *tam beatae passionis, necnon et ab inferis resurrectionis, sed et in caelo gloriosae ascensionis*.)

In addition to this highly teleological premise of all liturgy, there is also another equally traditional contribution which the eschatological emphasis can make to a theological explication of Christian sacraments that can help both in their being appreciated as credible and as their requiring that participants seek to experience in life what they have experienced liturgically – namely that sacraments always have a mission and justice dimension. The very fact that all contemporary liturgies contain euchological prayers which always point to what we do not yet possess (at least as fully as we might) and substantially worded intercessory prayers for what we need and that in liturgical prayer we seek for what we do not yet have, indicates that the liturgy always articulates our belief in a providential God who also challenges us to serve others as God serves us here and now through the sacraments themselves. The yearning for what is not yet fully revealed or for what we do not yet possess are clear indications of eschatology's intrinsic nature in both sacramental liturgy and in theology in general. The very fact that we pray for our needs in liturgy indicates that all human life and liturgy are provisional. Only in God's fullness will we be complete.

Such an eschatological recovery can also help to demonstrate how justice is intrinsically grounded in sacramental liturgy. The linkage of liturgy and social justice is by no means a contemporary fad or trend. The very fact that liturgy itself is eschatological grounds how the justice we experience in liturgy always leads us to yearn for its fulfilment and at liturgy we are always challenged to share with others the divine (and

---

14. For a useful summary and assessment of a number of theories of liturgical memorial, see, F. Chenderlin, *Do This As My Memorial*, Analecta Biblica, 99 (Roma: Biblical Institute Press, 1982).

15. See the helpful theology of worship by M. Micks, *The Future Present. The Phenomenon of Christian Worship* (New York: Seabury Press, 1970).

therefore qualitatively superior and all-encompassing) justice we have experienced in the liturgy itself.

Clearly this is commonly understood to be anthropocentric and thus oriented toward other humans. Yet it is the liturgical *orandi* itself which broadens any such perspective to include all things that dwell on the earth, the earth itself and the cosmos. The declaration of the fourth eucharistic prayer

> you formed man in your own likeness and set him over the whole world to serve you, his creator and to rule over all creatures[16]

is itself an explicit demonstration of the way the liturgy's *orandi* reflects the cosmos as well as humans, where humans take responsibility for the cosmos as stewards. The fact that the prayer articulates the place of humans in the *magnalia Dei* prayed in such blessing prayers is itself a reflection of how the earth is appreciated as the arena where humans live and work out their salvation, not only *from* the world but by being engaged as trustworthy stewards *in* the world. Again, any "other worldly" notions of salvation or of an anthropocentric notion of salvation are here placed in relation to the wider tapestry of the world as sacrament of God[17] and of the prayers in sacraments as reminders of our role in creation and our responsibility for it.

This is to suggest that sacramental liturgy is best appreciated theologically and spiritually as privileged means of experiencing God here and now and as a challenge for us to live and share with others what we ourselves have experienced liturgically. This means that social justice is not an option – it is an extension of what sacramental ritual enacts. Especially because the *lex orandi* consistently refers to the cosmos and all things on the earth, nature and humans themselves, that we rightly insist that justice refers to this good earth as well as to persons on it.

Ecology

Contemporary reflection on the environmental crisis often distinguishes between *environment*, meaning our living on this earth and the world as our surroundings, and *ecology*, which refers to our being "at home in the

---

16. The Latin reads: Hominem ad tuam imaginem condidisti,
eique commisisti mundi curam universi,
ut, tibi soli Creatori serviens,
Creaturis omnibus imperaret.

17. See A. Schmemann, *Sacraments and Orthodoxy* (New York: Herder & Herder, 1965) and the brief but helpful insights in T. Runyon, "The World As Original Sacrament," in *Worship* 54 (1980) 495-511.

world."[18] Another contribution which sacramental liturgy can make toward concern for preserving creation and our being at home in the world is that by its nature it combines both of these aspects and articulates how humans are both "at home" in the world as God's gift and also how humans are "pilgrims" who yearn for a new heaven and a new earth.

The very fact that sacramental liturgy uses symbols – of this earth or made by human hands from this earth – is an expression of *lex orandi* not only through texts but through texts placed in relation to the goods of creation. The euchological articulation of our belief in the God of creation and redemption is thus helpfully reflected in both the fact that we use symbols in liturgy and the way in which we use them: water for baptismal washing, bread and wine for eucharistic sharing, oil for anointing etc. But sometimes it is the use of the symbols in liturgy themselves that articulates the need for trustworthy stewards today simply because what we do liturgically clashes with what we now find in nature and the cosmos. This is especially true of the way symbols are to be used (enacted really) in the revised liturgy. We use water in baptism for washing, yet how much of this world's water is polluted? We are to immerse in water for the richer experience of washing and new life, but how often do political considerations over "water rights" mitigate notions about "new life" when some people do not have the water they need to sustain physical life? (The anthropological and cosmic premise of the use of water at initiation is that it is the only element in creation without which we cannot live.) We use bread and wine at the eucharist to remind us of all of God's gifts to us and of human ingenuity in manufacturing these central liturgical symbols to be shared in communion. The clash here is between the eucharistic species to sustain us on our pilgrim way and the fact that there are all to many places on this "good earth" where there is not enough food for people to live on. The liberation challenge about using "stolen" bread for the eucharist cannot but resonate with contemporary experience where all too many people simply do not have enough of the world's resources to live on – much less to use for the sacramental realization here and now of the kingdom of God to be fulfilled. Some here and now do not have enough of the resources of this world to live on much less to be sustained on them as signs of a better, richer, fuller life to come.

These actual human life experiences raise legitimate questions for sacramental liturgy, questions which challenge theologians to articulate the intrinsic relationship between sacraments and these kinds of crises in daily life. The issue becomes less one of fostering onto liturgy a political

---

18. From the Greek term *oikos*.

agenda than it does one of admitting the clash between what we profess sacramentally and how the symbols of the liturgy reflect the vision of creation to be shared in by all God's creatures. Again the contribution of sacramental liturgy here is not to overstress political action against the praise of God or to emphasize social involvement over against prayer. What the liturgy provides is an inclusive balance that requires our attentiveness to faith in the God who dwells with us in this world and to the requisite demands which faith in God places on us all in terms of service of each other. Liturgy as a balance of praise of God and service of each other helps ground our communal prayer which could otherwise become too concerned with either the heavenly or the earthly. By its nature, the liturgy always does both. Hence it serves as a central experience of "heaven on earth" and of the way we are then to share the goods of this earth with each other.

In a world that needs to reevaluate the distribution of the world's goods and how 'good' resources are polluted and devastated in nature, the doctrine of sacramentality comes full circle. This is to say that because we believe that God is discovered in all of life and on this good earth, then we need to be attentive to how this theological locus is revered and made more vibrant in our day by the celebration of sacramental liturgy itself. When probed from the perspective of *lex orandi, lex credendi,* sacramental liturgy expresses our belief in the God of redemption as well as the (same) God of creation. It offers praise and thanks for what is, while at the same time it begs for what is not yet – for example, equitable distribution of the world's goods and the eschatological banquet where all will feast superabundantly. Sacramental liturgy always leads us to this kind of full realization since it also names where and when equity in terms of the use of the goods of this world does not exist. Sacramental liturgy is therefore best understood both a means to lead to a more adequate distribution of the world's resources as well as the ultimate realization and experience of God's goodness in the kingdom. Sacramental liturgy thus offers a balanced and proper theological and ecclesial grounding of real human and world concerns, including (but certainly not limited to) environment and ecology. By its nature and structure, the *lex orandi* of sacraments avoids the either/or of God of creation and redemption, and it properly integrates creation theology and spirituality with the Catholic tradition. It respects liturgy as a theological source and underscores liturgy's challenges. Such are appropriate means whereby the church's contemporary sacramental practice can become the more credible without becoming too narrow ideologically or theologically.[19]

Conclusion

The premise of this article has been that sacramental liturgy, understood as the *actio ecclesiae,* defines Catholicism as a living tradition that enacts what it believes. Engagement in sacramental liturgy is crucial to foster awareness of the divine in the human and the response of humans to the divine in service to others: that is to persons and to the world. For credibility, for good liturgical theology and for adequate notions about sacrament, the church's *lex orandi* provide a most adequate, compelling and challenging theological source. The premise of *sacramentality* articulated here recovers a traditional paradigm for all sacramental engagement. A major contribution it makes to sacramental credibility is the way it bridges the 'sacred' and 'secular' aspects of human life in terms of God's transparency in human life and the way it draws us beyond the here and now toward a "new heavens and a new earth" (2 Pet 3,13). When such traditional concepts are recalled, such as the challenge which sacraments always offer and present day crises in our world, then it is logical that we can see in sacramental liturgy a clear locus for articulating a theology that necessarily includes eschatology and ecology. Because liturgy enacts the divine and articulates our beliefs, it can be succinctly argued that the doctrine of sacramentality needs sacraments, and for the sake of credibility sacraments themselves need to be understood as intrinsically "sacramental."

The Catholic University of America   Kevin W. IRWIN
Department of Theology
Washington, D.C. 20064

---

19. See, among others, K. Irwin, "The Sacramentality of Creation and the Role of Creation in Liturgy and Sacraments," in E. Pellegrino and K. Irwin (eds.), *Preserving the Creation. Environmental Theology and Ethics* (Washington, DC: Georgetown University Press, 1994) 67-111.

ROOT METAPHORS AND SACRAMENTAL PRESENCE IN A POSTMODERN AGE

At first glance, the conjunction of the terms 'Root Metaphor', 'Sacramental Presence' and 'Postmodernism' seems oxymoronic. The Postmodern Movement appears to question the very existence of roots or grounding. Instead, it seems to thrive on the theme of absence not presence. Consequently, two questions arise immediately. First, is there any way for Christian sacramentalists to converse with Postmodernism and still value the cultural reality and function of root metaphors? Second, can the general and specific claims for the salvific presence of divine love both within and without religious ritual behavior or worship be affirmed with at least relative warrants of adequacy? The initial phases of this paper will examine three different 'schools of metaphor' operating in theological thought and praxis.

1. Three Trajectories of Metaphor

The term "metaphor" entered the horizon of sacramental/liturgical theology from two different, but potentially intersecting trajectories. The dominant path emerged from continental linguistic studies emerging from the French Structuralists and more specifically with Ricoeur's analysis of metaphor in his interpretation theory and his later narrative theory.[1] A second path emerged from classical continental anthropological research, like that of Geertz and van Gnepp, but then took an American shift in Mead[2] and Turner.[3]

Both viewpoints are deeply interested in metaphor, but with a different emphasis and lens. The metaphor as linguistic school, which I

---

1. Cf. P. Ricœur, "Explanation and Understanding: On Some Remarkable Connections Among the Theory of the Text, Theory of Action, and Theory of History," in *The Philosophy of Paul Ricoeur: An Anthology of His Work*, ed. C Reagen and D. Stewart (Boston, 1978) 149-166; P. Ricœur, *Freud and Philosophy: An Essay on Interpretation* (New Haven, 1970); P. Ricœur, *Interpretation Theory* (Fort Worth, 1976); P. Ricœur, *Symbolism of Evil* (Boston, 1976); P. Ricœur, *The Rule of Metaphor* (Toronto, 1975); P. Ricœur, "Creativity of Language," in *Philosophy Today*, vol. 17 (2/4) 97-112.

2. Cf. M. Mead, *Kinship in the Admiralty Islands* (New York, 1934).

3. Cf. V. Turner, *The Ritual Process: Structure and Anti-Structure* (Chicago, 1969).

believe to constitute the predominant theological group, focuses on metaphor as word(s), speech or narrative stories. In this focus, metaphors and narratives both disclose and shatter perceptions and claims to truth in the midst of ambiguous experience.

The metaphor as action or behavior school, which I believe has fewer theological adherents, focuses on how expressed and experienced actions can constitute both sociability and comradeship in ritual communities. Metaphors trigger, express and mediate corporate and individual identity attained in being together through shared actions. They primarily aim at encouraging performance of the good, i.e., the undertaking ethical behavior and/or witness.

Both trajectories appear valid, valuable and worthwhile. Both can suffer distortion by extremism. Placed in creative tension, both can prosper and yield increased insight. The relationship of language metaphor and behavior metaphor seems to parallel the relationship of the true and the good. The true needs to be corrected and balanced by the good and the good, needs to be informed and corrected by the true. Without each others creative tension and balance, both perspectives can become distorted. Metaphor as language can slip into a logism or even nominalism. Metaphor as behavior can slide into utilitarianism, utopianism or emotivism. Language metaphor without event is hollow and easily collapses under pressure. Behavior metaphor without language is overwhelmingly ambiguous and chaotic. If, however, both language metaphor and behavior metaphor can be held in creative tension, a third metaphor, a metaphor of beauty might emerge. Ritual may be the privileged place where language and behavior converge and compliment each other, creating a different metaphorical expression. In ritual as metaphor of beauty, the dual trajectories of language and behavior may intersect and may discover a creative and comfortable home. Beauty expresses a dimension of the true *in figura*. Also, beauty calls forth an ethical imperative insofar as it witnesses to the good. A metaphor of beauty is always a real cultural particular and never an abstract universal. Yet, the particularly beautiful moves those who encounter it beyond its particularity to the 'more' it expresses and the behavior it witnesses and demands.[4] For example, Michelangelo's *Pieta*

---

4. Cf. J. Walgrave, *Unfolding Revelation: The Nature of Doctrinal Development* (Philadelphia, 1972) 119-164; J. Walgrave, *Geloof en Theologie in de Crisis* (Kasterlee, 1966).

 or *Mater Dolorosa* in St. Peter's Basilica discloses *in figura* the truth of a particular mother's love for her child, her heart pierced and broken as she once again cradles her babe in her arms. Potentially, this *figura* calls attention to our death, our broken heartedness, our confrontation with absence and ambiguity.

An Eleventh century illuminator disclosed a similar truth of a suffering Father holding the cross of his dead son who is nestled in his lap, his paternal eyes cast to the side unable to face the tragedy directly. This *Pater Dolorosus* is seated on the 'throne of grace' and linked by the Holy Spirit to Jesus in a Trinitarian outpouring of grief, suffering and brokeness. In both the *Mater Dolorosa* and *Pater Dolorosus,* a convergence of disclosed meaning and its invitation to ethical behavior give rise to a *figura* of beauty.

Adherents to either a Modern or Postmodernism world-view gravitate to different configurations of the triad: truth, goodness and beauty. This gravitational field is not imposed from without; rather, it emerges from within the very forces that constitute the Modern or Postmodern perspectives. Let us take Modernism as an example.

The Modern was born in the insidious imperialism of reason. Human reason debunked the medieval gods. Detached, sober and allegedly objectively verifiable scientific reason replaced mythological thinking. No longer was the human dependent on external forces and powers. Autonomous reason was self-sufficient and final. No longer was the human required to appease celestial powers. Autonomous reason through logical inquiry, analysis, critical reflection and planned application could crack the codes embedded in the universe and all its entities. Reason could, then, subject them to human manipulation and control through applied science or technology. Autonomous reason could establish its own clear goals and objectives. Clearly, the cosmos existed not for the mythological gods of old, but for those humans alive now, those who would seize and subject the cosmos to their plan and design. Autonomous reason could achieve these lofty goals under its own power. Industrious labor, ingenuity and intelligence were the prayerful mantras of Modernism. In sum, autonomy, individualism, self sufficiency and self finality, these were the foundations of Modernism.

It is not surprising that modernity would gravitate toward and afford primacy to the truth with a tiny nod toward the good (as a derivative of correct thinking and frequent application of various forms of natural law theory). Beauty was virtually forgotten. On the one hand, feeling, emotion, intuition, imagination and community were unfortunate lesser dimensions of human existence which should be suppressed or controlled. Interestingly, these human features were, frequently, classified as 'feminine traits and characteristics' which impeded true critical investigation and development. On the other hand, rational thinking, science and technology (male traits) were the proper productive paths to truth. Little value was to be afforded to these 'other', these 'different' dimensions of human existence. It was just a matter of time until they, too, were harnessed and controlled by reason and jettisoned as irrelevant impediments .

Power in modernity was might. It found its highest and densest expression in 'the nuclear armaments, the unnatural human instrument for global annihilation.' A global hierarchy was fashioned on the basis of amassed nuclear destructive power. Science for science sake almost  ended the rational life which created it. Interestingly, it was through the force of feeling, intuition, emotion and imagination that attention to the good, attention to concrete ethical interaction, was revived and the march to doomsday halted. The good sobers a drunk rationalism and calls attention to the limits of individualism in a world where community is woven into the very fabric of concrete existence.

It is difficult to identify the Modern's contribution to beauty. Perhaps, it is the architectural form of the skyscraper. In some ways, the modern skyscraper mimicked the Gothic cathedrals of medieval times. However, these edifices did not soar into the heavens to draw closer to the holy. These modern 'cathedrals' were temples worshiping human power and success. Human achievement surpassed the gods of old which were now dwarfed by the rewards of human ingenuity and work: wealth, power and self-determination. Evidence of this restructuring is seen in the image of St. Patrick's Cathedral dwarfed by the skyscrapers of Rockefeller Center in New York City.

2. The Postmodern Reaction

When Victor Turner proposed his dynamic interpretation of cultural development and alteration, he described structure (what a culture is) and anti-structure (what a culture might become) as indissolubly conjoined.[5]

---

5. V. Turner, *The Ritual Process: Structure and Anti-Structure*, 131-166.

Anti-structure is already present in the concrete existential culture as its possibilities for change and development. From Turner's horizon, Postmodernism was already present as possibility in the Modern cultural world-view.

Exactly, what is it that triggers the process of breach, crisis, redressive action and resolution that fuels the cultural shift? What is it that triggers the reaction/change toward the convictions of the modern and the eventual development of the alternative Postmodern?

Turner argued that profound cultural change flowed from a weakening or collapse of the cultural ritual process. Cultures express their conscious and unconscious beliefs and convictions in the central rituals which seek to induce the participants to interpret their experiences, questions, tragedies, joys etc. within the parameters of the persons, events and symbols woven into its metaphors, narratives and social behaviors. Through ritual participation, these fundamental aspects of cultural identity and rules for social behavior are expressed and maintained among the members of the culture. Change can emerge from a distortion of ritual so that the cultural metaphors are cloaked and their power rendered inaccessible and unknown. Change can also emerge because the metaphors and narratives become sterile and impotent, no longer evoking an adequate insight or sense of reasonableness, comprehensibility or meaningfulness that can address the actual concrete living experiences of the ritual participants. Most likely, both phenomenon are mutually interactive and play crucial roles in cultural transformation.

When Toffler's perspective in *Future Shock* and *The Third Wave* are taken into account, cultural change is magnified and intensified in our own times by unprecedented global communication, increased mobility and cross-cultural travel, and world-wide economic systems.[6] These factors and others have quickened, almost beyond imagination, the rate of change. The shaking of the foundations is intensified by its rapidity and comprehensive character. The rapid rate of change can transform from one of acceptance or resistance to a reaction of paralysis or numbness, a suspension of true human functions.

If my earlier assessment of the propensity of the Modern was to elevate the true above the good and the beautiful, with the correlative emphasis on autonomous rationality over intuition, feeling, imagination and a neglect of the aesthetic is correct, one would suspect that the anti-structural possibilities of the Modern would erupt in the arts, literature and architecture. These human activities, by the very nature of their goals and enterprises, embrace imagination, intuition and feeling. The

---

6. Cf. A. Toffler, *Future Shock* (London, 1991); A. Toffler, *The Third Wave* (London, 1991).

emergence of Postmodernism within architecture is documented commonly.

One of the clearest poetic critiques of The Modern and affirmation of Postmodern themes is in D.H. Lawrence's poem "Climb Down, O Lordly Mind":

> Climb down, O lordly mind.
> O eagle of the mind, alas, you are more like a buzzard
>
> Come down now from your preeminence,
> O Mind, O lofty Spirit!
> Your hour has struck
> Your unique day is over,
> Absolutism is finished, in the human consciousness too,
>
> A man is many things, he is not only a mind,
> But in his consciousness he is twofold at least:
> he is cerebral, intellectual, mental, spiritual,
> but also he is instinctive, intuitive, and in touch.
> The mind, that needs to know all things
> must needs at last come to know its own limits,
> even its own nullity, beyond a certain point.
>
> Thou art like the moon,
> and the white mind shines on one side of thee
> but the other side is dark forever,
>
> and the dark moon draws the tides also.
>
> Thou art like the day
> but thou art also like the night,
> and thy darkness is forever invisible,
> for the strongest light throws the darkest shadow.
>
> The blood knows in darkness, and forever dark,
> in touch, by intuition, instinctively.
> The blood also knows religiously,
> and of this the mind is incapable.
> The mind is non-religious.
>
> To my dark heart, gods *are*.
> In my dark heart, love is and is not.
>
> But to my white mind
> gods and love alike are but an idea,
> a kind of fiction.
>
> Man is an alternating consciousness.
> Man is an alternating consciousness
>
> Only that exists which exists in my own consciousness
> Cogito ergo sum.

> Only that exists which exists dynamically and un
> mentalized in my blood.
>
> Non cogito, ergo sum.
> I am, I do not think that I am.[7]

Lawrence, dramatically and powerfully, questions and rejects the reduction of human existence to detached autonomous absolute reason. He affirms affect, imagination, feeling, touch and blood. The mind's knowledge is limited. There are alternative means and roads to knowing which are not mental. Living existence is not completely contingent on thought. Existence, living and feeling are prior to and deeper than thought.

3. Root Metaphors and Postmodernism

Now, we are confronted with the question of whether root metaphors possess any function or value in a Postmodern world. Turner described root metaphors as cultural foundation points of reference through which living experience is refracted and interpreted. A Postmodern first impression would understand root metaphors as cultural or transcultural 'meta-narratives' and, legitimately, call into question their claims to universal meaning and absolute truthfulness. Every and any metaphor is specific and particular culturally. Meta-narratives, ultimately, succumb to the reality of unfettered pluralism and cultural particularity.

Alleged meta-narratives or master narratives are at least as destructive of tacitly accepted meaning systems as they are supportive. Ricoeur has insightfully recognized and articulated this view:

> ...we should have to say that metaphor not only shatters the previous structures of our language, but also the previous structures of what we call reality. When we ask whether metaphorical language reaches reality, we presuppose that we already know what reality is. But if we assume that metaphor redescribes reality, we must then assume that this reality as redescribed is itself novel reality. My conclusion is that the strategy of discourse implied in metaphorical language is neither to improve communication nor to insure univocity in argumentation, but to shatter and to increase our sense of reality by shattering and increasing our language. The strategy of metaphor is heuristic fiction, for the sake of redescribing reality. With metaphor we experience the metamorphosis of both language and reality.[8]

---

7. E. Murray, *Imaginative Thinking and Human Existence* (Pittsburgh, 1986) 118-119.

8. P. Ricoeur, "Creativity of Language," in *Philosophy Today* 17 (2/4) 97-112.

I would like to extend Ricoeur's insight by meditating on the creative disruptive power of metaphors as behaviors or symbolic actions.

From the horizon of the metaphor from the behavior school, action as disruption or action as cultural disobedience may penetrate deeper into the structures of a culture and evoke more rapid change than the change initiated through language. I am not attempting to lessen the importance of language as a critical and constitutive dimension of human existence and community. I agree that there is no thought without language. I have also argued, following Brinkmann, that language is performative; language is a type of behavior.[9] Now, I am pleading for a recognition that how we act, gesture and behave is also of critical importance. Yet, I propose that it is act, gesture and behavior that are prior to language and give rise to language. Language attempts to express the meaning imbedded in acts, gestures and behaviors.

Actions or behaviors are *per se* symbolic actions because there is in them an incarnating or enfleshing of meaning. Behaviors are always corporal, bodily. In these bodily actions, self is expressed, albeit with ambiguity and a need for further clarification. Erik Erikson has underscored this corporeal substratum of the *humanum* in his theory of personality development outlined in his "Ontogeny of Ritualization."[10] Ritual mediates meaning precisely in its bio-psycho-social rootedness, where nature invites nurture, where biological need of instinct becomes a possible vehicle for the exchange, sharing or transmission of social values and meaning systems.

Actions, gestures and behaviors which function as and within cultural metaphors are specific, culturally particular and contextualized as language metaphors. Behaviors share the ambiguity of language. Yet, because of their necessarily incarnate character, behaviors may have a potentially deeper anchor in truthfulness and reality than language. Fundamental behavior instincts for personal survival (e.g. eating, drinking, reproducing) and for social survival and control (e.g. marrying, policing behavior, caring for the sick, assigning male and female roles and duties) evidence cross-cultural witness. I would suggest that there are what might be called meta-behaviors (e.g. birthing, maturing, marrying, becoming sick, aging, dying, etc.) which traverse every culture and which every culture addresses in its ritual processes. The particularity marking

---

9. B. R. Brinkmann, "On Sacramental Man: II The Way of Intimacy," in *The Heythrop Journal* 14 (1974) 6; B. R. Brinkmann, "On Sacramental Man: IV The Way of Interiorization," in *The Heythrop Journal* 14 (1973) 281.

10. E. Erikson, "The Development of Ritualization," in E. Erikson, *The Religious Situation* (Boston, 1968) 711-733; E. Erikson, *Identity: Youth and Crisis* (New York, 1968) 91-141.

these behaviors arises not from the behavior *per se* but from the time, place, history and culture in which the behavior is unfolding.

Ritual by necessity inculturates meta-behaviors. Ritual surrounds them with the inter-textual narratives and actions which foster a particular heuristic scheme. Cultures propose particular behaviors which are to be embraced and followed by the members of the ritual community and which are to be avoided. In terms of our earlier triad of the true, the good and the beautiful, a focus on meta-behaviors will allow the good to be afforded a relatively significant place alongside the true. Ritual will aim at inducing, sustaining and supporting right action, good behavior as well as articulating what a particular culture judges to be true.

Perhaps from a vision of meta-behaviors, we can respond to our first question: can sacramentalists in dialogue with Postmodern insights value root metaphors? I believe an affirmative answer is warranted. A shift from understanding root metaphors, but as meta-behaviors, accompanied by culturally imbedded narratives and gestures, can affirm the universal phenomenon of ritual as a medium of meaning in every known culture while accounting for the legitimate identification by Postmoderns of the limits and conditions of all narrative and their metaphors. The great challenge looming in this perspective is inculturation.[11] How can rituals become inculturated in different cultures and the differences may not be the behaviors *per se*, but the narrative and metaphor schemes which limit the range of their interpretation?

4. Sacramental Presence and Postmodernism

Recently, Lieven Boeve has recounted the challenges of articulating a plausible understanding of sacramentality in a Postmodern horizon and his writing is a fine conversation partner in getting at the issue of sacramental present absence and Postmodernism.[12]

Boeve has suggested that many sacramental theologies remain premodern and mythic, irrespective of Post Vatican II developments. Further, he notes that a sacramento-theological recontextualization in full discussion with modernity remains to be fully undertaken.

After comprehensively summing up Lyotard's critique of master narratives and contemporary critical consciousness, Boeve comes to the crucial issue for sacramental/liturgical theology, the issue of 'presence' (and notice that the modifier 'real' is not employed in his presentation):

---

11. Cf. G. Worgul, "Inculturation and Root Metaphors," in *Questions Liturgiques - Studies in Liturgy* 77 (1996) 1/2.

12. Cf. L. Boeve, "Post-Modern Sacramento-theology: Retelling the Christian Story," in *Ephemerides Theologicae Lovanienses* 74 (1998) 326-343.

In short, a particular narrative cannot fully present the fundamental heterogeneity accompanying it (the ultimate which cannot be mastered or grasped), while at the same time heterogeneity can only be referred to within the limits of this particularity. Even though heterogeneity constantly escapes particular speech, it is only within this speech that the "other" can be spoken about. Heterogeneity, then, can no longer be referred to in terms of "presence," but only in terms of a "present absence." Heterogeneity cannot become present in thinking, language, signification, symbol or ritual, but it also cannot be postulated as simply absent. It can be evoked only as absence made present. In this regard, the "other" and the "self" cannot find each other in a higher; heterogeneity is in fact precisely that which in principle makes such identity impossible.[13]

Christian narratives must become 'open narratives' for the disruptive event within which the transcendent might enter (as present absent) and they must bear witness in a non-hegemonic way to this transcendent. Sacramental celebrations are condensed ritual celebrations by Christians of their open narratives and testimonies to God's interruptions and the call to conversion, openness and witness.

Boeve ends his interesting piece with a bold conclusion:

In the postmodern context the Christian narrative can regain contextual plausibility only by recontextualizing and reconstructing itself as an open narrative. In this regard, it must be able to take distance from premodern and modern ontological foundations, as well as from the modes of legitimation offered by modern philosophers of history. The sacramentality of life, clarified and celebrated in the sacraments, is no longer considered as participation in a divine being, nor anticipation of a self fulfilling development, but as being involved in the tension arising from the interruption of the divine Other into our human narratives, to which the Christian narrative testifies from of old. Sacramental living and acting thus presuppose the cultivation of a contemplative openness, and testify in word and deed to that which reveals itself in this openness as a trace of God.[14]

Clearly, Boeve understands and articulates well the key tenets of the Postmodern tradition. He correctly notes their challenge to the way sacramentality was conceived in the past. But, his proposal might limit sacramentality and sacramental behavior to being a mere witness to a trace of God, a present absent God, in the interruptive event attended to in contemplative openness.

Earlier, I suggested that the Modern's over-emphasis on reason lead to an exultation of the true over the good/ethics and the beautiful/drama/art/ritual. In the Postmodern's view, one discerns a tendency to emphasize witness or ethics which can lead to exultation of the good at

---

13. *Art. cit.*, 340.
14. *Art. cit.*, 343.

the expense of truthfulness which is abandoned and forgotten. Without truth and reason, the good and ethics must turn to opinion, pragmatism or utilitarianism to enlist some form of grounding or level of reasonableness. A distorted bulge appears in our triad but in a different sector.

Serious questions and issues of a theological nature are raised by this Postmodern vision. First, I would suggest that any tendencies towards its own hegemony and imperialism should be abandoned. Controlling this habit, which can affect all theologians, is irksome but necessary. A start might be prohibition of the word 'only' as seen in the above citation. If nothing else, Postmodernism (correctly) reminds us that there are many legitimate approaches and perspectives on human experience, all of which are inextricably bound by cultural particularity. 'Only' suggests the emergence of a meta-narrative which has been abandoned already.

Second, would not the use of the 'trace' image compel us to inquire about a background or *gestalt*? Without this larger, denser, field or medium, it is hard to imagine how an appearing trace might be detected or perceived. What is the field of reference or range of experience in which one finds or experiences this 'trace'?

Third, does a 'trace of God' adequately articulate what Christians claim to experience within and without their sacramental celebrations? Does the term, 'trace of God,' adequately, articulate the claim that the triune God who Father, Son and Holy Spirit is present?

Fourth, and as a corollary, how is presence to be understood in the present-absent 'trace of God'? Is this the trace of a thing as in the trail left by a disintegrating element in a nuclear reaction? Is it a power or a force, as is the gravitational anomalies witnessed in comets, which is motivating some physicists to postulate a 10th planet or twin star in our solar system? Is this a trace of a person, recognized because he/she has, decisively, redirected the course of history? Perhaps, it is on this issue of presence that the Christian tradition and Postmodernism take different roads.

The challenge of accurately articulating what Christians believe from their experience of God seems perennial. The community may have done better at identifying what are distortions of its faith than specific positive and complete expositions. For example: this is not a physical presence resembling a thing in a place; this is not a purely mental presence as a remembrance of a past and completed event; this is not an exhaustive presence which can fix, possess or control the divine; this is not a magical presence which can conjure up the divine through special words or actions.

The Christian tradition has also identified positive affirmations about God's sacramental presence. This is a presence of a mystery which is inexhaustible. This is the presence of the one and only triune God. This is a presence of God in freedom as gift. This is a real presence, i.e. an encounter with God present through word, minister, gathered community and sacramental symbol. This is an interpersonal presence, a true meeting of persons and a true exchange of selves.

Clearly, an affirmation that sacramentality and sacramental living give testimony in word and deed to the traces of God which appear in contemplative openness does not say enough to be proposed as an adequate articulation of Christian sacramental faith of action in a Postmodern context. This affirmation does remind the tradition that God is not a possession and that God is always the transcendent one, even in God's greatest immanence. It, also, reminds the tradition that its beliefs and professions of faith are inescapably bound to particular cultures and their contexts. Of great importance, it reminds the tradition that God's presence is always for the poor and the outcast, for the stranger and the voiceless, for those who are different and other. All these are embraced by God's love and welcomed.

Perhaps, if we shift from a metaphor of language to a metaphor of behavior, a more adequate contextual plausibility can be attained. Perhaps, actions of love, freely, shared with all are 'open' actions, revelatory actions in which we recognize not only the trace of the triune God, but this very God's enfleshment, incarnation and saving. Perhaps, our emulation of Jesus's suffering and dying for others in our feeding the hungry, clothing the naked, visiting the homeless, etc. is a real way to attain presence with this risen Lord and, in him, the Father and the Spirit. In entering into Jesus' Eucharist, we can find him present among us, as his Spirit gathers us for the breaking of the bread and the breaking of us, his body. Christian actions of love toward each other and all neighbors might not only disclose a trace of God, but also a vivid experience of God once again more present than absent in history.

5. Conclusion

In his fascinating essay, "The Great Disruption: Human Nature and the Reconstruction of the Social Order."[15] Francis Fukuyama indicates that the disruption of western civilization has halted and indicators of reconstruction are appearing in the social order. Religion has a role in the reconstruction. Fukuyama notes:

> A return to religiosity ... has already started to appear in many parts of the United States. Instead of community arising as a by-product of rigid belief,

---

15. Cf. F. Fukuyama, "The Great Disruption: Human Nature and the Reconstitution of Social Order," in *The Atlantic Monthly* (May 1999) 55-80.

> people will come to religion because of their desire for community. In other words, people will return to religion not necessarily because they accept the truth of revelation but precisely the absence of community and transience of social ties in the secular world will make them hungry for ritual and cultural tradition. They will help the poor or their neighbors not necessarily because doctrine tells them they must but rather because they want to serve their communities and find that faith-based organizations are the most effective means of doing so. They will repeat ancient prayers and re-enact age-old rituals not because they believe they were handed down by God but rather because they want their children to have proper values, and because they want to enjoy the comfort and the sense of shared experience that ritual brings. In this sense they will not be taking religion seriously on its own terms but will use religion as a language with which to express their moral beliefs. Religion becomes a source of ritual in a society that has been striped bare of ceremony, and thus is a reasonable extension of the natural desire for social relatedness with which all human beings are born.[16]

With Fukuyama, I think a new cultural age is in the making. The Modern Age of autonomous, self-sufficient and self-final reason has failed. Postmodernism has courageously exposed its flaws. It's important contribution may have already been attained. The emerging new age seems to be rediscovering the social, communal character of human nature. The emerging new age seems to recognize the importance of testimony and ethical behavior. Furthermore, the emerging new age seems to acknowledge the need for ritual as a means for expressing and living its foundational metaphors. Perhaps in the openness of this new age and in its gathering as a community in ritual, it will experience once again a God who is with us, for us and present to us. Perhaps in this emerging age, a range of proper balance and mutual interaction between the true and the good will disclose true beauty. For Christians, this beauty will be the figure of the crucified Jesus who in death become the risen Lord and Christ of Faith. Jesus' metaphor of behavior (his dying and rising) and his metaphor of language (disclosing the mystery of the Father and our mystery as God's children) explode in the metaphor of beauty: the divine Trinitarian life of love in which we are created, which is really but imperfectly present in sacramental life, by which we are called to live in this life and to which we are called in the life to come.

Duquesne University George S. WORGUL Jr.
Department of Theology
Pittsburgh, PA, 15282
USA

---

16. *Art.* cit., 80.

COMMUNICATION – SYMBOLS – SACRAMENTS

1. Introduction

There are three areas of investigation which have especially enriched research in dogmatic theology in the past decades and has led to a fruitful dialogue of theology with contemporary thinking and sciences: the changes in anthropology, the practice and theory of communications, and the linguistic and hermeneutical studies with their new evaluation of symbols.

1.1. The Anthropological Turn in Theology

Contemporary theological anthropology – far beyond a narrow christological framework – has initiated a fruitful dialogue with human sciences and prepared a real encounter between faith and reason, theology and science. According to the new concept of person, human beings are not only individuals, whose only desire is to become independent, autonomous beings. Rather, they are persons, in personal relationships, in communion. As such, freedom *from* everything and everybody cannot be the ultimate aim of human persons; they can only reach their genuine freedom and fulfilment by self-giving, by transforming themselves into gifts for the others, living in the unity of love with them.

1.2. Communication Theory

The insights of anthropology have been further developed by the recently born new human science of communication since no communion is possible without communication. The theory of communication was inspired partly by the recent technological revolution of information, partly by the new concept of human person as being in communion.[1] The

---

1. Cf. among others: M. Bangemann, *Europe and the Global Information Society. Recommendations to the European Council* (Luxembourg, 1994); *Europe's Way to the Information Society*. Updated version of the Action Plan, Updated version by 01/24/96. ISPO; R. A. Wauzzinski, "Technological Pessimism," in *Perspectives on Science and Christian Faith* (Indiana University, 1994) Vol. 45. N°2; D. Pullinger, "Information Technology: The Ethical Task," in *Gospel and Culture* (Newsletter 21, 1994); A. Keller, "Informationsgesellschaft," in *Stimmen der Zeit* 1 (1996); E. Galeano, "Notes on Inequality and Incommunication," in *Media Development* 43 (1996) 23; Communication

context of our communication age opens new possibilities for a fresh dialogue between communication science and theology. It is high time to elaborate the theology of communication and apply its insights for the interpretation of the history of salvation and also in our pastoral activity – an interpretation which sounds reasonable and perhaps healing even in postmodern thinking.

1.3. Sacraments as Real Symbols

The theology of communication runs parallel with the recent rediscovery of the sacraments as real symbols. (The Eucharistic debates in medieval thought show the fading of the clear concept of real-symbols: the distinction between the presence in truth /in veritate/ and the presence in mystery /in mysterio/ led to extremist views of Eucharistic presence: exaggerated realism on the one hand, and exaggerated /or rather, reduced/ symbolism on the other.) What will be said in the following is founded on Karl Rahner's "ontology of symbols." He states: "das Seiende ist von sich selbst her notwendig symbolisch, weil es sich notwendig 'ausdrückt' um sein eigenes Wesen zu finden."[2] Herein Rahner calls for a "theology of Christian symbolic reality" (eine Theologie der christlichen Symbolwirklichkeit).[3] Based on Aristotelian-Thomistic philosophy, Rahner states that the philosophical concept of symbol is derived from reality and its manifestation. "Das eigentliche Symbol (Realsymbol) ist der zur Wesenskonstitution gehörende Selbstvollzug eines Seienden im anderen."[4]

What seems to be lacking in this pioneer study is the *personal* aspect of symbols: what is the role of symbols in personal self-expression and in personal communication? Following recent inquiries of communication and of symbols, the present study takes communication by symbols as a matrix for a fresh understanding of the sacramental nature of the history of salvation and the sacraments as real symbols.

2. Communion and Communication

The pastoral instruction *Communio et Progressio* (1971) gave the basic magisterial-theological insight for the necessity of communication within the church and between the church and the world, claiming that no

---

as theological approach is excellently elaborated by A. Delzant, *La communication de Dieu* (Paris: Cerf, 1981); L.-M. Chauvet, *Symbol et sacrement* (Paris: Cerf, 1990) is the finest symbolic approach of the sacrament. The latter two books are widely used in my contribution.

2. K. Rahner, *Schriften zur Theologie* IV (Einsiedeln: Benziger Verlag, 1960) 278.
3. *Ibid.*, 309.
4. *Ibid.*, 290.

"communio" is possible without "communicatio." "Communication is more than the expression of ideas and the indication of emotion. At its most profound level, it is *the giving of self in love*. Christ's communication was, in fact, spirit and life."[5] The church is sent by Christ to convert humankind into a communion of love, in communion with the Triune God and with one another. This is the theological background providing the guidelines for our orientation in the following.

2.1. Revelation as Information or as Communication?

Divine revelation was seen for centuries as a sort of information given by God for our salvation. The dogmatic constitution on revelation *Dei Verbum* of Vatican II speaks about revelation on a much broader horizon. In revealing himself, God wants to communicate himself to humankind, "invite and receive them into his own company."[6] "By divine revelation God wished to manifest and communicate himself." The apostles, in turn, "were to communicate the gifts of God to all men."[7] As such, the concept of "information-revelation" has been replaced by the concept of "communication-revelation."

There are fundamental differences between information and communication. Information is a *one-way* transfer of data. Communication, by contrast, is mutual, happens in the form of a *"dialogue"*; it involves the reception of the message and as its follow-up the response given to it. Information is objective, *impersonal*, has little or no personal core in its message. Communication is much more *personal*, an "eye to eye," "hand to hand," "heart to heart" encounter of two (or more) persons, it presupposes, initiates or strengthens togetherness, a community of persons. *There is no real community without communication:* it is the life-giving breath of community. Love tends to union, says Thomas Aquinas, communication tends to communion. The peak point of communication is "the giving of self in love": the accomplished communion of those who want to donate themselves to one another.

The central message of Christ is that God loves us, because he himself is love. And he loves us in order to bring us to love one another. "God is love"[8]: a perfect communion of the three divine persons. The only one God is the Holy Trinity: God-Father, giving himself completely to his Son, to the extent of being one with him; God-Son, receiving completely his Father into himself, so that they are completely one divinity; and

---

5. P.C.I.S.C., *Communio et progressio*, 1971, in *Vatican Council II*, ed. A. Flannery (Dublin: Dominican Publications, 1975) 293-350. N° 11.
6. Vatican II, *Dei Verbum*, 1965, in *Vatican Council II*, ed. A. Flannery, 750-765. N° 6.
7. *Ibid.*, N° 7.
8. 1 Jn 1,1.

God-Spirit, the joyful result, the complete gift of the loving union between the Father and the Son. Human beings are created in the image and likeness of the Triune God, invited and taken up into that communion of love.[9]

2.2. God's Salvation: communion by loving communication

God is total love, total and mutual gift of the divine persons to one another. In other words: he is (they are) *total communication*. The Gospel of John begins as follows: "In the beginning was the Word, the Word was with God and the Word was God". This statement can be paraphrased as: "In the beginning was Communication". *This communication was extended outside God to humankind in the history of salvation*, a free initiative of God to embrace even human persons with his love, to invite them into his loving community. The dramatic change in the concept of revelation at Council Vatican II has led to the realisation that revelation cannot be separated from salvation, and salvation is our loving communion with the Triune God.[10]

This 'Communio-God' is announced by Jesus who established the perfect union between God and humanity in his own person. *Christ is the mediator and fulfilment of divine communication with humankind: God's total self-giving in love.* In him salvation is initiated and fulfilled at once: he is the perfect, personal union of humanity and divinity. In him, through him, with him we are all invited to be united with God. Instead of using the well-known dogmatic phrases, an attempt is made to give a communicative interpretation of this process.

2.3. We Seek to Give Answers to Three Questions:

How is communication realised: (1) in the immanent Trinity?; (2) in the economical Trinity, first of all in Jesus Christ?; (3) and in the church and its sacraments?

3. Immanent Trinity: Being as Communion

3.1. The Logos-symbol

The source and fulfilment of all community is the Holy Trinity. That is the only communion where communication (that of the divine persons) is complete and direct: they are one God in three persons. "Divine love is

---

9. Cf. Delzant, *La Communication de Dieu*, 302-320.

10. Cf. *Dei Verbum,* N° 2: "By his revelation the invisible God, from the fullness of his love, addresses men as his friends, and moves among them, in order to invite and receive them into his own company."

not a sterile symbiosis of lovers but an *élan* of perfect life wherein the love itself becomes a reality over and against the lovers with all the density of ontological personhood."[11] In the theology of the Trinity "a new ontology is developed: *for God to be is to be in communion.*"[12] The famous orthodox theologian Zizioulas builds his ontology of the person on the Trinity, speaking about the "ecstatic character of God, the fact that His being is identical with an act of communion."[13] "Love as God's mode of existence 'hypostasizes' God, constitutes His being."[14]

Because God exists forever, the Father begets his Son, the Logos forever. There was no time when God was just God without this inner ecstasy (as Arius and others had claimed). In his theology of symbol, Rahner speaks about Logos-theology as the peak-point of symbol-theology: the Logos is the Word of the Father, his perfect image, his self-expression. The Logos is the Symbol, the Word of the Father, begotten by him, in whom he perfectly finds himself.[15]

3.2. The Spirit-symbol

The mutual and complete giving of selves between the Father and the Son culminates in their bond, in their gift of love: the Holy Spirit, who is equally divine and equally person. If communication comes to its highest point in love, the only complete and unsurpassable communication is that of the Father and the Son in the Holy Spirit, who is the communication-in-person of the Father and the Son. Rahner does not go further in his explanation of the immanent Trinity by a theology of symbols, but it may be rightly added that the Holy Spirit is equally a Symbol: the bond (Augustine: "*vinculum*"), the gift (Augustine: "*donum*") of the mutual love of the Father and the Son: the perfect manifestation and expression of God's love.[16]

4. Economic Trinity: God's Salvific Plan with Humankind

"God is not a self-closed Absolute but a self-communicating Freedom."[17] He called human beings into existence in order to invite them to become parts and partners of his loving communion. There is, however, a gap

---

11. W. J. Hill, *The Three-Personed God* (Washington, DC: Catholic University of America Press, 1988) 75.
12. C. E. Gunton, *The Promise of Trinitarian Theology* (Edinburgh: T&T Clark) 39.
13. J. D. Zizioulas, *Being as Communion* (London: Darton, Longman & Todd, 1985) 44.
14. *Ibid.*, 46.
15. Rahner, *Schriften zur Theologie* IV, 292.
16. R. Haight, *Jesus Symbol of God* (New York: Orbis, 1999) 445-464.
17. Hill, *The Three-Personed God*, 76.

between the finite and the infinite, the created and the uncreated, the immanent and the transcendent. God created the world in complete freedom, setting the order of the world, but having to accept its rules with all the limitations belonging to it.

4.1. Symbols in Material-Personal Communication

Living in a material world human persons cannot communicate in such a direct and complete way as the persons of the Holy Trinity. As Rahner puts it, symbols are part of all existing beings as their manifestation. Symbols make knowledge and also communication possible.[18] Consequently, they are used first and foremost by persons and in personal communication. Conceptual-verbal communication is by its essence very limited. But there are other means available: symbolic words and various non-verbal "media": objects and gestures elevated to symbols, vehicles for "soul to soul" communication.

Symbols offer the greatest possible opportunity for personal communication and thus for relationship in our complex material-personal world. They can express the inner personal self and establish communication between persons. *Real symbols* – symbols which contain what they manifest – *connect persons to persons* and thus create communion. The condition of communication by symbols is the personal commitment of both the "sender" and the "receiver" of the symbolic message. God-Father committed himself totally and forever to humankind by "giving over" ("*tradidit*") his Son, Jesus Christ who is the perfect incarnation, the symbol of his love. The only adequate human response can be faith, the grateful acceptance of his gift.

In classical epistemology, symbols are less definite, less significant than conceptual-verbal definite statements, the correlation between reality and truth is not so clear as in the case of discoursive (discursive) concepts. In terms of personal communication conceptual language is accomplished and sometimes elevated by a symbolic (frequently non-verbal) language. Modern language theories describe different uses of words, some of them with much stronger re-present-ative power than more conceptual terms.

4.2. Unfolding Revelation by Symbols

In the economy of salvation God had to take into account the worldliness and historicity of human beings. According to Karl Rahner, transcendental revelation, God's personal self-communication "can only enter explicitly, reflectively, and thematically as an object into human

---

18. Rahner, *Schriften zur Theologie* IV, 286.

consciousness by virtue of an historical mediation. One *needs the symbolic mediation* of an external event or an objective and specifying medium."[19] In other words, even God was compelled to use a symbolic-sacramental language when he wanted to be revealed and communicated to human beings.

His mystery is revealed and realised *gradually in history*.

The *first phase* is *creation*: the universe can be seen as God's sacrament in a broader sense. Theologians speak about *natural sacraments* to be found both in nature and in human life.[20] The "sacramental world" shows God's existence as "communicative self", as A. Peacocke has stated and demonstrated extensively in his works.[21]

The *second step* is God's revelation with its fulfilment in Jesus Christ who is his incarnated word. Medieval theologians speak about *sacraments of the Old Testament*. The people of Israel was not only historical, but a sacramental-symbolic reality as well: as manifestation of God's grace, his loving care. Then, in the fullness of time, Jesus Christ is the highest density of God's presence in human history, his irrevocable commitment to humankind: he is *the realest symbol of divine love*, the perfect union of God and human beings in his person.

The *third phase* in the history of salvation is the historical presence of the risen Christ and his Spirit in the *church and its sacraments*: the centuries and millennia following the life and death of Jesus. A period which comes to an end at the final fulfilment of time with the second coming of Christ.

5. The Absolute Symbol of God: Jesus, the Logos of God

The term "symbol" is used in different senses. What is fruitful here is its personal-ontological meaning. It has been called concrete (vs. "conceptual") symbol by Haight, primary (vs. secondary) symbol by Rahner. In this sense *"Jesus is the concrete symbol of God."*[22] Rahner's ideas about the Logos-symbol have been widely analysed recently. J. H. P. Wong proposes "the twofold concept Logos-symbol as the key to synthesizing" the christology of Rahner.[23]

---

19. K. Rahner, *Foundations of Christian Faith: An Introduction to the Idea of Christianity* (New York: Seabury Press, 1978) 51-55. Cf. Haight, *Jesus Symbol of God*, 13.
20. T. Schneider, *Zeichen der Nähe Gottes* (Leipzig: St. Benno, 1981) 26.
21. A. Peacocke, *Theology for a Scientific Age* (London, 1993) 61. Cf. G. Predel, *Sakrament der Gegenwart Gottes* (Freiburg: Herder, 1995) 182.
22. Haight, *Jesus Symbol of God*, 14.
23. J. H. P. Wong, *Logos-Symbol in the Christology of Karl Rahner* (Rome: Vatican, 1984) passim; J. H. P. Wong, "Karl Rahner's Christology of Symbol and Three Models

5.1. The Incarnated Logos as the Earthly Presence of God

In what sense, then, can Jesus be called the symbol of God? "Jesus was one who mediated God, and people encountered God in Jesus." It is clearly a reciprocal and personal exchange: "people encountered God in Jesus, because Jesus mediated God."[24] But it must be clear that Jesus was a symbol of God not only in his actions, i.e. in a functional way, but also – first and foremost – in his being. Rahner understands Christ as the revelatory and salvific symbol of the Father, the humanity of Christ as the self-expression (Real-symbol) of the Logos: *"The incarnated Logos is the absolute symbol of God in the world*, which is unsurpassibly filled with the symbolised."[25] As such, the man Jesus Christ not only teaches about God, revealing his inner being, but re-presents, performs God, makes him present in his ecstatic love within the Trinity and "outside" it.

Jesus can never be separated from God whom he mediates – the term hypostatic union expresses this one-ness with the Father: they are equally of divine nature. At the same time, however, he is also true man. "The doctrine of two natures corresponds to the dialectical structure of Jesus as symbol of God,"[26] with an intrinsic tension between the finite and infinite: he is the symbol and sacrament of God. In the tradition of St. Augustine (*"ipsa assumptione creatur"*) Rahner holds that God "creates the human reality by the very fact that he assumes it as his own." Wong rightly remarks that "the twofold activity of constituting-retaining coincides with the process of symbolisation."[27]

5.2. Jesus: the Symbol

Jesus is the only perfect symbol, the utmost real-symbol possible. He contains and manifests the presence of God in his true human being, in his human history. He is the incarnated Logos, the sacrament of the world. The word "sacrament" is used in its classical meaning: *"sacramenta efficiunt quod significant et significant quod efficiunt."* The mystery of God who is love is revealed in him, i.e. is made historically present and manifest (in a descending move). At the same time, however, the mystery of the human person (who is finite, yet created in loving communion with God) is revealed in him: he is also the human "Yes" to God as response to God's affirmation of human people. "The whole of

---

of Christology," in *The Heythrop Journal* 27 (1986) 1-25, with extensive bibliography on the use of symbols by K. Rahner.

24. Haight, *Jesus Symbol of God*, 203.
25. Rahner, *Foundations of Christian Faith: An Introduction to the Idea of Christianity*, 251.
26. Haight, *Jesus Symbol of God*, 205.
27. Wong, "Karl Rahner's Christology of Symbol," 3.

history moves toward the self-communication of God to human existence. That union is fulfilled in God's presence to human existence in Jesus Christ, and in an absolute human acceptance in Jesus' death on the cross."[28] By his salvific act he made humans his sisters and brothers, the children of God, capable of joining him and approaching the God-Father (in an ascending move).

5.3. Symbolic Communication

In the person and life-story of the Christ-symbol, all the elements of real symbols are found:
- The full (divine!) but hidden presence of the symbolised (of God-Father in continuous dialogue with the Logos in the Spirit) – against the Arian view of Christ as "*deuterosz theosz.*"
- The full (material-human!) visible reality of the symbol manifesting (but also hiding) what is contained (of Jesus as true man) – as opposed to a docetist view of Christ.
- The full communicative dynamism of the symbol with the personal element of commitment:
  a) the self-emptying of the Giver entrusting (transforming, "depersonalising") himself to a symbolic existence and representation: the kenosis of Christ.
  b) the reception of the Giver by the Receiver who accepts the symbol in complete trust, "decoding", transforming ("repersonalising") it and thus comes into communion with the Giver.
  c) the (self-emptying) countergift of the Reciever to the Giver, a mutual exchange by which the personal union will be completed. The second and third move is realised by Jesus in his filial obedience unto death.[29]
  d) A final element can be added: the reception of the countergift, thus closing the circle of love: the acceptance of Christ's sacrifice on the cross, by his resurrection and exaltation.

5.4. The Evaluation of Symbolic Communication

Symbolic communication can be criticised as inadequate and insufficient. Still, one has to take into consideration the following:
- it belongs to our createdness and is the only way of access from God to created human beings, and viceversa, from humans to God, but also within humankind;

---

28. Haight, *Jesus Symbol of God*, 321.
29. Delzant, *La Communication de Dieu*, 143-152.

- the more so, because it belongs to the mystery of the Triune God. Theology warns us, humans, that divine mystery is mystery for ever, even in the final eschaton, when God will be seen "face to face." As Rahner phrases for the immediacy of the beatific vision "the humanity of Christ will have eternal importance."[30]
- it demands personal commitment which is the most important condition for any communion and which enables us to become more fully persons:
  a) between God and humankind, the self-emptying divine love and the self-emptying human faith, in a descending and ascending move (as referred to above),
  b) and similarly within humankind, becoming more fully human by becoming more and more members of a communion.[31]

6. The Historical Continuation of Christ-Symbol: the Church as Sacrament

Founded on the sacrament of Jesus (*Ursakrament*, original sacrament), the church may also, in a derived sense, be called the basic sacrament (*Grundsakrament*) of salvation.[32] "The church, in Christ, is in the nature of sacrament – a sign and instrument, that is, of communion with God and of unity among all men."[33] It is "the universal sacrament of salvation."[34]

6.1. Christ-sacrament and Church-sacrament

The risen Jesus is present in the church in different ways. And as Logos-christology may and should be accomplished by a Spirit-christology,[35] the traditional Christ-ecclesiology should be and partly has been recently accomplished by a Spirit-ecclesiology.[36]

---

30. K. Rahner, "Die ewige Bedeutung der Menschheit Jesu für unser Gottesverhältnis," in *Schriften zur Theologie* III (Einsiedeln: Benziger, 1962) 47-60, esp. 57.

31. Chauvet, *Symbol et sacrement*, 13-50.

32. This view is widely accepted in today's theology, and also introduced into the theology of Vatican II Council. Cf. *Catechism of the Catholic Church* (Washington, DC: USCC, 1994) N° 774ff.

33. Vatican II, *Lumen gentium*, 1964, in *Vatican Council II*, ed. A. Flannery, 350. N°1.

34. *Ibid.*, 407, N° 48.

35. Haight, *Jesus Symbol of God*, 445-466.

36. Y. Congar, *Sainte Église: Études et approches ecclésiologiques* (Paris: Cerf, 1963) 12.

Jesus is the real symbol of God's self-communication to the world. The church has the function of making historically present and tangible within the world this symbolisation of God's self-communication. (...) Only if the symbolisation of God's self-communication in Jesus continues historically can Christ continue to be a real symbol of God's presence for humanity.[37]

There is, however, a basic difference between the two symbols. "Christ is the real symbol and sacrament of God's presence. The church, however, is a symbol only insofar as it refers back to Christ and continues the symbolisation that has come to expression in him."[38] The sunlight of the world is Christ, the church is only like the moon: it reflects the light of the sun, Christ.[39]

The topic of the church as sacrament cannot be dealt with fully in the present paper. Only three aspects are to be mentioned insofar as they are relevant to the logic of this study.

6.2. Sent by Christ to Proclaim Salvation and Receive It

The church has a similar twofold function like Christ himself: it has to make God's salvific revelation be present in history (descending move of God's incarnated love), and it has to achieve the reception of God's gift and offer its own counter-gift in faith and love (ascending move of Christ crucified and risen), by the Holy Spirit. It must be the place of mutual exchange between God and humankind: the place for the incarnation of God's love and the place of human faith and worship, the meeting-point of "divine commerce" (*divinum commercium*). God's love needs our affirmation, the acknowledgement of his gift and our commitment represented by the countergift of faith, worship and love. The only perfect countergift was offered by Christ himself, and the church, the community of the faithful, joins to his offering, by personal commitment in faith and life.[40]

This double function is found in all aspects of the church's life, first and foremost in the service of the Word and the sacraments.

Firstly in proclaiming the Word of God and recieving it in faith. It cannot simply be a "herald"[41] proclaiming the message of God, as

---

37. F. S. Fiorenza, *Foundational Theology* (New York: Crossroad, 1985) 95. Cf. also *Systematic Theology* I, ed. F. S.Fiorenza & J. P.Galvin (Minneapolis: Fortress, 1991) 97.

38. Fiorenza, *Foundational Theology*, 95.

39. H. de Lubac, *Paradoxe et Mystère de l'Église* (Paris: Aubier, 1967) 32-35. De Lubac explains this "moonlike characteristic" of the church with rich references to the patristic age.

40. E. Schillebeeckx, *Christ, the Sacrament of the Encounter with God* (Kansas City: Sheed & Ward, 1963) 91-132.

41. A. Dulles, *Models of the Church* (New York: Image Books – Doubleday, 1987) 76-88.

revealed in Christ. The Creeds were originally called *symbola fidei:* the summary of revelation as mirrored in the faith of the church. The church becomes counterpart of God's self-communication as a believing and loving communion, expressing its faith in the liturgy and its love in the bond of communion and in the service of all. The church is not only ontologically holding and manifesting the presence of the graceful God, but also functionally, in its "*martyria, leiturgia, diakonia, koinonia.*"[42]

Secondly, the church cannot simply be an administrator of the sacraments. The sacraments are calls for an existential choice: the recipients have to open themselves to the grace contained within the sacrament.[43] The distribution of grace by sacraments cannot be compared to a humanitarian aid-action. The sacraments do not simply produce grace in a mechanical way (the causality-thinking of medieval theology – sacraments as instruments of grace – is surpassed in today's theological thinking and accomplished by the aspect of personal commitment: sacraments are by definition sacraments of faith!).[44] Rahner stresses the element of word even in the sacraments: the word which is proclaimed but which also makes a claim to be received in faith.[45] The sacraments call us to let the transforming power of God be effective in our lives.[46]

6.3. The Church as Trinitarian Communion

In post-Vatican II ecclesiology, the aspect of the church as communion is predominating. The church is not only a religious institution founded, but also a living communion of all those who believe in Christ, i.e. who have received the love of God and strive to make it really present and effective in their lives. The love of God can only be made present in a loving community. This community is called to become the real symbol of the triunal divine community as its continuous presence in history, as a constant call to salvation for all humankind and as a model of how to transform the life of individuals and of societies into loving communions.

Christ wanted his disciples to be one in spirit, imitating his one-ness with the Father. The communio, which is the church, finds its source and model in the communio which is the Trinity. "The vocation of the church

---

42. K. Rahner, *Handbuch der Pastoraltheologie*, I (Freiburg: Herder, 1971) 357.
43. O. Semmelroth, "Die Kirche als Sakrament des Heils," in *Sacramentum Mundi* IV, 1 (Einsiedeln: Benziger, 1972) 317. ("Zeichen ist, in dem die durch es zu vermittelnde göttlich-gnadenhafte Wirklichkeit mit Anspruch an die existentielle Entscheidung des Menschen herantritt, inh anrufend, dass er sich für die Aufnahme der im Sakrament enthaltenen Gnade erschliesse.")
44. L.-M. Chauvet, *Les sacrements* (Paris: Editions Ouvrières, 1993) 61-84.
45. E. Jüngel and K. Rahner, *Was ist ein Sakrament?* (Freiburg: Herder, 1971) 76.
46. M. Quesnel, *Sources des Sacrements* (Paris: Cerf, 1977) 125.

is to be a communion, a living source of Trinitarian relationships."[47] We may be reminded of Tertullian's phrase: "the church is the body of the Holy Trinity."[48]

If the church is built on relationships, then it must be communication. God communicates himself in the Word and in the Sacraments, and makes us capable of communicating with one another, to establish brotherhood and sisterhood within the church, and become a sign of communion and communication for the whole human family. We are all called to do our best to live in this communicative communion in the spirit of solidarity and service, in constant reconciliation, in a committed effort to improve the life of every person around us. It is not an abstract formula what has been said about the Triune God who is love: *communio in full communication*. It is proclaimed and practised by the church even if it is never fully achieved. Living fully human means to live in communion (i.e. in communication) with others both on the micro-level of private life and on the macro-level of social life.

6.4. The Two-fold Nature of the Church-sacrament

The Calcedonian formula of christology points out clearly the twofold – divine and human – nature of Christ. The terms are well-known: *aszünhutósz, atreptósz, adiairetósz, achorisztósz*: unconfused, immutable, indivisible, inseparable, unmixed, unchangable, undivided.[49] There are new attempts – or rather temptations – in and outside the church to forget about these essential conditions which are characteristics of all sacraments. Some want to see the church only as one human company among others; others want to divinize it by denying all its human faults and weaknesses; again others want to separate the two realities, distinguishing between a church of the saints (*sancti* and *sancta*) and a church of the sinners. The twofold nature of the church-sacrament may help us to accept the insufficiencies or even sins of the church while retaining our faith in the presence of Christ in it. The visible church as a socio-historical entity (with all possible human failures) is the sacramental symbol of the realm of God, the pledge and also effective presence of God's salvific will.[50]

---

47. *"The Sign We Give"* – a report on Collaborative Ministry, published by the bishops of England and Wales. Quoted by bishop Crispian Hollis in his lecture: "The Church as Communication," delivered in Rome, March 9th 1996.

48. Cited by de Lubac, *Paradoxe et Mystère de l'Église*, 74.

49. Denzinger-Schonmetzer, *Enchiridion Symbolorum definitionum et declarationum* (Freiburg-Roma: Herder, 1965) N° 302.

50. K. Rahner, *Über die Sakramente der Kirche* (Freiburg: Herder, 1991) 18-19.

7. The Sacraments of the Church – the Eucharist

Traditional theology restrained the "real presence" of Christ only to the Eucharist. Vatican II, however, enlarged this view: "Christ is always present in his Church, especially in its liturgical celebrations."[51] As such, Christ's presence in the Eucharist is not exclusive but eminent. In the last chapter two points are mentioned about the Eucharist as the focus-point of the life of the church: 1) Eucharist as sacrifice; and 2) Eucharist as banquet.

7.1. Eucharist as Sacrifice

Traditional theology gave a privileged position to the Eucharist, claiming that it is the only sacrament where Christ *himself* is present, not simply his grace. Contemporary theology of the sacraments considers this distinction to be insufficient and misleading: the grace of Christ cannot be present without him, and his real presence is not without his grace.

The traditional axiom is valid, but in a deeper sense: the Eucharist is the cultic symbol and manifestation of Christ's self-giving on the cross, of his proexistence. The last supper prefigured his death and resurrection, the Eucharist makes us capable of actualising this sacrifice, calling it into presence by commemorating it.

> In its narrative and in its ethics of compassion, the Christian community finds the presence of Christ in suffering. (...) It says in simplicity, in celebration and in action that God is there present, both revealed and concealed. (...) There God events anew in Christ and in his members.[52]

Scholastic theology compared the real presence of Christ in the Eucharist to his coming after his resurrection. The community celebrating the Eucharist commemorates the coming of the risen Christ, who arrives with his whole life, suffering and death, i.e. with his proexistential being, with his obedience and love. Real presence is essentially connected with his sacrifice. Anamnesis is not a repetition of Christ's sacrifice, it makes rather the risen Christ present in his self-giving "once and for ever."[53]

This anamnesis should be accomplished by the active participation of the faithful present. They have to "take part in the blood of Christ"[54]: receiving it in gratitude and returning it by their lives.

---

51. Vatican II, *Sacrosanctum Concilium*, 1963, in *Vatican Council II.*, ed. A Flannery, 5. N°7.
52. D. Power, *The Eucharistic Mystery* (Dublin: Gill and Macmillan, 1992) 304-320.
53. F.-J. Nocke, *Wort und Geste* (München: Kösel, 1985) 174.
54. 1 Cor 10,6.

7.2. Eucharist as Banquet

The Eucharist also prefigures the final banquet of the eschaton. The Lamb of God invites all humans to his divine banquet. Christ sacrificed his life for our salvation, but in his ecstatic dynamics of incarnation wanted to give himself as our daily bread, the bread of life for us, remaining with us and feeding us with his loving presence till the end of history. It is a special food, the bread of divine life for Christians: it has a transforming force for all those who participate in it making them similar to himself. "The accent must fall on the encounter of Christ and the Church in the act of the meal: this is where the center of gravity lies... The true sacramental sign in the Eucharist is the event of eating and drinking."[55] The central symbols of the table-communion – bread and wine – are transformed by "transsubstantiation." "The gift of the Spirit is God's own self-communication to those who are in communion with Christ."[56]

Our active participation in God's self-communication, in divine life, is nourished by the Bread of Life. The consuming of the Eucharist has a transforming power: the community itself becomes the body of Christ. We are transformed into the food we are receiving in Holy Communion. St. Augustine said: "If you are the body and members of Christ, it is your mystery which is placed on the Lord's table; it is your mystery you receive."[57] Divine self-communication will only be effective if it does not remain one-way information or donation but has its continuation by being received and reciprocally "counter-gifted" by the addressee of God's gift. This countergift is also caused by divine grace but cannot lack our own determination and moral effort to cooperate with it.

8. Conclusion: Symbolic Communication in Postmodern Age

The integral view of anthropology and christology proves that the way to full humanity leads through the openness and self-offering to the Other (God) and the others (human people). God has become a gift (a real-symbol) to us in Christ. Through him, with him, in him we have the opportunity and vocation to become gifts (real-symbols) to God and to others. The only language given to us as means of personal communication with God and human beings is the sacramental language of symbols.

---

55. H.U. von Balthasar, *The Glory of the Lord: A Theological Aesthetics* (New York: Crossroad, 1982) 573.
56. Power, *The Eucharistic Mystery*, 302.
57. Augustinus, *Sermo* 272. Cited by F.-J. Nocke, *Sakramententheologie* (Düsseldorf, Patmos, 1997) 162.

Karl Rahner has based his theology on the anthropological insight that full humanity is founded on being open to the absolute Mystery of God. This is fulfilled in Jesus Christ. The source and fulfilment of all communications is loving communion with the Holy Trinity. This is opened to created beings in Jesus Christ. Christ is the key symbol of all communications. His historical presence is upheld in his Body, the Church, the sacrament of salvation, the guarantee and model for sacramental communication.

The essence of human beings and the basic conditions of human life cannot be changed in any age. Our postmodern age is no exception. It is valid today and forever:

- being a person means becoming a person
- becoming a person means communication with others
- the highest form of personal communication is that by symbols
- all real human communication is essentially sacramental
- the only perfect symbol is Jesus Christ the sacrament of God
- the church and its sacraments offer us divine self-communication
- by genuine communication we can become ourselves by participating in God's salvific communication.

Postmodern thinking is an immense challenge to traditional humanitarian and Christian values. Whether it has a positive or a negative effect on Christianity and on humankind, depends on how it is faced and answered.[58] It may have positive effects by leading to a new self-awarenes and self-discipline, to a new intimacy,[59] and communication of the person. It may effectuate discernment between committed Christians and cultural or nominal Christians. It may refresh the ministry of the Word and sacrament. It may have a healing impetus on conservative bureaucratic pastoral and religious practices,[60] give a new meaning to the inculturation of faith and sacraments, to a contextual theology,[61] to a more committed and personal practice of faith in words, sacraments and service of others. It may lead to a Christianity more universal, i.e. Catholic, than before,[62] to a new type of pastoral activity,[63] to a new self-

---

58. K. Gabriel, *Christentum zwischen Tradition und Postmoderne*, Quaestiones disputatae, 141 (Freiburg: Herder, 1992) 163-201.

59. P. Koslowski, *Die postmoderne Kultur* (München: Verlag C.H.Beck, 1987) 45-48.

60. J. M. Mardones, *Postmodernidad y cristianismo* (Santander: Sal Terrae, 1988) 132-138.

61. S. B. Bevans, *Models of Contextual Theology* (Maryknoll, NY: Orbis, 1992) 1-22.

62. Mardones, *Postmodernidad y cristianismo*, 135.

63. U. F. Schmälzle, "Das neue religiöse Bewusstsein als pastorale Herausforderung," in *Religion und Glaube in der Postmoderne* (Nettetal: Steyler Verlag, 1996) 95-122.

identity and consciousness of Christians, to a communicative life of faith and of sacraments and of interpersonal interaction.

On the other side, however, postmodernity may be destructive as well. It is inclined to find a spirituality without religion,[64] a "religion without God,"[65] pluralism without a basic unity, communicative ethics or communicative activity without a solid transcendental foundation,[66] to satisfy excessive individual needs or, as another extreme, dissolve human persons in a senseless communication game.

Following the ideas of David Tracy, three elements are needed in a contemporary approach of symbolic worship:

> It will be *pluralist* to recognize the many voices of the community; it will be *conversational,* in the best sense, willing to listen, risking speech, and strengthening the interlocutors; it will be both *affirming* of our post-modern world and *critical* of its confusions.[67]

One more element, however, must be added without which no sacramental exchange is possible: it will be *communicative*, going beyond superficiality and sheer ritualism to achieve committed personal faith in the communion of believers.

The communicative approach of the sacraments as symbols can invite Christians today to make their communication more dynamic and effective, both on the horizontal (person to person) level and on the vertical (human-divine) level, and may help non-believers to give meaning to their lives and discover communication as the way to life, to a "more abundant life."

Sapientia Theological College for the Religious   László LUKÁCS
Ferenciek tere 7-8
H-1053 Budapest

---

64. T. W. Boyd, "Is Spirituality Possible Without Religion?" in *Divine Representations, Postmodernism and Spirituality*, ed. A. W. Astell (New York – Mahwah: Paulist Press, 1994.) 83-101.

65. H. Waldenfels, "Religion und christlicher Glaube – eine alte, ewig neue Spannung?" in *Religion und Glaube in der Postmoderne*, 77.

66. E. Arens, "Theologie nach Habermas," in *Habermas und die Theologie*, ed. E. Arens (Düsseldorf: Patmos, 1989) 11-38.

67. S. Happel, "Symbol," in *The New Dictionary of Sacramental Worship*, ed. P. E. Fink (Collegeville, MN: The Liturgical Press, 1990) 1244. Happel takes David Tracy's notion of an anological imagination as a guide in developing a contemporary style of symbolic worship. See D. Tracy, *The Analogical Imagination: Christian Theology and the Culture of Pluralism* (New York, 1981).

PERSONALLY SPEAKING: REFLECTIONS ON RELATIONAL THINKING FOR THE ECUMENICAL SACRAMENTOLOGICAL DIALOGUE

It is perhaps the saddest sign of Christian disunity that various Christian traditions have disagreed for so long about the central symbols of Christian unity, namely the sacraments of Baptism and Eucharist. True, the modern ecumenical movement has made great strides in bringing various viewpoints together and working toward what we might call a common Christian consensus, but a full consensus might yet be quite a ways off. While a great many churches recognize the validity of each other's baptism, a great many Christians can still not celebrate Eucharist together. And Ecumenical discussions still tend to falter on the same points they did almost five centuries ago, points like the substantial presence of Christ in the Eucharist or the sacrificial nature of the Eucharistic celebration. We have, however, progressed to the point where we seem to feel that these are issues to be talked about, not fought over.

While this progress has been occurring on the ecumenical front, another sort of revolution has been occurring on the theological front, namely, the contemporary philosophical turn toward language and away from metaphysics. Philosophers are exposing the depths to which all thinking – even our theological thinking – is tied to language and exposing also the pitfalls of tying our language and schemes of thinking too closely to some great metaphysical order of truth. In sacramentology, this has led to the rediscovery of the linguistic or symbolic nature of the sacraments and is challenging many traditional understandings of long-standing doctrines and dogmas. Some theologians have wholly embraced this new linguistic perspective and have taken theology down paths that only vaguely resemble those traditionally taken by the discipline. Others find themselves very leery of an anti-onto-theology that does away with all claims to normativity or any sort of ultimate truth.

And as the various high-level inter-church discussions continue and a barrage of new theological thinking is launched in the various academic journals and conferences, the Christian in the pew is still seeking what he or she has perhaps always been seeking – something that can anchor them to God and to the sacred in the midst of an increasingly secularising storm that surrounds them. It is in service to these latter that this article is intended.

I would like to begin this investigation by introducing what I mean when I use a phrase like "relational thinking" and how that interacts with the contemporary philosophical and theological turn toward language, particularly noting how it fills in a crucial missing piece. This particular piece is, I believe, nothing new, but in so many of our modern philosophical and theological reflections, it does tend to get lost in the shuffle. With this piece in hand, I would then like to turn briefly to the work of a few representative contemporary sacramentologists to see if we find evidence of relational thinking in their work. My intent in this section will not be to survey the entire range of sacramental thought but merely to demonstrate that hints of the relational thinking I will describe can be found across the sacramentological spectrum. Finally, given the presence of these hints, I would like to conclude with a few thoughts on the importance of recognizing this relational facet of sacramentology, and what that recognition might mean for our contemporary ecumenical sacramentological dialogue. Because the field of sacramentology is so large, I would like to limit the scope of my investigations to one particularly thorny sacramental issue – that of the presence of Christ in the Eucharist.

1. The Relational Ground of Language

One of the most exciting and fruitful trends in sacramentology has been the rediscovering of the symbolic power of language to create, which during the modern era was so often hidden behind the scientific power of language to describe. Insights concerning the narrativity of the sacraments, such as those of David Power, and on the understanding and power of symbol, such as we find in Louis-Marie Chauvet, are opening for us new vistas of understanding and hopefully better paving the way for greater mutual understanding of sacraments between the various Christian confessions. However, in our philosophical discussions on the importance and power of language, we often seem to be saying that language acts as something like the ultimate ground of human existing, that level below which (if anything can even be said to exist there) one could not possibly go. The problem with this is that it ignores the phenomenological fact that language itself is grounded in something else that both underlies and exceeds it, something with which every one of us lives out as the very core of our being.

Language, while unquestionably part of what it means to be human, is nevertheless an acquired tool. Language arises out of human interaction (what Ludwig Wittgenstein called *Lebensformen*), and we receive our language (and our thinking and our very possibility of self-hood) from the human community in which we are raised. A new baby has no language, but very few people would want to say that it is not human because of that. We instinctively recognize that "being human" is not a synonym for "being able to talk." Rather, as we can see in those first events of life (and perhaps even before in the womb), our humanity is grounded in being related to other human beings.

Humans are not sea-turtles, which are innately born with everything they need to be sea turtles even if they were never in their life to have contact with another of their species. Humans, however, require other humans to become fully human. True, the acquisition of language is an integral part of that, but it is only made possible because humans are first innately open to that human community and then immediately and without exception form a relational bond with that community.

These initial bondings (to mother, father or whomever) form the necessary foundation for all further development of a human child – including and perhaps most especially the development of thought and language. Where this is denied (as one might have seen in the impersonal orphanages found under communist regimes), human development (particularly language/thought development) will inevitably be arrested. Thus, as important as language is, one can only acquire it if one already has been accepted into a human relationship, if one has already been – if I might use this term – loved.

Language arises out of what I call "relational impulses." One foundational aspect of being human is that as a person grows to be more and more an individual, he/she is compelled to share the he/she-that-one-is-becoming with others. This, too, one can see by looking at children. The primary function of language, the one that first gets used, is not to describe the world or reality as such, but rather to share an experience. Children do not seem to talk in order to communicate information. They talk to share experiences, to experience the connection that communication brings. This is why a child can tell an adult about the same set of activities or observations many times and why he/she or she requires a response each time. When a child cries, "Look, Daddy, a bird," he is not primarily about the business of describing reality. The description of reality functions as an invitation for "Daddy" to share his experience of "bird," which is why "Daddy" is required to look at the bird and not just acknowledge the fact that the child has said something or conveyed information.

Language then is built on the foundation of something that I will call "human relationality" and functions primarily in furthering and fostering relationships. This relationality consists in a fundamental openness humans naturally have toward other humans, which naturally connects with the fundamental openness of other human beings to form something that we call a personal relationship. The shape, nature, and extent of this relationship will, in part, be determined by language, but there will always be an "relational excess" which eludes the power of words, as the very fact of relationship is built upon something that underlies (and therefore is inaccessible to) linguistic discourse.

It is as if all truly human existing is built around this core of relationship or relationality. And because language is dependant upon it, it often has trouble encompassing it. We cannot say in words what the bond between a mother and child is, nor do we fully describe a relationship when we hang a label on it such as "friendship." And who would think that one could replace the relational communication involved in the physical act of human sexuality with words or philosophical concepts? The best language can do is to point toward these relational anchors or relational impulses in which all human life is grounded. I call those facets of language that point back – though never really describe or circumscribe – the relational core of being human "relational vectors." Such vectors include words that are explicitly based on common interpersonal experience – words like "love," "trust" and "betrayal" – as well as those often implicit reminders that all words (from the specialized vocabulary of quantum physics to the lexical twists and turns of a mystic text) find their only home in interpersonal communication. Even when we talk to ourselves, we use the vocabulary and grammar acquired from our linguistic context.

If this is true of all language, then it must also be true for theology and the symbolic or linguistic communication of sacraments. Even religious language must ultimately be grounded in this relational core of humanity, and not immediately in some one-to-one correspondence with ultimate reality – whatever that may be. Of course, these relational "impulses" which ground language must find some expression in order to be communicated, but language itself neither arises out of nothing nor is given wholesale from the heavens. While this may present some problems for certain religions, Christianity (at least as it has classically understood itself) should have no problem with this, for Christian theology has very often and from the beginning understood itself as an attempt to articulate a very personal relationship or the encounter with God through Christ. And Christianity need not feel as though it must reach into some metaphysical world to do this because it has grounded its classical confession in the encounter with God through the historical person of Jesus of Nazareth. If this confession is valid, then Christianity itself is primarily about relationship – the personal relationship between God and humanity and the consequent relationships between humans themselves. Theology and the sacraments, then, have been and continue to be the "language" with which this relationship to God is conducted, arising from it, anchored it in, but never fully encompassing it or circumscribing it.

2. Relational Vectors and Current Positions in Sacramentology

If my thesis is correct, and the doing of Christian theology, including (perhaps even especially) sacramentology, consists in searching for appropriate means of expressing (and thereby bringing to the level of conceptual or performable reality) the essentially personal, relational impulses arising from the experience of God in Christ, then the "relational vectors" of theological and sacramental language ought to be in evidence everywhere Christian theology is done. I will now take a very brief look at just a few writers in whom we see these relational concerns at work. Again, I am not able here to do justice to the range of sacramental thought or the fine nuances of individual writers. My goal is simply to demonstrate that the relational view of language I have described above is really nothing new but can be found already at work in the enterprises of sacramentology if only we look for it. For this brief tour of the sacramental scene, we will look at what we might call the traditional Roman Catholic view, as represented by the writing of Colman O'Neill; the early post-Vatican II concerns of Edward Schillebeeckx; a contemporary and progressive Catholic approach as found in the work of Louie-Marie Chauvet; an Orthodox perspective given by the late Alexander Schmemann; and some Protestant thoughts, represented by Jean Calvin and by a few official statements of a few Baptist churches in response to the World Council of Churches Baptism, Eucharist & Ministry declaration (BEM). While these positions certainly do not exhaust the range of sacramental thinking, they should serve to show that hints of relational thinking can be found across the sacramentological spectrum.

In recent years, thinking about sacraments in the Roman Catholic church has undergone something of a change. Many voices are pushing for new – or perhaps better 're-newed' – understandings of the Eucharist. What drives this renewal? My suggestion is that it may be driven by a perception that the expression of the "relational vectors" found in the traditional doctrines as traditionally proclaimed is no longer adequate. As various sacramentologists have struggled with this fact, they have come to different conclusions. But a common dynamic may be seen at work in them.

Colman O'Neill's early work, *Meeting Christ in the Sacraments*, fairly represents, I think, a faithful and traditional Roman Catholic view of the Eucharist. There is a strong emphasis on the 'real presence' of Christ in the doctrine of transubstantiation (articulated in traditional Thomistic categories). And yet, O'Neill does not treat such understandings as if they were ends in themselves. His concern in promoting this doctrine is, precisely, relationship. "We have seen," he says, "the inter-personal relationship between God and man set up when the sacraments, through the mediation of Christ and the Church, bring grace to the faithful."[1] Later, he even appeals to something specifically non-philosophical or metaphysical in which to ground an understanding of the sacraments. "The Christian mind," he states, "grasps almost without reflection that the meaning behind the Eucharist is that it unites us to the person of Christ."[2]

In his *New Approaches to the Eucharist*, O'Neill spends a few pages defending a common-sense approach to the Eucharist which tries to get at the "pre-philosophical" nature of what is expressed in the dogmas of the church concerning the presence of Christ.[3] His appeal is specifically to a human experience which must be common to all otherwise people could not communicate. While he does not specifically speak of personal relationships here, they are clearly implied. Thus, while O'Neill here supports the Church's doctrine of transubstantiation, behind that doctrine one can perceive a truly "relational vector" at work.

We see a similar concern in the work of Edward Schillebeeckx, specifically in the epilogue that closes his *The Eucharist*.[4] Schillebeeckx states that "our attempts to thematise faith are secondary to our existential experience of the eucharistic event."[5] And earlier on the same page he describes this event in radically personal terms (as the self-giving of Christ to the believer). His plea is that we must seek to understand the Eucharist but that these understandings must be tested to see whether they can function as vehicles for "encountering the reality of faith."[6] I would simply here point out that this test is really a relational one, and that by identifying it as such we are able to deal with it more appropriately.

---

1. Colman E. O'Neill, *Meeting Christ in the Sacraments* (New York, 1964) 149.
2. O'Neill, *Meeting Christ in the Sacraments*, 182.
3. Colman E. O'Neill, *New Approaches to the Eucharist* (New York, 1967) 90-94.
4. E. Schillebeeckx, *The Eucharist*, trans. N. D. Smith (New York, 1968). Originally published as *Christus' Tegenwoordigheid in de Eucharistie* (Bilthoven, 1967). Page numbers for the original given hereafter in parentheses.
5. Schillebeeckx, *The Eucharist*, 156 (124).
6. Schillebeeckx, *The Eucharist*, 158 (125).

In building on the work of Schillebeeckx and in faithfulness to his concern, Louie-Marie Chauvet evinces these relational-linguistic sensitivities as well. In his book *Symbol and Sacrament*, Chauvet spends quite a few pages using the thought of Martin Heidegger to help his reader get beyond the sacramental impasse he sees as having been created by metaphysics and move the reader toward a better understanding of language (and thus of the symbolic nature of the sacraments). "Language," says Chauvet, "*creates*, creates 'things'."[7] Humans are possessed by language, are "formed in its womb."[8] For Chauvet, language necessarily implies distance, and this leads him to talk about something he calls, after Heidegger, "the presence of absence." "Thus, the Eucharist," he states, "seems to us the *paradigmatic figure of this presence-of-the-absence of God* outside of which the faith would no longer be the faith...."[9] Chauvet seems to be wrestling in his book with an over-emphasis on traditional formulations of transubstantiation on the presence of God, as if we could control God.[10] The reason that this seems to be a problem for Chauvet is that it fails to recognize the need for distance that is inherent in the very possibility of a true relationship. We cannot be "related to God" in any kind of personal way if we find ourselves completely ontologically united with God or control God as we would an object.

I am not sure, however, that Chauvet pays sufficient attention to the fact that absence is a consequence of presence and not the other way around, that the possibility of distance is itself built on a foundational, fundamental relational unity (what Paul Ricœur calls "that participation-in or belonging-to an order of things which precedes our capacity to oppose ourselves to things taken as objects opposed to a subject").[11] Nevertheless, Chauvet's approach evinces very relational concerns. He reminds us that the Eucharist is about being a part of the body of Christ[12] – which in Chauvet is much more appropriately interpreted as a relational concern rather than an ontological one. And he emphasizes the role of the community, even to the scandal of hinting at the presence of the Church as the Body of Christ in the Body of Christ that is the Eucharist.[13] He seems to work very hard to affirm the relational quality of the Eucharistic

---

7. Louis-Marie Chauvet, *Symbol and Sacrament: A Sacramental Reinterpretation of Christian Existence* (Collegeville MN, 1995) 89.

8. Chauvet, *Symbol and Sacrament*, 87.

9. Chauvet, *Symbol and Sacrament*, 405.

10. See here Chauvet's whole discussion on the radical resistance of the Body of Christ in the Eucharist. Chauvet, *Symbol and Sacrament*, 402-404.

11. Paul Ricœur, "Toward a Hermeneutic of the Idea of Revelation," in *Harvard Theological Review* 70 (Jan-April 1977), 24.

12. Ricœur, "Toward a Hermeneutic of the Idea of Revelation," 388.

13. Ricœur, "Toward a Hermeneutic of the Idea of Revelation,", 390.

event; he simply differs from his more traditional Roman Catholic colleagues on the best way to formulate and articulate the shape of this relationship – not the fact of the relationship itself or the relational impulse that grounds the symbolic communication of the Eucharist.

Resonances of these relational concerns about the Eucharist can also be found outside the Roman Catholic fold, another piece of evidence to support the idea that relational concerns enter the picture at some point before the thematisations and rationalizations of the faith that seem to make for denominational differences. In responding to what he sees as the Eucharistic crisis in the Church, the Orthodox theologian Alexander Schmemann reflects on various aspects of the sacrament in the posthumously published book *The Eucharist*. From a thoroughly Orthodox and pastoral perspective, Schmemann pleads throughout the book for a recovery of the very personal realities that constitute the Eucharist, realities such as the mutual dependence of the celebrant and the people during the Eucharist,[14] the importance of sacrifice as an expression of the intense yearning for God that is at the core of religion,[15] or the idea that the Church and her sacraments are ultimately about an encounter with the kingdom of God and not a doctrine *per se*.[16] Throughout the book, Schmemann pleads for a sacramentology that moves away from the bookish, scholastic concerns that have held it captive for so long and back to the personal realities of the relationship between Christian, Church and God. For Schmemann, good theology is about "uncovering the meaning and essence of this unity."[17] In other words, the relationship of the Christian and Church to God is the foundation upon which the edifice of theology is built. Theology that does not serve this, would not be worthy of the name.

Protestant sacramentology, lacking any kind of unified official doctrine, varies widely, and yet I think here too sacramentology at its best is driven by attempts to avoid the obstacles and preserve the essentials of the personal encounter with God in the Eucharist. For the reformer Jean Calvin, the sacraments were explicitly a medium of communication for an already-existing relationship between God and man. In the sacraments, God testifies to his good will to us and we in turn testify to our piety toward him.[18] Communication serves the relationship, but the fact that, for him, it follows (i.e., in no way produces) the relationship does not belittle the encounter with Christ to be found in the Eucharist.

---

14. Alexander Schmemann, *The Eucharist: Sacrament of the Kingdom* (New York, 1987) 14.
15. Schmemann, *The Eucharist*, 102.
16. Schmemann, *The Eucharist*, 242.
17. Schmemann, *The Eucharist*, 12.
18. Jean Calvin, *Institutes of the Christian Religion*, vol 2 (London ,1962) 491.

> To all these things [the assurances of our faith] we have complete attestation in this sacrament [Eucharist], enabling us certainly to conclude that they are as truly exhibited to us as if Christ were placed in bodily presence before our view, or handled by our hands.[19]

In their various responses to the World Council of Churches declaration on Baptism, Eucharist and Ministry, many different churches of the Baptist tradition reveal how important personal categories are to their sacramental understanding.[20] The Baptist Union of Scotland speaks of Eucharist as an occasion to rejoice in the presence of the Lord and as a "precious meeting place with the Lord."[21] Their reservations against the highly sacramental language of BEM seem to stem from their belief that a focus on the sacraments inhibits the broader relationship Christ has with his people in all worship and service to him. American Baptists likewise speak of the Eucharist as an occasion of Christ's presence and likewise express similar fears of how an emphasis on the rite of the Eucharist distracts from the true focus of God.[22]

Of course, this overly brief survey does not at all exhaust all possible positions. I believe that you can find relational vectors at work in the positions of Lutheran and Anglican churches, which tend to mediate between the Roman Catholic and Protestant doctrines described above. One could even find such vectors at work in the Quaker non-sacramentalist position, as they seem to believe that any physical mediator (such as bread or water) might distract from what is really at issue – i.e., the encounter with God in worship.[23] If there really is a pervasive concern for personal-relational reality in sacramentology, then this will have implications for both sacramentology in general and for the ecumenical dialogue.

3. Implications of Recognizing These Common Relational Vectors

There are two implications that I would like to draw from the discussion above, and one possible objection to it with which I would like to deal. The first implication concerns the way the ecumenical dialogue now tends to be conducted. One example of this is the way in which the World Council of Churches has officially reacted to the many responses of denominations to the 1982 BEM declaration. On the particularly sticky

---

19. Calvin, *Institutes of the Christian Religion*, 558.
20. Max Thurian (ed.), *Churches Respond to BEM*, vol 3 (Geneva, 1987) 230-263.
21. Thurian (ed.), *Churches Respond to BEM*, 243.
22. Thurian (ed.), *Churches Respond to BEM*, 257-263.
23. See the responses of the Quakers of Netherlands (297-299) and the Canadian Yearly Meeting of the Religious Society of Friends (300-302) in *Churches Response to BEM*, vol 3.

point of the presence of Christ in the Eucharist, the WCC suggests that if the various positions could better clarify themselves, then that would move the dialogue forward,[24] as if simply by changing our language we would find out that we really agree on this point after all and that all these centuries we've been fighting over nothing. For myself, I think this line of dialogue has already reached a dead-end. The WCC asks the Roman Catholic church to clarify what it means by "transubstantiation."[25] That seems rather an odd suggestion because it seems to me that the Roman Catholic church is already quite clear on what it has traditionally meant by the concept. It is a basic (and from the Vatican's point of view non-negotiable) understanding of the Eucharist that is simply at odds with the basic understandings of other churches, such as the Baptist and Presbyterians positions. More clarification is not going to miraculously bring about more agreement.

However, if relationship is what grounds our language (and thus our systems of clarification), and so many churches and sacramental writers already seem to be concerned with the preservation and maintenance of this relationship, then it would seem that many of us already agree on the most important point, the "what" of sacramental theology and language. Where we differ is on the "how," how this relationship is best fostered and preserved. This fact, if recognized, might go a long way toward demonstrating that some of the unity we are still desperately seeking is already there right under our noses.

A second implication of the relational understanding of sacraments concerns the relationship between the relationship with God, perhaps even best called "faith," and the various expressions given it. If what we have is a *fides quaerens intellectum*, and we share a common *fides*, then there is no reason we cannot share a common table. In matters of relationship, one does not tend to make understanding of the relationship the crux on which the relationship rises or falls. Just ask teenagers about their parents or most spouses about their partners. And what does a baby understand about his relationship to his father. A lack of understanding will certainly influence the way in which the relationship develops when it comes to that, but of itself it does not call the relationship itself into question, because personal relationships are built on something that goes deeper than our conceptual understandings or our ability to articulate them.

But I hear immediately the question coming, "How can you possibly know what kind of relationship you have until you put it into words? And if we all use different words, how can we know that this supposed

---

24. *Baptism, Eucharist & Ministry 1982-90: Report on the Process and Responses*, FO, 149 (Geneva, 1990) 117.

25. *Baptism, Eucharist & Ministry*, 117.

relationship we are talking about is exactly the same?" These are good questions, but to ask them is to miss entirely the point of what I am trying to say. Those questions are epistemological ones, important ones at that, but as questions of knowledge they enter into the fray after the questions of relationship have already been decided. As I have said before, personal relationships do not rise or fall on epistemological concerns.

Does this mean that anything goes, that we, for example, should open up the Eucharist to everyone regardless of their beliefs? Of course not. Relationships do have their parameters, their normativity. A father and husband cannot just do whatever he likes. But the parameters of what he can and cannot do arise from within the unique relationships that he holds and are not imposed by an external conceptual system (though he might use such a system to explain why he acts as he does). Relationships are governed by a more relational than philosophical logic. We live all of our lives outside libraries and classrooms according to this logic. Sometimes we understand it conceptually, sometimes we do not but bow to its dictates anyway. And it is in the context of such logic that those conceptual systems arise and back to that logic that they are primarily directed. And where relationships are at issue, it is enough that we try to understand, and try again and again, even though definitive conclusions may forever be beyond our reach.

Perhaps the British poet T. S. Eliot said it best when he speaks about the struggle of the enterprise of language in his *Four Quartets*. If Christianity is about relationship and the Eucharist is about encounter, then the job of theology and sacramentology will never be completed. But then completion is not the issue. It is rather through our halting attempts at understanding, our failures, and our attempts to find better understandings – in other words, through the struggle of theology – that we live out intellectually the relationship to God through Christ that is the very ground of our being.

Eliot writes:

> ...every attempt
> Is a wholly new start, and a different kind of failure
> Because one has only learnt to get the better of words
> For the thing one no longer has to say, or the way in which,
> One is no longer disposed to say it.
> ...And what there is to conquer
> By strength and submission, has already been discovered
> Once or twice, or several times, by men whom one cannot hope
> To emulate—but there is no competition—
> There is only the fight to recover what has been lost
> And found and lost again and again: and now, under conditions

That seem unpropitious. But perhaps neither gain nor loss.
For us, there is only the trying. The rest is not our business.

"East Coker," V, *The Four Quartets*, T.S. Eliot

Africa Nazarene University　　　　　　Timothy James CRUTCHER
PO Box 53067
Nairobi, Kenya

SECTION TWO

EXPOSING EUCHARISTIC FACES

PRESIDING AT THE EUCHARIST: SACRAMENT OF THE ECCLESIAL CHRIST

One of the most discussed items in liturgical studies is undoubtedly the sacramental place and function of the ordained minister in the Eucharist. How can we theologically characterise his position within the liturgical assembly? In recent times, liturgists have discussed this topic fiercely. Interesting in this regard, for example, was the discussion between Sarah Butler and Susan Wood in *Worship* some years ago.[1] Most of the time, the question has focused upon the acting of the priest *in persona Christi* and *in persona Ecclesiae*.[2] Since Vatican II it is common knowledge that the priest acts *in persona Christi* as well as *in persona Ecclesiae*;[3] his ministry is both christological and ecclesiological. The question is rather how these two realities are related to each other? Is it because the priest represents Christ that he is also able to represent the Church? Does he act

---

1. S. Wood, "Priestly Identity: Sacrament of the Ecclesial Community," in *Worship* 69 (1995) 109-127; S. Butler, "Priestly Identity: Sacrament of Christ the Head," in *Worship* 70 (1996) 290-306; L. J. Welch, "Priestly Identity Reconsidered: A Reply to Susan Wood," in *Worship* 70 (1996) 307-319.

2. For the origin of these terms we refer to B. Marliangeas, "'In persona Christi' – 'in persona Ecclesiae.' Note sur les origines de ces expressions dans la théologie latine," in *La liturgie après Vatican II. Bilans, études, prospective*, ed. Y. Congar *et al.*, Unam Sanctam, 66 (Paris, 1967) 283-288; Idem, *Clés pour une théologie du ministère. In persona Christi – in persona Ecclesiae* (Paris, 1978); Idem, "In persona Christi, in persona Ecclesiae," in *Spiritus* 70 (1978) 19-33.

3. See, for example, *Presbyterorum Ordinis* n° 2.

in persona Ecclesiae because he represents Christ? Or do we have to say that the priest first of all represents the community, and therefore he acts *in persona Christi*? In that case, the *in persona Ecclesiae* would be the ground for the *in persona Christi*.

In official Roman documents, the priest who presides at the Eucharist is seen as operating first of all *in persona Christi*. His acting *in persona Ecclesiae* is based upon his acting *in persona Christi*. It is because he is the representative of Christ, and this on the ground of his ordination, that he is also able to be the representative of the community during the Eucharist.[4] It is our conviction, however, that such a theology runs the risk of clericalism. Too much stress is laid on the liturgical minister as the '*sacerdos*', the one who has the power to consecrate as a sort of '*alter Christus*'. In that way, the gap between the assembly and the presiding priest is widens.

Therefore, we prefer another definition of the liturgical minister. We are convinced that the ecclesiological representation comes first, and that the acting of the priest *in persona Christi* is based upon his role as representative of the community. In our view, the priest who presides at the Eucharist is the 'sacrament of the ecclesial Christ'. It occurs to us that this is a much better characterisation of the priest in our postmodern context. But what do we really mean by saying that the priest is the 'sacrament of the ecclesial Christ'?

1. Sacrament of the Ecclesial Christ

Jesus Christ is the first subject of the liturgical act during the Eucharist (*Sacrosanctum Concilium* nr. 7; *Presbyterorum Ordinis* nr. 5). He is the primary subject. Through baptism, all Christians share in the priesthood of Jesus Christ (*Lumen Gentium* nr. 31). The celebrating community is the body of Christ. Therefore we can say that also the community is the subject of the liturgical act.[5] Christ being the primary subject, the community is the secondary subject.[6] Accordingly the celebrating assembly, as living body of Christ and Temple of the Holy Spirit, is the integral subject of the liturgical activity, as Yves Congar had already said

---

4. For example in *Inter Insigniores* (1976). See also *Pastores dabo vobis* n° 16 (1992) and the New Cathechism of the Catholic Church n° 1553 (1992).

5. "Träger der Liturgie ist darum die ganze zum Gottesdienst versammelte Gemeinde, in der die Kirche als der fortlebende Christus in Erscheinung tritt." R. Kaczynski, "Die Leitung von Gottesdiensten durch beauftragte Laien," in *Wie weit trägt das gemeinsame Priestertum? Liturgische Leitungsdienst zwischen Ordination und Beauftragung*, ed. M. Klöckener and K. Richter (Freiburg, 1998) 145-166, 149.

6. O. Nussbaum, "Die Liturgie als Gedächtnisfeier," in *Freude am Gottesdienst. Aspekte ursprünglicher Liturgie*, ed. J Schreiner (Stuttgart, 1983) 201-214, 211-212.

in the 1960s.⁷ Evidence can be found in the several Eucharistic prayers which are all formulated in the plural form.⁸

Within that context, what then is the function of the presiding priest? First of all, he represents the assembly. We can call him a sort of 'collective' or 'corporative' personality. As an individual, he represents the whole community which has come together and he acts on behalf of that gathered community. In this one man, the whole group is included. As such, he is the crystallisation point. In his acting and in his speaking, it is the community itself which acts and speaks.⁹ Thus, we can say, that the one who presides over the community acts first of all *in persona Ecclesiae*. This means that the difference between the minister and the people in the church does not lie in the fact that the first one is acting *in persona Christi*, and the others are not. No, everyone acts during the Eucharist *in persona Christi*, because through baptism all share in the priesthood of Jesus Christ.¹⁰ The difference between minister and believers is that the first one acts *in persona Ecclesiae*. In the prayer to God he represents the whole celebrating assembly.

But the question is of course: if the priest acts first of all *in persona Ecclesiae*, can we also say that he acts in a certain way *in persona Christi*? The answer is yes. Representing the assembly, the priest also acts in the Eucharist *in persona Christi Capitis*, he acts as head of Christ's body, which is the Church.¹¹ But the only reason why he can act *in persona*

---

7. Y. Congar, "L'ecclesia ou communauté chrétienne, sujet intégral de l'action liturgique," in *La liturgie après Vatican II. Bilans, études, prospective*, 241-282.

8. P. M. Gy, "Le 'nous' de la prière eucharistique," in *La Maison-Dieu* 191 (1992) 7-14; H. Legrand, "Le rôle des communautés locales. Dans l'appel, l'envoi, la réception et le soutien des laïcs recevant une charge ecclésiale," in *La Maison-Dieu* 215, 3 (1998) 9-32, 15.

9. S. Wood, "Priestly Identity: Sacrament of the Ecclesial Community," 114: "By virtue of ordination the priest sacramentally represents the ecclesial community. This means he stands in the stead of the community, stands for the community, becomes a type of corporate personality in which the community recognizes itself; in short, he is a sacramental sign of the community."

10. "The fundamental ability to represent Christ is given to all Christians." J. Baldovin, "Liturgical Presidency: The Sacramental Question," in *Disciples at the Crossroads: Perspectives on Worship and Church Leadership*, ed. E. Bernstein et al. (Collegeville, 1993) 27-44, 39; "Reflecting on the teaching and experience of Vatican II, theologians and canonists realize that all of Christ's faithful, by reason of baptism, act in persona Christi." J. P. Mcintyre, "In Persona Christi capitis," in *Studia Canonica* 30 (1996) 371-401, 373.

11. The expression *in persona Christi Capitis* was also used in *Presbyterorum Ordinis* nr. 2. Pope Pius XII also used this expression in *Mediator Dei* (1947): "Christifideles autem per sacerdotis manus Sacrificium offere ex eo patet, quod altaris administer personam Christi utpote Capitis gerit, membrorum omnium nomine offerentis." *Acta Apostolicae Sedis* 39 (1947) 521-595, p. 556. This is a better way to speak about the christological representation of the priest. Adding the word *Capitis*, the bond with the community as Body of Christ is more strengthened. See: D. Power, "Representing Christ

Christi Capitis is because he acts *in persona Ecclesiae*. His christological representation is based upon the fact that he represents the local community which gathers for the celebration. This view is shared by several contemporary theologians. Susan Wood for example points out: "In recapitulating the ecclesial community, the ordained minister acts in persona Christi."[12] The late Edward Kilmartin held the same opinion: "The priest first represents (denotes) the Church in its sacramental activity and secondly represents (connotes) Christ the Head of the Church."[13] Similarly, David Power writes: "It is because he acts in the name of the Church, and by his actions mediates its faith, that the priest also represents and acts in the person of Christ (...). The priest therefore, by being a symbol of the Church in its dependence on Christ's headship, is a symbol of the headship itself."[14] In the words of John Baldovin: "The priest acts 'in persona Christi Capitis' insofar as he acts 'in persona Ecclesiae', and not vice versa."[15]

But how, then, we should we understand this christological representation? Certainly not as if the priest were a sort of *'alter Christus'*. In that way, there would no longer be a difference within the christological representation of the priest. In no way the priest as symbol of Christ can coincide with Christ Himself. Therefore we would prefer to say: acting *in persona Christi Capitis*, the priest reveals in a symbolic way that it is the risen Christ himself who leads the celebrating congregation, He who is the Head of the assembly. The priest reminds the community that Christ is the first subject of the liturgical activity, and that the congregation is his actual Body. In the ordained minister, the assembly sees what it really is: the Body of the risen Lord. Therefore, the priest is a symbol and an icon of Christ. In a symbolic way, he reveals the identity of the assembly. He shows explicitly to the celebrating community what it really is. That is why we can say that he is the 'sacrament' of the community.[16] Kilmartin wrote:

> Presiding over the community priests represent the whole Church and so connote Christ's activity. They act in the name of the whole Church and so

in Community and Sacrament," in *Being a Priest Today*, ed. D. Goergen (Collegeville, 1992) 97-123, 110; Idem, "Church order: The Need for Redress," in *Worship* 71 (1997) 296-309, 300.

12. S. Wood, "Priestly Identity: Sacrament of the Ecclesial Community," 126.

13. E. J. Kilmartin, "Bishop and Presbyter as Representatives of the Church and Christ," in *Women Priests: A Catholic Commentary on the Vatican Declaration*, ed. L. Swidler and A. Swidler (New York, 1977) 295-302, 297.

14. D. Power, *The Christian Priest: Elder and Prophet* (London, 1973) 112-113.

15. J. F. Baldovin, "Concelebration: A Problem of Symbolic Roles in the Church," in *Worship* 59 (1985) 32-47, 36.

16. Cf. the title of the article of Susan Wood: S. Wood, "Priestly Identity: Sacrament of the Ecclesial Community," in *Worship* 69 (1995) 109-127.

serve as transparency for the grounds of unity and activity of the whole Church: Christ and the Holy Spirit.[17]

Elswhere he has pointed out:

> The official servant of the unity of the Church, much in the way of a father of a family, becomes in a special way transparency for the grounds of the unity of the Church: Christ.[18]

By acting *in persona Ecclesiae*, the priest becomes transparency for the identity of the community. He reminds the community that it really is the body of Christ, and for that reason, he also acts *in persona Christi Capitis*.

We can even say more. By presiding at the Eucharist, not only does the priest reveal the identity of the assembly, but he also brings it about. In that way, he is both *révélateur* and *opérateur*[19]. By reminding the community that she is really the Body of Christ (*révélateur*), he also invites this same community to become (*opérateur*) what it is, the Body of the risen Lord. Together with Louis-Marie Chauvet we can say:

> En présidant l'eucharistie au titre de son ordination, le ministre exerce une fonction sacramentelle de 'sym-bole', c'est-à-dire de 'révélateur' (il donne à voir) et d' 'opérateur' (il donne à vivre en donnant à voir) de ce qu'est la communauté et de ce qu'elle fait: elle est Église du Christ animée par l'Esprit, et elle agit, par la communion de l'Esprit, comme corps du Christ qui, comme à la dernière Cène, continue de prendre le pain, de rendre grâce et de le lui offrir comme sa propre vie.[20]

This means that the Christ who is represented by the priest is not an imaginary Christ, but rather the living Christ who is incarnated, by means of the Holy Spirit, in his ecclesial Body.[21] The Christ represented by the priest is the Christ who is sacramentally *present* on earth 'as the Church'.[22] The Christ represented by the minister is the ecclesial Christ, namely the Risen Christ who transforms the community into His Body through the Spirit. There can be no immediate representation of Christ by the leader of the Eucharist, but only of the Christ mediated by the

---

17. E. J. Kilmartin, "Bishop and Presbyter as Representatives of the Church and Christ," 298.

18. Idem, "Apostolic Office: Sacrament of Christ," in *Theological Studies* 36 (1975) 243-264, 259.

19. L.-M. Chauvet, *Les sacrements. Parole de Dieu au risque du corps* (Paris, 1993) 5-17.

20. Idem, "Le ministère de présidence de l'eucharistie," in *L'Eucharistie. Jésus offert – Jésus vivant* (Paris 1981) 21-38, 32.

21. Idem, "Les ministères des laïcs: vers un nouveau visage de l'église?" in *La Maison-Dieu* 215, 3 (1998) 33-57, 45-46.

22. P. Fink, "The Sacrament of Orders: Some Liturgical Reflections," in *Worship* 56 (1982) 482-502, 486.

assembly. In other words, the one who presides at the Eucharist is the 'sacrament of the ecclesial Christ'.

Still, something more needs to be pointed out. By stating that the priest acts first of all *in persona Ecclesiae* during the Eucharist, we mean that he does so during the entire Eucharistic celebration, also during the Eucharistic prayer which includes the institution narrative. Therefore, we cannot agree with Dennis Ferrara,[23] according to whom the *in persona Christi* is also incorporated in the *in persona Ecclesiae*, except during the institution narrative. At that moment, says Ferrara, the priest no longer acts any more *in persona Ecclesiae*, but only *in persona Christi*.[24] This happens in an apophatic way. The priest must disappear so that Christ may become present at that particular moment.[25] Based upon the theology of the Eucharistic prayer, we are convinced that the priest acts *in persona Ecclesiae* during the institution narrative as well. To claim that the priest acts *in persona Ecclesiae* during the Eucharistic prayer, but *in persona Christi* during the institution narrative, would overemphasize the institution narrative. This latter would then become a magic formula and not longer a mere narrative within the Eucharistic prayer. Since the whole Eucharistic prayer is consecratory, and not only the institution narrative,[26] we are convinced that the priest always acts *in persona Ecclesiae* during the Eucharist, also when he recites the institution narrative. But this acting *in persona Ecclesiae* is of course an acting *in persona Christi Capitis* as well, because the priest officially represents the assembly of which Christ is the Head.[27]

---

23. D. Ferrara, "Representation or Self-Effacement? The Axiom 'In Persona Christi' in St. Thomas and the Magisterium," in *Theological Studies* 55 (1994) 195-224; Idem, "The Ordination of Women: Tradition and Meaning," in *Theological Studies* 55 (1994) 709-719; Idem, "In Persona Christi: A Reply to Sara Butler," in *Theological Studies* 56 (1995) 81-91; Idem, "In Persona Christi: Representation of Christ as Servant or Servant of Christ's Presence?" in *CTSA Proceedings* 50 (1995) 138-145; Idem, "In Persona Christi: Towards a Second Naiveté," in: *Theological Studies* 57 (1996) 65-88; Idem, "In persona Christi. Valeur et limites d'une formule," in *La Maison-Dieu* 215, 3 (1998) 59-78.

24. Ferrara finds evidence for this in the writings of Thomas Aquinas: *Summa Theologiae* III, quaestio 82, articulus 7, ad 3.

25. "And the point I am making is that in the formal constitution of the sign the priest's role is not representational but apophatic: in the quotation of Christ's words of institution by way of anamnesis, the I of the priest steps aside in order to let the 'I' of Christ appear, the persona of the priestly narrator gives way visibly to the persona of Christ." D. Ferrara, "Representation or Self-Effacement?" 213.

26. A. Verheul, "De consecratorische waarde van het eucharistisch gebed," in *Donum Amicorum aan Lukas Brinkhoff bij zijn 60e verjaardag* (Trier, 1979) 40-56; Idem, "La valeur consécratoire de la prière eucharistique," in *Questions Liturgiques* 62 (1981) 135-144.

27. Cf. E. J. Kilmartin, "The Catholic Tradition of Eucharistic Theology: Towards the Third Millennium," in *Theological Studies* 55 (1994) 405-457, 440-441.

2. Advantages of an Ecclesiological Approach

We have opted in favour of an explicit ecclesiological approach of the ordained minister acting in the Eucharist, whereas the official Church is rather inclined to choose the more christological point of view. In our position, the christological characterisation of the priest is not dropped out but incorporated within the ecclesiological definition. Such a stance entails many advantages. One advantage, for example, is the fact that in that way an important argument against the ordination of women can be overcome. *Inter Insigniores* says that women cannot become priests, because they are not able to act during the Eucharist *in persona Christi*. There is no natural resemblance between a woman and Christ. But when we say that the ordained minister in the Eucharist acts first of all *in persona Ecclesiae*, then this argument of *Inter Insigniores* no longer holds. A woman can represent the assembly as well as a man, and therefore both a woman and a man can represent Christ the Head of the community.[28]

Another important consequence of the ecclesiological approach to the ordained minister in the Eucharist, is the fact that presiding at the Eucharist and being the pastor of a community are closely intertwined. It is theologically very difficult to preside at the Eucharist in a community one is not the pastor of. If we say that during the Eucharist the ordained minister acts *in persona Christi Capitis* just because he also acts *in persona Ecclesiae*, then we have to add: only those who are representing the community in the totality of its religious life can also lead this community in its Eucharist.[29] The leader of the community has to be the leader of the Eucharist as well because the Eucharist is the source and the summit of the Christian life of the community (*Sacrosanctum Concilium* nr. 10; *Lumen Gentium* nr. 11). In other words, leadership in the community cannot be separated from leadership in the Eucharist. This of course puts into question the pastoral practice of many parishes in our countries where, due to the lack of ordained ministers, lay people have the responsibility of a community, whereas an ordained priest has to come from outside for the Eucharist. One has to be aware of the fact that this is an anomaly. David Power states this very clearly: "It would betray the early sense of Church not to see that Eucharist and community are reciprocal realities and that celebrating the Eucharist is essential to being

---

28. H. Legrand, "Traditio perpetuo servata? The Non-Ordination of Women: Tradition as Simply or Historical Fact?" in *Worship* 65 (1991) 482-508, 502-504.

29. R. Michiels, "Het ambt in de kerk van morgen," in *Pastoraal ambt in een priesterarme kerk*, ed. R. Michiels and W. Van Soom, Nikè-reeks, 24 (Leuven, 1990) 107-166, 125, 128 & 136; E. Van Waelderen, "De plaats van ambt en bediening in de gezamelijke opbouw van de geloofsgemeenschap", in *Collationes* 9 (1979) 292-328, 309.

pastor of the community."[30] Therefore, the one who leads the community also has to be the one who presides at the Eucharist of this community. In the 1970s, Karl Rahner, dealing with the problem of pastoral assistants, already defended this position.[31]

A final important advantage of the ecclesiological approach to the ordained minister in the Eucharist is the fact that it fits better in the postmodern context in which we are now immersed. A christological characterisation of the ordained minister makes it almost possible to point out where Christ is present in the Eucharist, namely in the ordained minister who presides at the Eucharist *in persona Christi*. He is almost an '*alter Christus*'. But in a postmodern context, such an over-emphasis of the presence of Christ in the Eucharist is very problematic. A postmodern sacramentology is very watchful against affirming the presence of God and Christ in the holy symbols.[32] God and Christ are present as well as absent. We can come in the vicinity of God, but we cannot encompass him totally, because our words and our thoughts are too deficient for such a great mystery.[33] This is at work in the Eucharist as well. There, Christ is both present and absent. A strong christological approach of the leader of the Eucharist does not do justice to the absence of Christ in the Eucharist, overlooking, the radical difference of Christ. It is a theology which lays too much accent upon the presence of Christ while overlooking his absence.[34] And such a theology is problematic for postmodern men and

---

30. D. Power, *The Eucharistic Mystery: Revitalizing the Tradition* (New York, 1992) 79. See also: H. Legrand, "The Presidency of the Eucharist According To the Ancient Tradition," in *Worship* 27 (1979) 413-438, 432: "For the ancient tradition, whether we refer to the liturgical texts having the most authority or to canonical texts, the presidency of the eucharistic assembly appears as the liturgical dimension of the pastoral charge."

30. K. Rahner, "Pastorale Dienste und Gemeindeleitung," in *Stimmen der Zeit* 195 (1977) 733-743, 742: "Der Pastoralassistent müßte also die seiner tatsächlichen Funktion entsprechende Beauftragung erhalten. Entspricht diese Funktion den Aufgaben eines Diakons, dann sollte er sakramental zum Diakon geweiht werden. Ist die Funktion eines Pastoralassistenten faktisch die eines Gemeindeleiters, dann sollte er die Priesterweihe erhalten, weil die Trennung zwischen der Funktion des Gemeindeleiters und der Funktion des Eucharistievorstehers wesenwidrig ist."

32. L. Leijssen, "De kinderdoop en de éne initiatie. Een (postmoderne) sacramentologische reflectie," in *Nieuw leven. Rituelen rond geboorte en doop*, ed. G. Lukken and J. De Wit, Liturgie in beweging, 1 (Baarn, 1997) 216-230, 223.

33. Therefore, Marion always crosses out the word 'God' in his works. See J.-L. Marion, *Dieu sans l'être* (Paris, 1991). For a short commentary on the works and thoughts of Marion, see D. Power, *et al.*, "Current Theology. Sacramental Theology: A Review of Literature," in *Theological Studies* 55 (1994) 657-705, 688-693.

34. "All theoretic claims of church authorities to possess the authority of God and to act in God's place, as vicar, as representative, 'in persona Christi', negate the difference between the holiness of God and the divinely willed profanity of every created thing." M. Collins, "The Public Language of Ministry," in *Official Ministry in a New Age*, ed. J. H. Provost, Permanent Seminar Studies, 3 (Washington, DC, 1981) 7-40, 37.

women. Openness to the transcendental is lost, the attention for the difference has disappeared. Everything is clear and filled in. A rigorous christological theology gives the impression of not being aware of the restriction, contingency and particularity of all our speaking about God and Christ. It seems to neglect the inadequacy of the symbolic representation of Christ by the priest. What we have to do is to try to bear witness to the transcendence in a non-hegemonic way, making use of our fragmentary words, images, stories, symbols and rituals. We have to make space for the coming into presence of the transcendental.[35]

It is our conviction that the ecclesiological approach to the ordained minister in the Eucharist is the best way to let this happen. When the priest acts *in persona Christi Capitis* as a consequence of his acting *in persona Ecclesiae*, his representation of Christ has to be decoded throughout the celebrating assembly. Such an approach to the ordained minister is less hegemonic and takes into account the radical difference of Christ. In no way can the priest represent Christ in a direct way. Only because he presides over the celebrating assembly, the ecclesial body of Christ, is the priest able to act symbolically as the Head, that is Christ. The mediation of the community must certainly not be overlooked.[36] Christ's presence in the priest has always to be decoded through the assembly. In this way, the aspect of immediacy is brought into a proper and fecund perspective.

Faculty of Theology
Katholieke Universiteit Leuven
Sint-Michielsstraat 6
B-3000 Leuven, Belgium

Gino MATTHEEUWS

---

35. J. Bloechl and S. Van den Bossche, "Postmoderniteit, theologie en sacramentologie. Een onderzoeksproject toegelicht," in *Jaarboek voor Liturgie-onderzoek* 13 (1997) 21-48, 41.

36. Cf. L.-M. Chauvet, *Les sacrements*, 56: "une rencontre du Christ vivant qui n'est pas possible que moyennant la médiation concrète d'une Église."

PREACHING IN A POSTMODERN CONTEXT

Introduction

"The split between the Gospel and culture is undoubtedly the drama of our time," so claims John Paul II in his exhortation *Ecclesia in America*.[1] One scene from this drama has been described by Cardinal Godfried Danneels of Mechelen-Brussels, Belgium. He claims that the major problem facing Western society as it moves into the third millennium is religious indifference.

> People have the impression that they don't need God to be happy. ... He is irrelevant to many people. I think there is a blind spot in the eye of modern people that doesn't allow them to see the importance of God ... (They) are not against the Church ... they simply say 'Why the Church?' 'Is it useful?' 'Does it give me something more than I can have by normal life?' That is the problem![2]

The challenge to the Church, as we enter the third millennium, is to ask what difference does it make in one's life to believe in God and to worship with the church?

The announcement for this conference states that people do not always recognize themselves in the language and structures of traditional religions, thus theologians are called to a renewed reflection on sacramental presence. As part of a renewed reflection, John Paul calls for a "new evangelization," i.e., a serious effort to inculturate preaching in such a way that the Gospel is proclaimed in the language and in the culture of its hearers.[3] A postmodern approach to preaching, "what some have called 'A New Homiletic'," provides one means to foster such a renewed reflection and is vital for a new evangelization.

In the first place, preaching is sacramental. As St. Paul writes, "Faith comes through hearing"(Rom 7,10). Sacraments signify the presence of God within the community of believers, and preaching serves to express

---

1. John Paul II, Post-Synodal Apostolic Exhortation, *The Church in America* (Boston: Pauline Books and Media, 1999). Here he quotes Pope Paul VI, *On Evangelization in the Modern World, Apostolic Exhortation Evangelii Nuntiandi* (Washington, DC: United States Catholic Conference, 1975).
2. An interview with Cardinal Godfried Danneels, *Church Magazine* 3 (1999) 17-22.
3. John Paul II, *The Church in America*, 111.

verbally the effects of grace within the assembled community and calls the members of the community to a transformation. The hearers who have encountered the Word of God are invited to respond to the Lord. While current Catholic homiletics emphasizes the conversational nature of the homily, the conversation heard in much preaching today sounds rather one-sided. From a theoretical standpoint, preaching today still follows the deductive method of modern rhetoric whereby the sermon moves from the mind and heart of the preacher to the ears of the listeners. If this is the case, the sermon is constructed by rationalistic and propositional logic, and the authority for the proclamation rests with the preacher.

The New Homiletic as proposed, for example, by David Buttrick, Fred Craddock, and Richard Eslinger, employs the postmodern critique of Western rationality and of the appeal to foundations.[4] It shifts the method of composing a sermon from propositional logic to an emphasis on the experience of the congregation. In this way the method shifts from a deductive to an inductive one. It serves to remind us of the presence of Christ within the assembly. It relocates the authority of preaching from the preacher to the community of listeners who are in dialogue with the Scripture and with their culture.

We find the roots of the New Homiletic in ancient rhetoric, specifically with the rhetorical devices of 'invention' and 'persuasion.' The first device holds that the nature of truth is something to be discovered, or 'invented.' This is to say that the truth of the proclamation may be discovered through the dialogue of preacher and congregation. The second device reminds us that rhetoric is the art of dialectical persuasive reasoning. For the ancient rhetoricians, rhetoric was not concerned with the communication of information, *per se*, and surely not with flowery eloquence, but essentially with the transformation of the listener.

Religion is by its nature persuasive, not merely propositional. I propose that for preaching to communicate effectively a sacramental presence in a postmodern context, the Church should heed the method of the New Homiletic in order to uncover the presence of Christ within the community. In addressing the role of preaching for the drama of our time I will consider three points. First of all, the Postmodern challenge to the church; second, to briefly review John Paul's exhortation to show how he addresses this drama, especially in his emphasis on the need for believers to encounter Christ; third, I will focus a response to this challenge through the medium of liturgical preaching.

---

4. D. Buttrick, *A Captive Voice: The Liberation of Preaching* (Louisville: Westminster/John Knox Press, 1994); F. Craddock, *As One Without Authority* (Nashville: Abingdon Press, 1979); R. Eslinger, *A New Hearing: Living Options in a Homiletic Method* (Nashville: Abingdon Press, 1989).

1. The Postmodern Context

Postmodernism defies definition. However, David Power, in his book, *Eucharistic Mystery*,[5] offers a description of postmodernism. He explains that while we cannot analyze its components we can identify some of its aspects. For instance, postmodernism professes a disillusionment with the achievements of the Enlightenment. Despite the great attention that modern society has given to the human subject, we have not achieved a deep understanding of the person or of the social order. Our technological advances have not brought progress and prosperity to the world, instead they have wrought much environmental damage. The atrocities of the twentieth century, especially the Holocaust, have disrupted the myth of human progress and the belief in divine providence. The result is that there is no comprehensive myth or philosophy that offers a coherent explanation for the whole of reality.

Postmodernism seeks to transform in local ways the way we understand ourselves in relation to modernity and to contemporary culture and history.[6] Its primary purpose is the critique of Western rationality, the legacy of the Enlightenment, and the centered subject. Postmodernism invites us to go beyond the modern world-view initiated by Galileo, Descartes, Bacon and Newton.[7] In transcending this world-view postmodernism challenges the assumptions which have directed the inquiry of knowledge since the Enlightenment, such as separating issues of fact from value, differentiating scientific inquiry from humanistic inquiry and the driving concern for certainty and control.[8] This modern world-view becomes like the proverbial air we breathe: it so permeates our culture and our way of proceeding that we barely notice it. According to William Willimon,

> (M)odernity, and the liberalism it spawned, enforced a closed epistemology in which all knowledge was self-derived, readily available to anyone, anywhere ... . [It] claimed that everything in the world is capable of being known, 'grasped' by anyone who is 'reasonable.' There is nothing

---

5. David Power, *Eucharistic Mystery: Revitalizing the Tradition.* (New York: Crossroad, 1995) 10.

6. George Aichele, et. al., *The Postmodern Bible* (New Haven: Yale University Press, 1995) 9.

7. David Ray Griffin and Huston Smith, *Primordial Truth and Postmodern Theology* (Albany: State University of New York Press, 1989) xii.

8. Robert Stephen Reid, "Postmodernism and the Function of the New Homiletic in Post-Christendom Congregations," in *Homiletic* 2 (1995) 5.

miraculous, gifted or unavailable to the knower. nothing essential to be added to the natural world from outside the natural world.[9]

In a word, there is no need for grace. The proponents of postmodernism invite us to consider how much we are influenced by the modern, scientific, mechanistic and economic view of life, a view that celebrates the capacity to know, control, and manage.

The optimism and self-assuredness of the modern period has been tempered by the onslaught of World War I, and the devastation of humanity throughout the twentieth century. These atrocities continue to the end of the millennium with the war in Kosovo and in East Timor, as well as with the earthquakes in Turkey and Taiwan. The theological question of the twentieth century would appear to be "where is God?" Indeed, our age seems to be characterized by the absence of God.

2. Pope John Paul II and the "New Evangelization"

To respond to this drama Pope John Paul II calls for a "New Evangelization," which is not merely a re-evangelization but one that he says is "new in ardor, methods, and expression." The starting point for his program of a new evangelization is an encounter with the living Lord. Such an encounter, he says, is the way to conversion, communion, and solidarity. "A fresh encounter with Jesus will make all members of the Church ... aware that they are called to continue the Redeemer's mission in their lands."[10]

This notion of encounter with God was seriously discussed some thirty years ago by the Dutch Dominican, Edward Schillebeeckx.[11] He describes this encounter as the intimate relationship between God and the person: God discloses Himself through revelation and the person devotes himself or herself to God's service through religion. Thus religion is essentially a personal relationship with God. Because God initiates this relationship, in humility condescending to meet the person, the person lives in a graced "condition of active and immediate communication with ... the living God."[12] Schillebeeckx warned of the danger of losing this sense of intimacy in religion. This warning applies to liturgical preaching as well as to sacramental worship.

---

9. William Willimon, "'Suddenly from Heaven There Came a Sound': Pentecostal Preaching at the End of the Twentieth Century," in *Journal for Preachers* 21 (1998) 15-21, at 19.

10. John Paul II, *The Church in America*, 14, 18.

11. E. Schillebeeckx, *Christ the Sacrament of the Encounter with God* (New York: Sheed & Ward, 1963).

12. *Ibid.*, 3-4.

The mechanical approach to sacraments, focusing upon the physical categories "sacrament as substance," renders the faithful mere passive recipients of sacramental grace. Herein sacramental worship becomes an automatic process: the worshipers "put in" their prayer and devotion; in return for their devotion they "get grace." This mechanical approach does away with the need for a personal response. When we approach the liturgy in a mechanical way, "putting in prayer in order to take out grace," we forsake the intimacy of God's loving relationship with humankind. We are not saved simply by hearing God's word or by consuming the communion bread but by personally responding to the Word of God and to the offer of Christ's flesh for all. God initiates the offer of salvation and we respond. The response to Christ is symbolized through the community gathering around the table and sharing in the Eucharistic meal. Only from a genuine, heartfelt response can we "become what we eat," one with Christ and with one another. The sacramental encounter, an intimate relationship between God and a person, requires a personal response. A person must either accept or reject God's offer of salvation, but one cannot remain indifferent in the presence of God's invitation.

Ideally, a person is transformed in the process, similar to those who were transformed by a personal encounter with Jesus, as we read in the Scriptures.[13] An encounter with the living Lord is a transforming experience. The purpose of the encounter, then, according to John Paul II, is to "move from a faith of habit to a faith which is conscious and personally lived. The renewal of faith will always be the best way to lead others to the truth that is Christ."[14] The encounter is important to bridge the gap between the Gospel and culture. The encounter with the living Lord will provide the experience of an intimate relationship with God. It is only through the light of this experience that one can answer the question "Why do I need God? Of what use is the Church?" Here we find the importance of preaching for John Paul II. In his words, "It is indispensable that all remain united to Christ by means of a joyful and transforming *kerygma*, especially in liturgical preaching."[15] Note: liturgical preaching should convey a "joyful and transforming *kerygma*." It is not merely doctrinal or instructional preaching, but preaching that has the power to transform the faithful.

---

13. John Paul II, *The Church in America*, 19.
14. *Ibid.*, 118.
15. *Ibid.*

3. A New Homiletic

Here is where the lessons of postmodernism come to bear. Rhetoric in general, and preaching in particular, have been greatly influenced by the rationalist mindset of the Enlightenment. Modern rhetoric overturned classical rhetoric by focusing on the logical content of a speech and discouraging the expression of feeling or passion. However, if liturgical preaching is to bring about a new evangelization and provide an opportunity for a personal encounter with the Lord, then we should heed the advice of those who currently call for a "new homiletic," i.e., a return to classical rhetoric, and a preaching that is more inductive than deductive.

The problem was stated succinctly by two diverse Christian thinkers two centuries ago. The Danish philosopher, Soren Kierkegaard, once opined, "There's no lack of information in a Christian land; something else is lacking, and this is a something which the one man cannot directly communicate to the other."[16] Also, Jonathan Edwards, the revivalist Puritan preacher from colonial Massachusetts, emphasized the rôle of passion in the spiritual life: "Our people do not so much need to have their heads stored, as to have their hearts touched; and they stand in the greatest need of that sort of preaching that has the greatest tendency to do this."[17]

3.1. The Decay of Rhetoric

I will begin the discussion of the new homiletic with a brief look at the transition in the history of rhetoric. Rhetoric is the theory and practice of purposive discourse.[18] The purpose of rhetoric, in the classical tradition, was to persuade an audience of a particular viewpoint or to reaffirm a standing policy. This was accomplished through the application of accepted strategies and techniques designed to move the listener or reader to agree with the speaker or author. There were two schools of thought concerning these strategies and techniques. On the one hand, members of Plato's Academy argued from abstractions aspiring to the ideals of knowledge (*episteme*). On the other hand, the Sophists aspired to move the listeners through the persuasion of opinion (*doxa*). The Sophists stressed the speaker's effect on the audience rather than the content of the speech. Language was considered to be more of a form of power rather than a conveyance of ideas. Sophistic rhetoric was primarily concerned

---

16. Cited in Fred Craddock, *Overhearing the Gospel* (Nashville: Abingdon, 1978) 120-123.

17. J. Edwards, *Treatise Concerning Religious Affections*, 1746, cited by Alan Jacobs, "Preachers without Poetry," in *First Things* 95 (1999) 49-54.

18. Richard Lischer, *Theories of Preaching: Selected Readings in the Homiletical Tradition* (Durham: Labyrinth Press, 1987) 209.

with the effective use of language in order to create an experience for an audience.[19] The rules of rhetoric devised and developed in ancient Greece and Rome were codified in rhetorical manuals and influenced the Western intellectual tradition through the fifteenth century.[20]

3.1.1. The Early Christian Period

The development of early Christian preaching is discussed by Thomas Carroll in his book *Preaching the Word*.[21] I will summarize here. Early Christian preaching was somewhat influenced by the ancient Greek rhetorical form of the *diatribe*, referring to a learned discussion. This form of discourse developed during the decline of the Hellenistic Age. In this confusing and fearful time the speaker, striving to win the attention of the audience, would need to engage the listeners in a dialogue, speaking with them in familiar terms while guiding them along a hopeful and practical path. Delivered by a skilled speaker, the diatribe was a discourse that retained the mannerisms of animated conversation.

The early Christian church adopted this form of rhetoric, filtered through Jewish worship. This is to say that Jewish preaching was strictly related to a tradition of Sacred Scripture and expressed within the cult of the synagogue. For the early Christians the most significant element in the proclamation of the Word was prophecy. Prophecy asserted itself as a compelling Word of God placed on the lips of the human herald. A prophetic preacher spoke to the present situation with divine authority, enabling the Christian community to understand their particular situation as a manifestation of the historical revelation.[22] An example of this is Jesus' first sermon in the synagogue at Nazareth.

The preachers of the early Church, besides being prophetic, maintained the conversational quality of the diatribe. Hence the preaching event came to be called a "homily." Origen is the first to use this term for preaching, as he titled one of his works, "Homilies on Luke."[23] Generally speaking, this term connotes "a being together" or "communion;" a "meeting of minds and hearts." When applied to public speech it acquired the meaning of conversation or familiar discourse. Following the model of Jesus as preacher, the Church Fathers throughout Greece and Rome preached on Scripture in a prophetic and homiletic manner. They brought into being a unique type of rhetoric. The homily

---

19. Robert Stephen Reid, "Postmodernism and the Function of the New Homiletic in Post-Christendom Congregations," 9.
20. George Aichele, et. al., *The Postmodern Bible*, 149-56.
21. Thomas K. Carroll, *Preaching the Word* (Wilmington: Michael Glazier, 1984).
22. *Ibid.*, 17.
23 Origen, *Homilies on Luke; Fragments on Luke*, translated by Joseph T. Lienhard (Washington D.C.: Catholic University of America Press, 1996).

saw its culmination in two outstanding preachers, Origen and Augustine. Origen's preaching was noted for its prophetic quality which he delivered in a conversational style. Augustine was a masterful teacher, proclaiming the Word of God in an accessible manner so that all could grasp and respond to the message. Although he preached in a cathedral his homiletic style created the mood of an intimate conversation.[24] Augustine applied the rules of rhetoric to his preaching. Borrowing a scheme from Cicero he taught that preaching has a three-fold purpose: to teach, i.e, to instruct the faithful in the doctrine of the Church; to delight, i.e., to inspire them with a desire to follow Christ's teaching; and to move, i.e., to motivate the listeners to translate their desire into action.[25]

The era of preaching in a prophetic and homiletic manner concluded during the papacy of Gregory the Great. This was a period of transition: Christianity moved from the age of the Fathers to the age of the Church. During the great Gregorian reform we find the decline of the Word in the Roman tradition. Gregory encouraged the practice of reading a patristic sermon at Mass, which eventually became the norm for much of Christian worship. This use of ancient sermons in a living worship contributed to the decline of preaching. The faithful no longer benefitted from the exposition of Scripture, a message that would help them to understand their lives and their present day concerns in light of a living tradition. Preaching had lost its prophetic voice.[26]

3.1.2. The Modern Period

The advent of the modern period brought about a decline of interest in rhetoric, a situation which has lasted into our era. One of the main causes of the demise of rhetoric was the modern philosophical notion of the unicity of truth, that truth could be known only through analysis and demonstration. One of the main culprits in the demise of classical rhetoric is Peter Ramus, the sixteenth century educational reformer and logician, who was appointed Professor of Eloquence by Henry II in 1551. In his movement of educational reform he found it necessary to divorce the study of content from the study of form or feeling. This separation eventually resulted in two separate discourses: poetry and science. Poetry concerned itself with the ways in which we express feelings, "the

---

24. *Ibid.*, 196.
25. Augustine writes: "A certain orator has said, and said truly, that an eloquent man should speak in such a way that he teaches, pleases, and persuades.' Then he added: 'to teach is a necessity, to please is a satisfaction, and to persuade is a triumph.' Of these three, the ... teaching depends upon what we say; the other two depend upon the manner in which we say it." *Christian Instruction*, IV:26, in *Writings of St. Augustine*, vol. 4, ed. John J. Gavigan (New York: CIMA Publishing, 1947) 192-193.
26. Thomas K. Carroll, *Preaching the Word*, 220.

discourse of the human spirit." Science concerned itself with analysis and demonstration in order to verify what is true. Rhetoric became associated with poetry and eloquence, and was thought of as mere ornamentation.[27] Its focus shifted from persuasion to narration, from social to personal contexts, and from discourse to literature. Under the Western philosophical idea of the "unicity of truth" rhetoric was reduced to an instrument for transmitting theological, philosophical and cultural texts.

The emphasis on the unicity of truth brought about a major shift in the understanding of the role of public speaking. Before the Middle Ages speech was primarily an event in sound. During the Middle Ages, with the development of abstract thought, as well as the invention of the printing press, the focus of oral communication shifted from sound to sight, from the aural to the visual; dialectic replaced rhetoric. Speech and hearing was no longer an event but the means for the conveyance of information. Here we find the reification of knowledge. Now knowledge is treated like a commodity, a thing to be acquired by one person and passed onto another. An example of this can be found by considering three terms used repeatedly by Peter Ramus and his disciples to describe the activity of discourse: 'stored', 'key', and 'place'. Knowledge is something that is 'stored' under special topics or 'places' (from the Greek *topos*, meaning place), and certain ideas provide the 'keys' to unlock the places and retrieve the store of knowledge.[28] This approach to knowledge is heavily influenced by visual and spatial imagery. Just as the words, ideas and topics are laid out on a textbook page, so too should they be organized in a speech. There is now a geometrical and mechanical quality to communication. Ramist rhetoric replaced voice with vision. For him, the processes of personal communication do not play any necessary role in intellectual life since they provide no means for understanding or for the discovery of the truth. For Ramus, dialogue and conversation become mere nuisances. Even though rhetoric is concerned with expression and communication, and presumes the three components of speaker, subject matter, and listener,[29] Ramus renounced the possibility of discovery

---

27. To be sure, eloquence in public speech has always been suspect. For example, Cicero warned "though wisdom without eloquence is of little service to states, yet eloquence without wisdom is frequently a positive injury, and is of service never." Richard Lischer, *Theories of Preaching: Selected Readings in the Homiletical Tradition*, 212.

28. Walter Ong, *Ramus, Method, and the Decay of Dialogue* (Cambridge, MA: Harvard University Press, 1958) 315.

29. Aristotle writes: "Of means of persuading by speaking there are three species: some consist in the character of the speaker; others in the disposing of the hearer a certain way; others in the thing itself which is said, by reason of its proving or appearing to prove the point." *Aristotle's Treatise on Rhetoric also the Poetics of Aristotle*, ed. Thomas Bucklry (London: Henry A. Bohn, 1850) 12.

within this speaker-listener framework; the discovery of truth is restricted to a dialectical world.[30]

Peter Ramus accordingly distinguished between poetic and scientific discourse, expressing a grave distrust for the former. In his words:

> (W)hen a thing is to be taught perspicuously, the method will consist in various homogeneous enunciations ... . But when the auditor is to be deceived by pleasure or in some other way, some of these homogeneous items have to be put aside, such as the great luminosities of definition, partitions, and transitions, for certain heterogeneous things, such as digressions from the matter and delaying over the matter. But most of all, the order of things from the beginning has to be reversed, and antecedents have to be put after consequents... . This is what the poet does as a major part of his tactics, when he sets out to sway the people, the many-headed monster. He deceives in all sorts of ways. He starts in the middle, often proceeding thence to the beginning, and getting on to the end by some equivocal and unexpected dodge.[31]

Ramus criticizes those orators who are more interested in delighting and moving the listeners rather than teaching them. Poetry still has its place, namely for children for whom it is like the formula fed to infants who are not yet capable of digesting the solid food of logic.

Ramus calls attention to the structure of the piece to be presented. The scientific structure of a presentation moves from the general to the specific, the universal to the singular, the antecedents to the consequents, from what was commonly known to what needs to be understood. This scientific structure studies the arts following the path of analysis and synthesis. By the arts we refer to the study of medicine, law, and theology, for example, each one "a collection of propositions and general observations looking to some useful end in life."[32] Analysis, literally "a breaking up of the whole into its parts," distinguishes the individual subjects to be understood. Synthesis reverses this procedure, showing the activities of the individual subjects in relation to the end.

The emphasis on the scientific structure of a presentation held sway over preaching. The Puritans prided themselves on the "plain sermon," a simple and straightforward delivery of the word unencumbered by flowery eloquence. This style called for an opening of the text by analysis, preaching according to a method which cites doctrine and provides a well-reasoned argument. Also, the Calvinists found a companion with Ramus due to his distrust of words and his teaching that eloquence was but a necessary evil for a recalcitrant audience. Their

---

30. Walter Ong, *Ramus, Method, and the Decay of Dialogue*, 288-289.
31. *Ibid.*, 253.
32. *Ibid.*, 232.

dislike of drama found expression in his abolishing of college student plays, part of his educational reform.[33]

It would appear then that both sacramental worship and the preaching of the Gospel suffered a similar problem: the reification of the event. In sacramental worship the focus shifted away from the event of the meal. The liturgy suffered from a de-emphasis of the activity of sharing the food and drink, the central action around which the community establishes its identity. The focus of reverence then shifted to the elements of bread and wine themselves which many people came to think were imbued with magical powers. The emphasis on participation in the sacramental event was replaced with an emphasis on receiving or simply gazing upon the sacramental material. With the emphasis on the material elements of the Eucharist, rubrics were established to insure the proper and fitting distribution of the host by the priest to the communicant. The Church moved from the physical activity of gathering and sharing a meal, which marked them as a community of disciples, to more of a mental activity of seeing and believing in the presence of Christ.

Likewise, with preaching, the Church moved from a dialogue between preacher and congregation, to a monologue, a format resembling a classroom lecture: the wise preacher imparted his knowledge through a carefully structured format to a patient and passive audience. The medieval sermon followed the model of the university curriculum, devised to communicate knowledge in the most efficient, scientifically structured, way.

3.2. The New Rhetoric

The new rhetoric seeks to restore the principles of classical rhetoric which were taught by the ancients. I believe that this new rhetoric will help to achieve the "new evangelization" called for by John Paul II. Again, this new evangelization is not a re-evangelization. It is not a matter of adding more information to what we already know. Rather, it is more of a process of uncovering the meaning of what we already know and then responding to it. The two steps here "uncovering and responding" are matter for the two devices of classical rhetoric, invention and persuasion.

According to the principle of invention, the nature of truth is something to be discovered.[34] It requires the creative arrangement of a given subject into discursive themes which are appropriate for the subject and

---

33. *Ibid.*, 284-287.
34. The English word "invention" is derived from the Latin *inventus*, meaning to come upon, meet with, discover.

the audience.[35] In other words, the individual themes are arranged in an order such that it would be most likely to make an impression upon the hearer.[36]

This allows for a shift from rationalistic and propositional logic because the speaker intends to create an experience for the listeners in the communicative event. The difference is that what is ordered is the experience rather than the ideas in order to produce a "re-happening" of the biblical story for a contemporary audience.[37] Invention is concerned with the ordering of a speech in such a way that both speaker and audience embark upon a discovery of truth.

Following the principle of persuasion, the speaker links the ideas being presented with an emotional appeal. *Pathos* is the prime motivating force for action. In order to persuade an audience, reason must be accompanied by an appeal to emotion. There is a rationality of the emotions. Conscious rational thought is never fully in charge in human interaction. We might say that "meaning happens" in a rhetorical situation, rather than that meaning is given by the speaker to the hearer. True meaning is encountered through the human interaction in a rhetorical situation.[38]

Here we find the close relationship between rhetoric and religion. The primary motive of rhetoric is not communication but transformation. The literature of the Bible is not without its eloquence, the purpose of which is to persuade the audience. In defending the use of eloquence for preaching, Augustine points out that "A good listener warms to a Scripture passage not by diligently analyzing it but by pronouncing it energetically..."[39] Both rhetorical devices of invention/discovery and persuasion lead to an encounter of the faithful with the word of God.

Another way of fostering this encounter is through the use of inductive, rather than deductive, preaching. Deductive preaching follows a propositional method, structured around several points through which a speaker lays out a particular situation, offers evidence to support his/her position, and through a rational argument attempts to persuade the audience into a particular way of thinking, or towards a specific course of action. Examples of this are found in the courtroom where a lawyer pleads his/her case, or in congress where a senator argues for the passage of a bill. Preaching of this sort was codified in the Middle Ages with the

---

35. George Aichele, et. al., *The Postmodern Bible*, 159-160.
36. Francis Fenelon, "Natural Communication," in Richard Lischer, *Theories of Preaching: Selected Readings in the Homiletical Tradition*, 228.
37. Robert Stephen Reid, "Postmodernism and the Function of the New Homiletic in Post-Christendom Congregations," 7-8.
38. George Aichele, et. al., *The Postmodern Bible*, 167.
39. *Christian Instruction*, IV:21.

ars praedicandi, a manual of sermon design and construction. The complex arrangement found in the manual was greatly influenced by the scholastics with their Aristotelian logic rather than by the rhetoric of Cicero and Augustine.[40]

A deductive sermon moves from a general principle or point of doctrine to a particular application for the listener. It employs an authoritarian method and presumes a passive audience whose members accept the authority of the speaker to interpret the text and apply it to their lives.[41] The problem with the deductive method of preaching today is that much of the audience has become desensitized to the message. Citing Kierkegaard again, "There's no lack of information in a Christian land ..." We have, already, an adequate store of information. What is lacking is the meaning for the individual, and this meaning cannot be directly communicated to another. In the words of the poet T.S. Eliot, "We know too much and are convinced of too little."[42] The Gospel has become an all-too-familiar story and this familiarity fosters the habit of faith against which John Paul II warns.

Both the desensitized state, and the habit of faith, form a barrier to an encounter with God. In order to create a situation in which an encounter is possible we should approach preaching through an inductive manner. Instead of beginning with a proposition based upon a point of doctrine, the inductive method begins with human experience, i.e., the relationship of the audience to the text.[43] The shape of the inductive sermon differs significantly from the propositional structure of the deductive sermon. Robert Waznak describes this shape as moving from an opening disequilibrium (or conflict) through escalation (complication) to a surprising reversal (*peripetia*) into a closing denouement.[44]

Following this scheme, the inductive sermon resembles a narrative rather than a logical argument. The narrative's structure provides order and meaning as one moves from conflict to resolution. The structure of the narrative helps to recreate the Gospel story as an event rather than as a lesson from the past. It is in the narrative's developing of characters and in the unfolding of events that the listeners are moved to participation as they "experience" the Gospel for themselves. We participate in a narrative because we appropriate the experiences of others. The story

---

40. Richard Lischer, *Theories of Preaching: Selected Readings in the Homiletical Tradition*, 219.
41. F. Craddock, *As One Without Authority*, 54-55.
42. T. S. Eliot, "A Dialogue on Dramatic Poetry," in *Selected Essays, 1917-1932* (New York: Harcourt, Brace & Company, 1932) 32.
43. Robert Waznak, *An Introduction to the Homily* (Collegeville: Liturgical Press, 1998) 24.
44. *Ibid.*, 141.

provides a context for our own personal narrative.[45] Preacher and congregation walk a journey together in the discovery of the meaning of the Scripture text. With the inductive sermon the preaching authority comes from the engagement of the preacher with the congregation through the expression of a shared experience: a shared longing or desire, what we are searching for in common.

If the preacher succeeds in engaging the listeners, they will be moved to participate in the preaching event. They will identify with certain experiences and thoughts which they find analogous to their own. It is the general similarity of human experiences which makes communication possible.[46] A sermon that is presented inductively is told like a narrative rather than sounding like an argument. Inductive preaching which resembles a narrative enables the proclamation to become an event in which both preacher and congregation encounter the Word of God.

Conclusion

The postmodern situation poses a challenge to the meaning of Christianity for today. In following the Lord's command to take this message to the ends of the earth (Mt 28,19-20) the Church now incorporates many and diverse cultures. The challenge for our Church entering the third millennium is indeed how to be all things to all people. If the Church is truly "catholic," i.e., universal, then we will be able to meet the postmodern challenge of this new era. I believe that the call of John Paul II for a "new evangelization" moves us in the right direction, disposing us for an encounter with Christ. This encounter will foster a renewed relationship with the living Christ, inspiring believers to respond in faith and compassion to God and neighbor. An ancient Gospel text pleads for a fresh hearing for those who wait in silence for a word from the Lord, for those concerned with world peace, proper stewardship of the planet, justice for the oppressed, and salvation for humankind.

Liturgical preaching is a significant means for fostering a new hearing. A preacher who is attuned to the experiences and needs of the congregation will allow the liturgy to become a faith-filled event rather than a formulaic rite, one in which the worshipers experience an opportunity to encounter Christ. In this way an all-too-familiar text may surprise and stimulate the assembly to renew their pledge of faith. A new age calls for a new hearing.

Fordham University Thomas J. SCIRGHI, S.J.
The Bronx, New York

---

45. Craddock, in Richard Lischer, *Theories of Preaching: Selected Readings in the Homiletical Tradition* (Durham: Labyrinth Press, 1987) 257.
46. *Ibid.*, 252.

"SUNDAY CELEBRATIONS IN THE ABSENCE OF A PRIEST":
A POSTMODERN READING

In "The Eucharist Today: Problems in a Postmodern World," the opening chapter of *The Eucharist Today*, David N. Power refers to a disillusionment today that is often looked at in the context of a postmodern world. This disillusionment results from the fact that there is no all-encompassing explanation or "myth" that serves to give meaning to life in either a sacral or profane sense.[1]

Indeed, it is the "attitude towards, and use of, grand narrative,"[2] according to Jean-François Lyotard, that differentiates the modern and the postmodern. The modern relies upon some grand narrative that ultimately provides an explanation and an understanding of everything. The postmodern, however, puts no faith in any form of a grand narrative.[3]

And the reason why the postmodern relates to metanarratives in this way is because these metanarratives are judged to be dependent on their own presuppositions. Lyotard, with reference to the disillusionment noted above by Power, stresses that the postmodern principle is fundamentally supportive of a system that is open to interpretation and meaning. Much of today's disillusionment is the result of systems which are closed, totalitarian, or based upon a premise that is justified through a ficticious consensus. The "expert" is one who promotes the same closed system (homology), while the inventor is always seeking that which is different (paralogy), as opposed to the same old thing.[4]

Power goes on to comment that a postmodern critique questions the premise that language simply serves in an instrumental fashion to express meaning. Indeed, language is not something over which one has absolute control. Ironically, control has been exercised by those who want only the *same* consistent interpretation to emerge, suppressing or silencing any

---

1. D. Power, *The Eucharist Mystery, Revitalizing the Tradition* (New York: Crossroad, 1995) 10.
2. S. Sim, *Jean-François Lyotard* (Hertfordshire, GB: Prentice-Hall, 1996) 31.
3. J-F. Lyotard, *The Postmodern Condition: A Report on Knowledge*, transl. G. Bennington and B. Massumi (Minneapolis: University of Minnesota Press, 1984) xxiii-xxiv.
4. J-F. Lyotard, *The Postmodern Condition*, xxiv-xxv.

different interpretations. All of this relates to a need to study a particular text in this way.[5]

Power's observations deserve to be studied carefully. For as I will show below, the postmodern, specifically from the point of view of Lyotard, does not give priority to language over thought, inverting the modern project, but warns of the danger that the non-postmodern reader is not only constituted as a subject, but in such a way that the reader is subjugated by this knowledge apparatus.

Jean-François Lyotard is clearly not calling for a return to, or a renewal of, the modern project. Rather, he is calling for something different. And what he has to say has important consequences for how one reads a text, or more precisely, a ritual text.

Wlad Godzich, in his article, "Afterword: Reading against Literacy," succinctly highlights Jean-François Lyotard's call for "Literacy."[6] Godzich first presents what takes place, following Lyotard, when one reads a text. The words of a text are not simply repeated by the reader in a homologous fashion, but the reader's voice is taken over, "invaded" in a paralogous manner, such that the self is aware of itself as invaded.[7]

Godzich then goes on to highlight the difference between an oral culture and a written one. In an oral culture, it is always through the voice of *another* that one has access to the vast *memoria* of a culture's foundational myths and stories. But in a written culture, one is dispossessed of one's own voice by a text, which has no voice, so that it may now relate to one by means of one's own voice. The written text, through the appropriation of one's own voice, actually constitutes one as a subject, for the subject was not "there" before the written text, but is constituted "after."[8]

And this, then, is precisely the problem in postmodernity: to learn how to read. But it is gaining literacy not in the way of the modern project of so-called functional literacy, but in the way that Lyotard presents in *Le Différend* and develops in *The Postmodern Explained*.[9] From this there are two moments of great importance for Lyotard. Godzich first explains that the modern premise is that of the autonomous

---

5. D. Power, *The Eucharist Mystery*, 11.
6. W. Godzich, "Afterword: Reading against Literacy," in J-F. Lyotard, *The Postmodern Explained, Correspondence 1982-1985* (Minneapolis, 1993) 109-136.
7. W. Godzich, "Afterword: Reading against Literacy," 131-132.
8. W. Godzich, "Afterword: Reading against Literacy," 132-133.
9. W. Godzich, "Afterword: Reading against Literacy," 134. See J-F. Lyotard, *The Postmodern Explained*, and, also, J-F. Lyotard, *The Differend: Phrases in Dispute* (Minneapolis, 1988). In addition, see L. Boeve, "Bearing Witness to the Differend, A Model for Theologizing in the Postmodern Context," in *Louvain Studies* 20 (1995) 362-379, and L. Boeve, "Critical Consciousness in the Postmodern Condition: New Opportunities for Theology?" in *Philosophy & Theology* 10,2 (1997) 449-468.

subject who comes already fully constituted to the act of reading. The postmodern premise, however, is that the "child" (that is, the opposite of the autonomous subject) is constituted as subject in and through the act of reading, but then as a result is led to a belief in a prior subject. The written term, postmodern, accurately expresses the reality that the *post* always occurs *before* the modern, in fact, is a condition allowing for the emergence of the modern.[10] Secondly, the frequent campaigns for literacy that abound are promoting the modern project in an extreme way. The assumption is that the autonomous subject is capable of solving any problem. But paradoxically, rather than exercising control over knowledge, the subject is in fact subjected to a knowledge apparatus and becomes its servant. Lyotard describes this arrogance of the expert who thinks that she or he knows (or can know) everything as similar to that of the teenager, whose life is characterized by impatience. By contrast, a child does not presume to be an expert and consequently exhibits an attitude of patience. The great danger is that the modern project will seduce one out of her or his childhood with empty promises of control that in fact lead to being controlled for the rest of one's life.[11]

In place of consensus, Lyotard sees dissensus. The modern project always aims for consensus, that all arrive at the same conclusion by reading in a homologous way. But reading for postmodernism results in what Lyotard calls an unresolvable dissensus. Here one is described as a heteronomous subject in contrast to the modern autonomous subject.[12]

Bill Readings summarizes Lyotard's approach to reading by pointing out that the act of reading is in fact more of a rewriting, and not at all an attempt to reflect "what" the text is saying. He emphasizes that as readers one writes *after* rather than about texts. And it is this that in reality proclaims their irrepresentable difference, what Lyotard describes as their differend.[13]

---

10. W. Godzich, "Afterword: Reading against Literacy," 134-135. Note, also, that the original French title of *The Postmodern Explained* is *Le Postmoderne expliqué aux enfants* [emphasis mine] (Paris: Editions Galileé, 1988).

11. W. Godzich, "Afterword: Reading against Literacy," 135-136.

12. W. Godzich, Afterword: Reading against Literacy," 133. See, also, J-F. Lyotard, *Just Gaming* (Minneapolis, 1985).

13. B. Readings, "Jean-François Lyotard," in *The Johns Hopkins Guide to Literary Theory & Criticism*, ed. M. Groden and M. Kreiswirth (Baltimore/London: Johns Hopkins University Press, 1994) 478-479.

The Phenomenon of Pastoral Leadership Being Entrusted to Someone Other Than a Priest

Phillip Murnion and David DeLambo have recently provided an update of the increasing phenomenon in the United States of pastoral leadership being entrusted to someone other than a priest. Documentation indicates that in at least four hundred and fifty parishes in the United States, or possibly as many as six hundred, pastoral leadership has been entrusted to someone other than a priest. Overall, about two-thirds of those entrusted with this leadership are women religious. The remaining one-third is equally divided between ordained deacons on the one hand, and laywomen and laymen on the other. During the most recent five-year period studied, there was a 12% decrease in the total number of parish priests, and during the same five-year period, a 65% increase in the number of persons who are not priests being entrusted with the responsibility of pastoral leadership.[14]

Pastoral leadership itself involves many varied duties and responsibilities. My focus limits itself to that which is in many ways the most public and prominent aspect of this leadership: the event of worship, and most particularly, the Sunday celebration itself. It is within the context of this phenomenon of pastoral leadership being entrusted to someone other than a priest that I focus even more specifically on the ritual text for these Sunday celebrations.

One normally hears that the justifying reason for this overall phenomenon is the decrease in the number of priests. But it is often added that this "solution" is seen only as something that is temporary, and not a sign nor a symptom of any substantive changes. I am not so sure that this is the case. Rather I would argue that these Sunday celebrations can be, and in many cases, will be read in a very different way – one that brings a very significant change. It all depends upon one's perspective: whether one is reading this ritual text from a modern perspective or from a postmodern perspective.

Sunday Celebrations in the Absence of a Priest

In 1997, The Liturgical Press (Collegeville, Minnesota) published *Sunday Celebrations in the Absence of a Priest: Leader's Edition*. It is identified

---

14. P. Murnion and D. Delambo, *Parishes and Parish Ministers: A Study of Parish Lay Ministry* [A Study Conducted for the Committee on the Laity of the National Conference of Catholic Bishops with the Support of the Lilly Endowment, Inc.] (New York: National Pastoral Life Center, 1999) 10-12. See, also, P. Murnion, "The Potential and Anomaly of the 'Priestless Parish'," in *America* 170 (January 29, 1994) 12-14.

as an official publication that was prepared and approved for use by the U.S. National Conference of Catholic Bishops.[15]

As the Decree notes,[16] while the National Conference of Catholic Bishops approved in plenary session on 7 November 1989 the publication of this ritual, it was not in print until eight years later. A notable feature of the ritual is that it is published in a bilingual format, with Spanish and English text facing each other for the entire ritual, including five of its six appendices.[17] The official Spanish text of the *Directory for Sunday Celebrations in the Absence of a Priest* published by the Vatican Office of the Congregation for Divine Worship is absent from the ritual. In this instance the text is still seeking to exercise control over the reader. The consequence is that exclusively Spanish-language readers are excluded completely from an encounter with the Vatican text. Thus, not even functional literacy, which is fundamentally a *modern* project, is possible for Spanish-language readers.

My interest is to focus on *Sunday Celebrations in the Absence of a Priest* in a postmodern context. This means that the text is not given priority as something which exists in an independent, objectified manner. Nor does it mean that the reader, the subject, must seek to "understand" and probe the text in order to draw out the truth. That would be a modern approach. Rather, in a postmodern context, one sees the reader as one who is constituted as a subject in the very act of reading the text. It is, to use another expression, seeing the act of reading as an *event*, existential in character, radically historical, such that the reader brings to the reading all that one is, at that moment. The reader gives her or his own voice to

---

15. National Conference of Catholic Bishops, Committee on the Liturgy, *Sunday Celebrations in the Absence of a Priest: Leader's Edition* (hereafter *Leader's Edition*) (Collegeville MN: The Liturgical Press, 1997): "prepared by the Committee on the Liturgy, National Conference of Catholic Bishops" and "approved for use in the dioceses of the United States of America by the National Conference of Catholic Bishops," cover page.

16. In *Leader's Edition*, National Conference of Catholic Bishops, United States of America, DECREE: "In accordance with the provisions of n. 41 of the *Directory for Sunday Celebrations in the Absence of a Priest*, promulgated by the Congregation for Divine Worship on 2 June 1988, *Sunday Celebrations in the Absence of a Priest: Leader's Edition* was approved for use by the members of the National Conference of Catholic Bishops in plenary session on 7 November 1989. On 1 January 1994 *Sunday Celebrations in the Absence of a Priest: Leader's Edition* may be published and used in those dioceses where the diocesan bishop has given authorization for Sunday celebrations in the absence of a priest. Given at the General Secretariat of the National Conference of Catholic Bishops, Washington, DC, on 14 September 1993, the feast of the Holy Cross." [Signed] † William H. Keeler, Archbishop of Baltimore, President National Conference of Catholic Bishops, [Signed] Robert N. Lynch, General Secretary.

17. Appendix VI is the full text, in English, of the Directory for Sunday Celebrations in the Absence of a Priest [hereafter Directory] published on 2 June 1988 by the Vatican Office of the Congregation for Divine Worship.

the text so that it may speak. The text has no power or control over the *postmodern* reader. To see it otherwise would be an affirmation of the text as a grand – or petite! – narrative.

The reader encounters a complex text. There are two chapters, *Morning and Evening Prayer [with Holy Communion]* and *Celebration of the Liturgy of the Word [with Holy Communion]*.[18] Preceding these two chapters is the *Introduction*, which delineates the norms and guidelines for the implementation of the Ritual.[19] And following these two chapters are the appendices. Appendix I consists of *General Intercessions;* Appendix II, *Acts of Thanksgiving;* Appendix III, *Prayers of the Day and Prayers After Communion for Sundays, Solemnities, and Feasts of the Lord;* Appendix IV, *Additional Prayers after Communion;* and Appendix V, *Blessings*.[20] What is also significant is what the reader does not encounter.

In the *Introduction,* paragraph number 44, notes that paragraph 45 of the Vatican *Directory* provides two alternatives for the thanksgiving. However, the National Conference of Catholic Bishops has eliminated any choice[21] by excluding the option that involves placing the ciborium with the eucharist on the altar, kneeling before the altar, and then reciting or singing a psalm or a litany.[22] It is an interesting omission on the part of the National Conference of Catholic Bishops. The reader is prevented from giving a voice to this passage.

The opening paragraph of the *Introduction* is itself a quotation from the Vatican Council II document on the liturgy, *Sacrosanctum concilium* which speaks of the apostolic tradition of the church's celebration of the

---

18. NCCB, Committee on the Liturgy, *Leader's Edition*, "Chapter I: Morning and Evening Prayer [with Holy Communion]" = "Capitulo I: Oracion de la mañana y de la tarde [con la sagrada comunión]," 34-101; "Chapter II: Celebration of the Liturgy of the Word [with Holy Communion]" = "Capitulo II: Celebración de la liturgia de la palabra [con la sagrada comunión]" 102-143.

19. NCCB, Committee on the Liturgy, *Leader's Edition*, "Introduction" = "Introducción" 12-33.

20. NCCB, Committee on the Liturgy, *Leader's Edition*, "Appendix I: General Intercessions" = "Apendice I: Plegaria universal" 144-151; "Appendix II: Acts of Thanksgiving" = "Apendice II: Acción de gracias" 152-197; "Appendix III: Prayers of the Day and Prayers after Communion for Sundays, Solemnities, and Feasts of the Lord" = "Apendice III: Oraciones del dia y oraciones despues de la comunión para los domingos, solemnidades, y fiestas del Señor" 198-337; "Appendix IV: Additional Prayers after Communion" = "Apendice IV: Oraciones adicionales despues de la comunión" 338-347; "Appendix V: Blessings" = "Apendice V: Bendiciones" 348-357. [Appendix VI is the official Vatican text in English only, "Directory For Sunday Celebrations in the Absence of a Priest," 359-375.]

21. NCCB, Committee on the Liturgy, *Leader's Edition*, 31, number 44.

22. NCCB, Committee on the Liturgy, *Leader's Edition*, 374, number 45.

paschal mystery every Sunday, the day of the Lord's resurrection.[23] The postmodern reader is constituted as the one who celebrates the paschal mystery. And this paschal mystery in itself is constituted in and through the act of faith of the believer. It is to continue, indeed, to promote the celebration of the paschal mystery which is the claimed reason for the publication of this text.

The Importance of the Sunday Celebration

According to the text, the ultimate purpose of Sunday celebrations in the absence of a priest is expressed in a two-fold reason: the continuation of the weekly gathering of the faithful, and the preservation of the Christian Sunday tradition.[24] But for the reader, the ultimate purpose is not to maintain a ritual tradition, but to enable an *event*. The text further emphasizes that even when a priest cannot be present for Sunday Mass, it is of the highest importance that the community gather to celebrate the Lord's resurrection.[25] But for the postmodern reader the resurrection of the Lord is not a commemoration of some past occurrence. It is an *event*, the coming-into-existence-anew, of all those who profess this faith. The reader, with all of one's brokenness, alienation, and individuality, as well as one's wholeness, communion with and relatedness to others, is constituted precisely in and through this celebration.

For identity reasons, among others, the earliest Christian assemblies took place on the day *after* the Jewish Sabbath, what is accurately described as a post-Sabbath *event*. The postmodern reader centers on the meaning of these assemblies, and not on the particular day of the week on which it may occur. Thus, for the postmodern reader, the *Sunday* celebration is equal in significance and meaning whether it occurs on a Saturday, a Monday, or a Wednesday.

Looking at the text itself, from a *modern* perspective, there is no explicit statement at any point in the *Introduction* which refers to the possibility that this weekly gathering might take place on Saturday evening or any other day. It presupposes that it would take place only on Sunday itself. And when the text states that "normally" there should be

---

23. NCCB, Committee on the Liturgy, *Leader's Edition*, 13. The quotation is from article 106 of *Sacrosanctum concilium*. The English translation is one that is the work of Joseph Rodgers, which itself "owes a great deal to the translation made by Clifford Howell, S.J.," and which has also been "considerably revised by Austin Flannery" [A. Flannery, ed., *Vatican Council II: The Conciliar and Post Conciliar Documents* (Collegeville, 1975) 1, note a].

24. NCCB, Committee on the Liturgy, *Leader's Edition*, 15, number 8.

25. NCCB, Committee on the Liturgy, *Leader's Edition*, 15, number 10.

only one such assembly in a particular place and on a particular Sunday,[26] the postmodern reader would have no concern in this *event* being "repeated" as one *"event"* followed by another. To the postmodern reader, it is never an instance of the "same" celebration being repeated at different times.

For the postmodern reader, what is important is the act of *gathering*, focusing on the assembly itself. The reader views the gathered assembly as a full subject, *in persona Christi*, in whom Christ is constitutively present. To be even more precise, the reader does not come to the assembly as a full subject, but is so constituted in the very act of its assembling as a faith community. The text itself, however, stresses something different. It views the assembly in a more passive, essentialist fashion. The text describes the assembly with regard to what can be done for the assembly: giving the assembly holy communion and always proclaiming the scriptures to the assembly. And while Christ is described as present in the gathered assembly, one wonders if the presence of Christ is seen more as a kind of residual presence.[27] This same attitude is fostered in the directive that cautions that the faithful should not be deprived of the Sunday lectionary readings nor the seasonal liturgical prayers.[28]

It is also explicitly stated in the text that one must make sure that the faithful do not confuse Sunday celebrations in the absence of a priest with eucharistic celebrations.[29] Such warnings in fact disclose for the reader the hegemonic interests of the text to maintain control. For the reader, however, it is she or he who gives a voice to each ritual text. And the consequent result is not a harmonious consensus, but a dissensus that is rooted in heterogeneity. As noted above, the "expert" is one who promotes the same closed system (homology), while the inventor is always seeking that which is different (paralogy), as opposed to the same old thing.[30]

Through a postmodern reading there is present this dissensus which is inevitable, and indeed, necessary. The Vatican *Directory*, however, provides this interpretation. It says that one should regard the celebration (the text, in fact, uses the word "sacrifice") of the Sunday Mass as the only true actualization of the paschal mystery of the Lord, as well as the most complete manifestation of the church.[31] And then there follows a

---

26. NCCB, Committee on the Liturgy, *Leader's Edition*, 17, number 11.
27. NCCB, Committee on the Liturgy, *Leader's Edition*, 23, number 26.
28. NCCB, Committee on the Liturgy, *Leader's Edition*, 23, number 25.
29. NCCB, Committee on the Liturgy, *Leader's Edition*, 17, number 12.
30. J-F. Lyotard, *The Postmodern Condition*, xxiv-xxv.
31. NCCB, Committee on the Liturgy, *Directory*, 366, number 13. This passage is incorporated, almost literally, into the *Introduction* of the *Leader's Edition*, 13, number 4.

quotation from a major text, something of a grand narrative, the Second Vatican Council document, *Sacrosanctum concilium*, which purportedly provides the theological foundation for this previous statement. But, in point of fact, the quote from the Second Vatican Council document on the liturgy is not specifically about the Eucharist, but about *Sunday*, referring to the fact that other eucharistic celebrations should not take precedence over the Sunday eucharistic celebration.[32] The misapplication of one text by another text demonstrates the unrestrained drive for control that is so apparent. In contrast, the postmodern approach allows both the Sunday eucharistic celebration and the Sunday celebration in the absence of a priest to exist, as it were, side by side, not seeking to subjugate one to the other.

The text states that the Communion Rite is both an expression of communion with Christ and with his members as well as an accomplishment of this communion. And then it notes that this communion with others is particularly the case with regard to other Christians who have taken part that same day in the eucharistic celebration.[33] For the postmodern reader, however, what stands out is that communion unites one to Christ and, consequently, to all other Christians, not singling out those Christians who have or have not participated that day in the Sunday eucharist. In a similar way, the postmodern reader notes a shift in *before* and *after*, but not in substance. For in the Eucharistic liturgy, thanksgiving always precedes communion, in the *Sunday Celebration in the Absence of a Priest*, communion may precede thanksgiving. Yet the text proposes its own interpretation, stressing not union with Christ and others, but union to the eucharistic sacrifice.[34]

The Event of Leading

Looking again to the text, the leader is, by definition, not a priest, but that does not mean that the leader is not one who is ordained. Rather, the *Introduction* states that a deacon is particularly recognized as one to lead

---

But there is a significant difference. The *Leader's Edition* hides or masks the attempt to control the reader by changing "that the sacrifice of the Mass *be regarded* as the only true actualization of the Lord's paschal mystery ...." to "that the sacrifice of the Mass is the only true actualization of the Lord's paschal mystery..." [emphasis mine].

32. NCCB, Committee on the Liturgy, *Leader's Edition*, 13, number 4.

33. NCCB, Committee on the Liturgy, *Leader's Edition*, 27, number 36. Again the term "eucharistic sacrifice" is used in reference to the Sunday Mass.

34. NCCB, Committee on the Liturgy, *Leader's Edition*, 31, number 45. For example, when holy communion is distributed at the end of either Morning or Evening Prayer, then some type of a thanksgiving prayer or litany would follow the reception of communion, 31, number 43.

these Sunday celebrations.[35] It further delineates that it actually belongs to the deacon in and of himself to be a leader of prayer, a proclaimer of the gospel followed by the homily, and one who gives holy communion.[36] For the reader, however, the key question is not to ask to whom these various functions belong. It is the act, the *event* of leading that is significant. Continuing on, the text states that if neither a deacon nor a priest is available, the bishop is the one who is to appoint non-ordained persons to lead these celebrations.[37] Again, for the reader, the appointment of a leader by someone is not a key issue. What an authority beyond the assembly does, does not bring the assembly into existence. Rather, it is the assembly itself which constitutes itself with a leader that it receives. The text is concerned with external authority issues. For example, the Vatican *Directory* indicates that it is the parish priest (pastor) who is to appoint laypersons to lead these celebrations.[38] But in the ritual text approved by the National Conference of Catholic Bishops it states that the actual pastor of the parish does not have competence to appoint leaders for these celebrations, but must simply recommend persons – and there is no certainty that the pastor's recommendation will be accepted. The bishop is the only one who is authorized to appoint them as leaders. The message is very clear. This is one more example of the kind of control that is eschewed by a postmodern reading.

The text first focuses on the leader who is a deacon. The deacon, in the absence of a priest, is to carry out the normal sequence of activities for the Sunday celebration that involves leading the prayers, proclaiming the gospel, and giving communion.[39] Yet, what erases any doubt about the preeminent place given by the text to the deacon is that he is to *preside* over the Sunday celebration, using the presidential chair.[40] This is in complete contrast with how the role is described of the leader who is a layperson. Again, for the reader, this is no more than a rearranging of deck chairs on the *Titanic*. One final point that the text states with regard to the deacon is that he, in a way that is identical for one who is not a deacon, is to be one of a number of various persons who each contribute to the realization of the celebration.[41]

When both priest and deacon are absent, then, according to the text, the bishop appoints non-ordained persons who are entrusted by him to

---

35. NCCB, Committee on the Liturgy, *Leader's Edition*, 19, number 18. The language refers to leading "Sunday assemblies."
36. NCCB, Committee on the Liturgy, *Leader's Edition*, 19, number 18.
37. NCCB, Committee on the Liturgy, *Leader's Edition*, 19-21, number 21. These non-ordained are described as either "lay" or "religious."
38. NCCB, Committee on the Liturgy, *Leader's Edition*, 370, number 30.
39. NCCB, Committee on the Liturgy, *Leader's Edition*, 19, number 19.
40. NCCB, Committee on the Liturgy, *Leader's Edition*, 19, number 19.
41. NCCB, Committee on the Liturgy, *Leader's Edition*, 19, number 20.

lead these Sunday celebrations.[42] For the postmodern reader, however, any trust that is present is not a consequence of an assessment and subsequent approval of the individual by the bishop. The trust itself is constituted in the event of leading these celebrations.

The text states that those non-ordained who are appointed are recognized as competent to lead such Sunday celebrations based upon their own baptism and confirmation.[43] But what precisely does it mean to speak of these leaders who carry out their responsibilities based upon their baptism and confirmation? From the point of view of the text, one would look to another text, the *Roman Ritual* of the *Rite of Christian Initiation of Adults*. In the opening paragraphs of the *General Introduction* of this text, it speaks first of baptism and then confirmation, noting that baptism both incorporates one into Christ and forms all the baptized into God's people.[44] And confirmation is seen as making one more into the image of the Lord, and consequently capable of bearing witness to him to all people.[45] But again, for the reader, baptism and confirmation are not things that happen to you. In and through the *event* of baptism and confirmation, one is continually constituted as one who is being united with Christ and who is being formed into God's people, as well as one who is being made into the image of Christ. And each one who is being made into the image of Christ evidences the radical heterogeneity of each one who is an image of Christ. Indeed, one's sacramental initiation through baptism, confirmation and the eucharist is a sharing in Christ's paschal mystery.[46] But, again, this paschal mystery is not seen as a commemoration of some past legitimating occurrence. One's own paschal mystery, not identical with the paschal mystery of Christ, is

---

42. NCCB, Committee on the Liturgy, *Leader's Edition*, 19-21, number 21.

43. NCCB, Committee on the Liturgy, *Leader's Edition*, 21, number 21. And there is a footnote referring one to the *Codex Iuris Canonici*, canon 230, n. 3. It is of interest to quote this reference in *Code of Canon Law*, Latin-English Edition (Washington, DC: 1983) 77: "When the necessity of the Church warrants it and when ministers are lacking, lay persons, even if they are not lectors or acolytes, can also supply for certain of their offices, namely, to exercise the ministry of the word, to preside over liturgical prayers, to confer baptism, and to distribute Holy Communion in accord with the prescriptions of law."

44. NCCB, Committee on the Liturgy, *Christian Initiation of Adults*, Revised Edition, Liturgy Documentary Series, 4 (Washington, DC: United States Catholic Conference, 1988), 7, number 2. This new edition of the *Rite of Christian Initiation of Adults*, which is the official English translation of the 1972 *Ordo Initiationis Christianae Adultorum* promulgated by the Holy See, was confirmed by the Apostolic See on 19 February 1988 and its use became mandatory as of 1 September 1988, as indicated in the Forward of the publication, 1-2.

45. NCCB, Committee on the Liturgy, *Christian Initiation of Adults*, Revised Edition, 7, number 2.

46. NCCB, Committee on the Liturgy, *Christian Initiation of Adults*, Revised Edition, 7, number 1.

nonetheless united to his pashal mystery and, through him, to the paschal mysteries of all others.

As was affirmed earlier with regard to the assembly itself, Christ is truly present in the active gathered assembly and in the Scriptures that are proclaimed, even when the reception of holy communion cannot take place. This emphasizes the gathered assembly as the full subject – or, more precisely, being constituted as a full subject in the very *event* of gathering – *in persona Christi*, in whom Christ is constitutively present. Consequently, what is affirmed with regard to the entire assembly is, *ipso facto,* true of each one who is a constitutive member of the assembly, including the one who is leader. Thus, while the text establishes and reinforces an exclusive approach, the reader gives voice to a radically and fundamentally inclusive approach.

In a particularly key guideline, the text states that while those appointed carry out their responsibilities in virtue of their baptism and confirmation, there are two criteria identified as essential in the implementation as to who are to be chosen. One's way of life must be consistent with the Christian gospel, and it must be expected that one will be found acceptable by the community itself.[47] In other words, there are two questions that must be answered in the affirmative: 1) whether one is faithful to the life initiated in the sacraments of baptism, confirmation and the eucharist, and 2), whether it is expected by the proper authority, that is, the bishop – that one is acceptable to the community. For the postmodern reader what is necessary are not criteria for being chosen, but the *acceptance* of this individual by the assembly. To exercise this responsibility of leading, one must not only be living the Christian faith with personal integrity, but one must also be *accepted*, in the classical sense of reception, by the community if that leading is to truly take place. Once again, there is a remarkable emphasis placed on the role of the assembly itself. Thus, the fundamental relationship between the one leading and the assembly is not one of control, in either direction, but an acceptance of mutual heterogeneity. With regard to the text, it is also extremely interesting that although the Vatican *Directory* emphasizes that a non-ordained person who leads an assembly does so as one among equals, nowhere does it appear in the ritual text.[48] One additional directive in the text emphasizes the collegial nature of this leadership, by stressing, in the identical language referring to the deacon who is leader, that the non-ordained leader is to be one of a number of various persons that each contribute to the realization of the celebration.[49]

---

47. NCCB, Committee on the Liturgy, *Leader's Edition*, 21, number 21.
48. NCCB, Committee on the Liturgy, *Directory*, 372, number 39.
49. NCCB, Committee on the Liturgy, *Leader's Edition*, 21, number 24.

The text, in a very controlling fashion, states that the layperson is not to "use words that are proper to a priest or deacon" and is to omit anything that would be associated with the Mass, so as not to give the impression that one is an ordained person.[50] In addition, the layperson is never to use the presidential chair,[51] but as the *Directory* specifies quite clearly, the layperson uses a non-presidential chair that is clearly located outside the sanctuary itself.[52] And there is an even stronger directive given with regard to the relationship between the layperson and the altar. The only time that the layperson is to stand at or near the altar is for the rite of communion.[53] Indeed, the layperson who is a leader takes a subservient role to that of the altar itself. After placing the eucharistic bread on the altar for communion, she or he is to retreat back to her or his chair located outside the sanctuary. From there, one leads all in the Lord's Prayer, and then there follows the sign of peace. Only then does she or he go back to the altar to invite all to receive communion. In contrast to this, the deacon remains continuously at the altar.[54]

It is the postmodern reader who gives a voice to the non-priestly leader in a way no different from giving a voice to the leader who is a priest. The gestures, the words, and the symbolic actions constitute in a heterogenous manner the reality of the sacramental event.

There is another significant directive in the text about the relationship between the lay leader – indeed, the deacon as well and the altar. It is in reference to the Act of Thanksgiving, specifically at a celebration of the Word of God. The leader – and it would appear to be true for both a deacon as well as a non-ordained leader – is obligated to lead a prayer of thanksgiving with one's back turned to the assembly, as everyone together faces the altar.[55] While the text literally obligates the leader to turn one's back on the assembly, in contrast what is significant for the postmodern reader is the constituting of this assembly as persons who are directed dynamically toward each other.

A Response

The modern and postmodern approaches to reading are clearly different. The text, for the modern reader, represents a voice, an authoritative voice that explains, justifies, and – in an ultimate way – controls how something is understood, indeed, how something is to be understood. But

---

50. NCCB, Committee on the Liturgy, *Leader's Edition*, 21, number 23.
51. NCCB, Committee on the Liturgy, *Leader's Edition*, 21, number 24.
52. NCCB, Committee on the Liturgy, *Directory*, 373, number 40.
53. NCCB, Committee on the Liturgy, *Leader's Edition*, 21, number 24.
54. NCCB, Committee on the Liturgy, *Leader's Edition*, 33, number 47.
55. NCCB, Committee on the Liturgy, *Leader's Edition*, 31, number 44.

reading in postmodernism results in an unresolvable dissensus.[56] There is no single legitimizing grand narrative that grounds all understanding. For example, in regard to the study of this ritual text, one must conclude that another ritual text, namely, the Sunday eucharistic celebration, cannot be accepted as a meta-narrative that would explain and give meaning to *Sunday Celebrations in the Absence of a Priest*. Nevertheless, in a rather interesting twist, while the postmodern seeks to de-absolutize the modern subject, nonetheless, the postmodern itself returns to the subject, emphasizing in this instance that all reading is in fact more of a rewriting and not an attempt to reflect "what" the text is saying.[57] In fact, one writes *after* rather than about texts.[58]

A postmodern critique of understanding is important and needed. There are many signs, some simple, others grand, that question one of the presumptions of the modern project, namely, that human beings are capable of solving any problem.[59] Among the simple signs that cause one to be less confident about human capabilities was the so-called Y2K crisis that generated so much concern. Among the signs that are much greater is the continuing disparity that one finds among human beings on every level throughout our world. At the same time, postmodernity is rightly suspicious of the subject being or becoming the servant of the "knowledge apparatus," however that apparatus might be configured.

Conclusions

A postmodern reading of *Sunday Celebrations in the Absence of a Priest* must be a reading not about the text, but *after* the text. And it must then result not in writing about the text, but what one writes *after* the text. A postmodern reading of *Sunday Celebrations in the Absence of a Priest* leads one to a theological affirmation of the extremely important constituting of the Church as *Event*.

It is important to both recognize and to accept the fundamental heterogeneity of *Sunday Celebrations in the Absence of a Priest* as well as the heterogeneity of the Sunday eucharistic celebration. Each bears witness to the diversity of lived faith in our postmodern world. Believers are called to an active and dynamic faith that is not uniform and identical to the faith of others, but one that is rooted in heterogeneity. The leadership of these *Sunday Celebrations in the Absence of a Priest* is exercised

---

56. W. Godzich, "Afterword: Reading against Literacy," 133.
57. W. Godzich, "Afterword: Reading against Literacy," 134-135.
58. W. Godzich, "Afterword: Reading against Literacy," 132-133.
59. W. Godzich, "Afterword: Reading against Literacy," 135-136.

by both non-ordained and ordained, women and men, married and celibate. And this difference is the hallmark or our postmodern world.

It is the coming together, the constituting of an assembly, that historically and dynamically actualizes and manifests the church, the basic sacrament, the *Grundsakrament* in the terminology of Karl Rahner. As I have developed in another place, [60] the affirmation of the Church as *Grundsakrament,* as well as the equivalent term *sacramentum,* is used in the context of the Church's relationship to the world – and specifically to the postmodern world – and not primarily as descriptive of the constitutional structure of the Church. It refers both to the grace of God precisely where that grace is not manifested in its full ecclesial expression, and also to the church inasmuch as it is the manifestation of God as grace in its social and historical fullness. The church is claimed to be the historical continuation of Christ's existence – a claim that cannot be legitimated in any absolute sense. Jesus Christ, and he alone, is claimed to be *Ursakrament,* the definitive pledge of God's salvation in whom salvation is accepted, and so, realized.

Xavier University of Louisiana   Jerry T. FARMER
Department of Theology
1 Drexel Drive
New Orleans, LA
USA

---

[60]. J. Farmer, *Ministry in Community: Rahner's Vision of Ministry* (Leuven: Peeters Press/Eerdmans, 1983) 117-119.

THE SACRAMENT IS THE MESSAGE: ON THE MEDIATION OF LITURGY THROUGH THE ELECTRONIC MEDIA

Media transform the reality they intend to communicate. This is true for any medium of communication, for communication itself involves a transformation.[1] The situation becomes more complex when one medium intends to communicate another medium, as is for example the case in the broadcasting of liturgy through the electronic media. At first glance, this complex form of communication seems to raise no significant problems. A message in one medium is in itself a reality, and can thus be transformed into a new message in another medium. When for example Lady Diana was buried, the whole western world watched the ceremony and thought it was good. A problem arises, however, when the original message is to be preserved, in this case that the message of the liturgical celebration must remain unchanged. In order to preserve the original message, you need to have control of the transformations caused by the second mediation, that is the broadcasting. And indeed, the first problem that is met in the broadcasting of liturgy has to do with control. Who has the authority over the process of liturgical mediation: is it the broadcasting station or the celebrant, or is it the bishop or the conference of bishops? I do not want to go into that question now. I would, however, like to get an idea of the problems of control itself. For even if the matter of authority is solved, the question remains whether the authority has the *power* to control the process of mediation. In a recently begun Dutch research project, we plan to investigate the problems of the mediation of liturgy.

In order to understand the nature of the problem, we will make two moves. First, we will differentiate the liturgy and the media, and we will observe and interpret their individual qualities. Second, after their separation we will re-connect them in order to observe and interpret their

---

1. Cf. W. M. Speelman, "On Liturgical Enunciation as the Transparence of a Coming Truth," in *Acta semiotica fennica II: On the borderlines of semiosis*, ed. E. Tarasti (Imatra: ISI, 1993) 79-91; Idem, "Traditie als het schijnen van waarheid. Een semiotiek van de traditie," in *De Onvoltooid Verleden Tijd. Negen bijdragen tot een bezinning op traditie*, ed. R. J. Peeters, W. M. Speelman, N. Wiskerke (Tilburg: Tilburg University Press, 1992) 81-98.

connection. Finally, we will evaluate their connection in the broadcasting of liturgical celebrations. In the following I will try to present the trajectory of this investigation. Because we have only recently begun, most data have been taken from literature, whereas our project will involve observations of concrete broadcast celebrations.

1. **Differentiation of Liturgy and Electronic Media**

In their differentiation, both the liturgy and the electronic media will be approached as forms of communication. In such an approach, a model of communication is needed. We will use the semiotic model developed by Greimas and his Paris School. There is not space here to present this model here more extensively than to say that both liturgical celebrations and medial broadcasts can be described as discourses and that discourses can be described on several levels of signification.[2]

Since both liturgy and media can be described as discourses, they can also be differentiated. And indeed, according to most authors, liturgical celebrations and medial broadcasts are radically different. I will try to describe their differences in terms of qualities. In **[Figure 1]** an example of such a description is given. The qualities will be sought for with the help of the semiotic model mentioned, the different realizations of these qualities will be sought for with the help of literature, and the interference (see below) will be observed in concrete broadcasts of liturgical celebrations.

I will give you a brief description of the differentiation on the level of enunciation. The first difference between the two media is their *intention*. Liturgy intends to *illuminate* the world in the light of the Holy, whereas the media intend to *illustrate* the world in the light of the factual. Liturgical communication can be described, like all sacred discourses, as a *gesture*.[3] It has the intention to *transform* the world by putting it in a new light. Some authors seem to misunderstand the liturgical form of communication by approaching it as an interaction between the faithful.[4]

---

2. For an elaborate description and use, see: W. M. Speelman, *The Generation of Meaning in Liturgical Songs* (Leuven: Peeters, 1995).

3. A. J. Greimas, "Conditions d'une sémiotique du monde naturel," in *Du Sens. Essais sémiotiques* (Paris: Seuil, 1970) 49-91.

4. Cf. H. E. Thomé, *Gottesdienst frei Haus? Fernsehübertragungen von Gottesdienst* (Göttingen: Vandenhoeck & Ruprecht, 1991).

Figure 1.

Reality / Quality	Liturgy	Electronic media	interference (broadcasting of celebration)
Intention	Illumination	Illustration	illumination or illustration?
Communication	Transformation	Transmission	transformation or transmission?
Effect	Sanctification (*benediction*)	Connection (reality as a potential relationship)	what is the intended effect?
Semantic character	Sacramental	Imaginative	what semantic character?
Enunciation	Physical presence and active participation	imaginative presence and receptive participation	what kind of presence and participation?
Discursive level	faithful actors, consecrated space, holy time	observing actors, mediated space, 'carved' time	what kind of actors, times and spaces?
	biblical figures and themes	medial figures and themes	what kind of figures and themes?
Narrative level	Structure based on scripture and sacrament	structure based on myth and image	what narrative structure?
	biblical and traditional values	values of present-day culture	what values?
	Salvation as isotopy	happiness as isotopy	what isotopy?
Deep level	Presence and Participation	representation and reproduction	what forms of being and of doing?

But actually the celebration tries to temper the interaction in order to make room for a transcendent orientation: *an orientation towards the divine*. The media, on the contrary, do not want to change the world, but intend to communicate it as it is.⁵ They form a kind of market-place or forum, where the society *communicates with herself*.⁶

Because of their different intentions, the liturgy and the electronic media have a different *semantic character*.⁷ The liturgical reality is essentially *sacramental*. As a sacramental reality, liturgy cannot be mediated through ideas or images. The sacrament does not mediate an image: it does not give you an idea of Jesus' life and appearance, but it communicates Him as a tangible presence, affirming that He is here. Sacraments communicate a material reality which presents a being. This, by the way, is also true for the icons, which seemingly illustrate holy figures, but intend to present the Holy in a *material* reality. The medial reality on the other hand is essentially imaginative (according to some authors 'illusive' or 'fictional'). The media communicate an imaginary representation of beings. Media cannot mediate things. The image is not a tangible presentation: it does not affirm that Jesus is here, but presents an idea of his looks and existence. The media are not focused on the material reality of a being, but on its ideal reality, whereas its material existence is being masked or even cut.

The sacramental vision of reality presents the world as a material being. It affirms that we will not only spiritually but also physically be resurrected, and that Christ is not only spiritually here but also in this corporal community and in this bread and wine, and that the Word of God is not only spiritually on earth but that it has been incarnated in the flesh. The sacramental vision presents the world as matter, and intends to *sanctify* that matter by illuminating it in the light of the Holy.⁸ The media, by contrast, intend to present the real world. We know, of course, that in fact they create their own reality, masking the real world. But we also know that this is true for any form of communication. Ferdinand de Saussure has shown that our natural language gives us the world also by masking it with images (*images acoustiques*). The media give us the

---

5. An elaboration of this difference shows that the liturgical form of communication concentrates on competence and performance, whereas the second form of communication concentrates on manipulation and sanction/veridiction. See W. M. Speelman, "On Liturgical Enunciation".

6. R. A. White, "Religion and Media in the Construction of Cultures," in *Rethinking Media, Religion, and Culture*, ed. S. M. Hoover and K. Lundby (London: Sage, 1997) 37-64. Referring to names like Geertz, Turner, Bell and Grimes, White approaches both religion and media as places where a culture communicates with herself. I have problems with this approach, not because it is wrong, but because it tends to overlook a fundamental difference between a religious and a non-religious form of communication. I see the first as primary receptive, the second as primary reflexive.

7. See: W. M. Speelman, "Het ware licht. Theologie van de liturgie in de media," in *Jaarboek voor Liturgie-onderzoek* 16 (2000) (is still forthcoming).

8. Vatican Council II, *Constitution on the Liturgy — Sacrosanctum Concilium*, art. 61.

factual in a *fictional representation*. The important question is in how far this fictional representation is capable of conveying the essence of the real world.⁹ And what matters here is not so much the fictional nature of the message, but its *intentional nature*. Communication is a matter of intentions. The intention of medial communication is a potential *connection* between an individual's life and any possible reality in the world. The media intend to connect. Think of telephone numbers or symbols, emblems, badges, logos: they are all fictional representations of people, created with the intention to connect them. The semantic character of the media is imaginative, and its intention is to connect reality.

Sacramental communication demands that the faithful are physically *present* and participate *actively*. The church, however, does not deny that other forms of presence and participation can also be effective. An intended or desired presence and participation (cf. *spiritual communion*) is considered a meaningful form of engagement as well.¹⁰ The media on the other hand, demand an imaginative presence and a receptive participation. Thus the intentions of the media can be understood as orientation away from the material towards a true and ideal reality. It is as if the media want to say that things are not what they seem, but that through their appearance they point at their true nature. According to the philosopher Kees Vuyk, this is a theatrical view of reality, and he explains this theatrical view as a 'potentialization' of our daily lives. The theatrical view sees the factual reality as a potential one: fiction shows that the facts could have been and can be different.¹¹

2. The Interference between the Liturgy and the Electronic Media

After recognizing how liturgy and media can be differentiated, I would like to reflect on their connection. What happens when liturgy and media are connected in the broadcasting of a liturgical celebration? Will the liturgical qualities govern the medial ones, or vice versa? Is the broadcasting a mere image of the liturgy or does it indeed transmit a

---

9. W. Sanders, "Gottesdienstübertragung in Hörfunk und Fernsehen der ARD," in *Liturgisches Jahrbuch* 36 (1986) 142-154, quotes Josef Burbach: "[der Fernsehregisseur] muß alles, was das Auge sieht, in mediale Bilder umsetzen und übersetzen, um so zum Wesen vorzustoßen."

10. Cf. *Sacerdotium ministeriale*, n°4: *Enchiridion documentorum instaurationis liturgicae*, n°4782. An important question is raised by Hans-Bernhard Meyer, who says that a presence and participation which is only intended cannot be called a liturgical activity, but is an act of personal devotion. See also Th. Lentes, "Liturgie und Gottesdienstübertragungen im Fernsehen. Liturgiewissenschaftliche Reflexionen," in *Communicatio Socialis* 20 (1987) 217.

11. K. Vuyk, *De esthetisering van het wereldbeeld* (Kampen: Kok, 1992) 81f, 186.

celebration? We do not yet know the answers to these questions, but of course we have expectations. Our hypothesis is that both the media and the liturgy are to be approached as *operations*. Media and liturgy are not things, but operations in operation, working works (in German: *Wirklichkeiten*). When operations are being connected, they interact. The result of their interaction can be called an interference (cf. *inter-ferre*: bearing in between, or *s'entreférir*: striking each other?). In their interference, operations work upon each another: they either reinforce, or harmonize or strike each other dumb.[12] Some authors say that liturgy and the media reinforce one another, due to the fact that they have much in common (White: border-experiences, Schilson: shows).[13] Other authors think that the media strike the liturgical movement dumb, due to the fact that they are so radically different (Meyer, Metz, and so on).[14] Our investigation of liturgical celebrations on the radio and the television intend to find out what kinds of interference really happen.

The investigation aims at a precise description of the interference. For such a description, we need a model. Now, if liturgy and media are forms of communication which intend a certain reality, they can be said to make propositions. Propositions can be described with the help of the so-called logical square.[15] **[Figure 2]** The square of opposition is very old, going back to Aristotle, and organizes all possible propositions. You can propose A (A), or deny it (non-A), or you can propose the opposite of A (B), or deny the opposite of A (non-B). In figure 2, this square of opposition is represented together with the possible operations, which are represented by the arrows.

---

12. P. Post, "Feast as a Key Concept in a Liturgical Studies Research Design," in *Christian Feast and Festival. The Dynamics of Western Liturgy and Culture*, Liturgia condenda, 10 (Leuven: Peeters, 2000) (forthcoming)

13. R. A. White, "Religion and Media in the Construction of Cultures" (footnote 6); A. Schilson, "Liturgie – die bessere Show? Das 'Medienreligiöse' als Herausforderung an die Kirchen," in *Communicatio Socialis* 29 (1996) 33-53. Schilson depicts the tendency of the electronic media to take the place of the liturgy, where it concerns the communication of the religion of the society. In many aspects, the programs on television look like liturgy: they dramatize our reality, reconcile us with each other, forgive us, witness our marriages, reflect our existence, promise us heaven and eternity. According to Schilson the liturgy should sanctify the electronic media, so that *its* message will be transmitted (the electronic media have no message of their own). This, however, is only possible when the liturgy learns to communicate in the grammar of the electronic media.

14. H.-B. Meyer, "Gottesdienst in audiovisuellen Medien," in *Zeitschrift für Katholische Theologie* 107 (1985) 415-438; J.B. Metz, "Kirchliche Kommunikationskultur. Überlegungen zur Kirche in die Welt der Massenmedien," in *Communicatio Socialis* 24 (1991) 247-258.

15. See 'Quadrat, logisches', in *Historisches Wörterbuch der Philosophie*. Bd. 7 (Darmstadt: Wissenschaftliche Buchgesellschaft, 1989) cc. 1733-1736.

Fig. 2

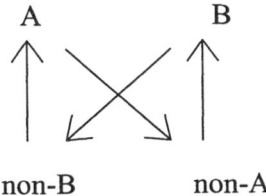

3. The Four Constructions of Reality

This abstract scheme must be adapted to the specific kinds of matter we are dealing with: liturgy and media. In the adaptation that we would like to propose, liturgy and media are approached as constructions of reality. Both liturgy and media are dealing with reality by proposing a certain vision on it. **[see Figure 3]** Our adaptation of the square of opposition, accordingly, differentiates four constructions of reality,[16] in which

A = the truth as the appearance of being (it appears to be what it is)
non-A = the illusion as the denial of the truth in the non-appearance of being (it appears not to be what it is)
B = the lie as the appearance of non-being (it appears to be not what it is)
non-B = and the sacrament as the denial of the lie in the non-appearance of non-being (it appears not to be not what it is)

Figure 3.

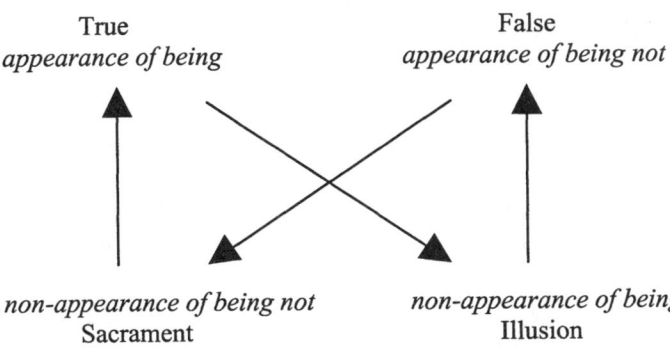

---

16. See W. M. Speelman, "The Plays of Our Culture," in *Jaarboek voor Liturgie-onderzoek* 9 (1993) 65-81; Idem, *The Generation of Meaning in Liturgical Songs*, (Leuven: Peeters, 1995) 24-27.

The first position is the reality in which things are what they seem. This is the reality of normal everyday communication, in which things are intended to be what they are. *When blood appears to be blood indeed, we have a true reality.* In everyday communication things are said to be what they are, so that we may believe that there is something like a true reality.

The second position is the negation of this reality in the illusion. This is what we intend to do in theater and in entertainment. In the imaginary reality, things are not supposed to be what they seem. *The illusion allows an actor to make us believe that tomato ketchup is blood.* In entertainment we are segregated from our everyday experience, and brought into a situation of freedom. In this imaginative reality we are able to reflect on our everyday life and become aware of it as a *potential* reality: things could have been different, and thus *can* be different. The illusion gives us the opportunity to put our life in perspective and to make connections.

The third position is the unmasking of the illusion. This is what we do in science or in court. The scientific operation is a diagnosis, a looking through the illusion. *The diagnosis of the falsehood is that the blood used in theater is not blood at all, but ketchup.* Science falsifies illusions in order to make clear distinctions between what is true and what is false in reality.

The fourth position is the reality proposed by the sacraments. The sacrament masks the falsehood in order to give it the time it needs to tell the truth it intends to tell. *The sacrament denies that the wine in this cup is not blood, but only wine. The sacrament says, that it is indeed wine but as wine the blood of Jesus.* The intention of this sacramental proposition is to open the real reality for the divine. As the sacrament opens the reality for the divine, there is a difference between the first position in the square and the 'fifth': the affirmation of reality *after* the sacramental proposition sees reality in the light of the divine.

4. What is the Position of Liturgy - What is the Position of Media?

The description of the complex communicative situation of one medium communicating another medium is possible with the help of this square. Now it is very important to describe the connection between liturgy and media in a liturgical celebration precisely. For example, when we compare liturgy and the media in culture, the liturgical celebration as a sacramental reality can be situated on the bottom-left position, and the television- and radio-programs (stories) as imaginative realities can be situated on the bottom-right position of the square. **Figure 4** visualizes a possible description of an event in the life of Jesus, and the different constructions of reality in which this event appears.

Figure 4.

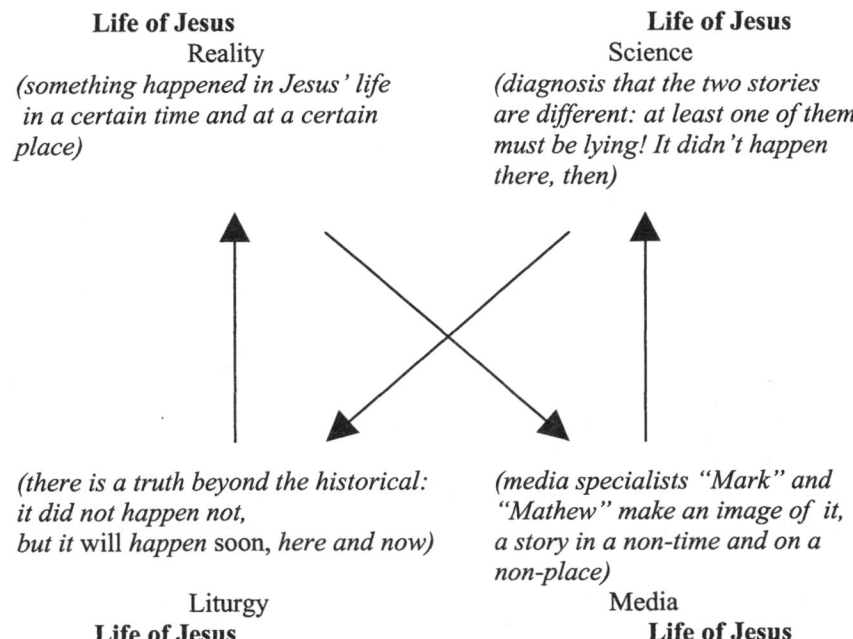

It is very important to notice that there is a difference between *starting* at the top-left position (a historical event in Jesus' life) and *arriving* at the top-left position (realization of that event in our lives) after having heard the stories, having unmasked the illusions in them and having denied their falsification in a liturgical re-reading.

The situation becomes more complex, when we describe the liturgy *in* the media. When a liturgical celebration is transmitted in the media, liturgy is to be approached as a *program* next to other programs in the media, for example plays, discussions and documentaries. Recent studies in communication, by the way, show that the electronic media have developed to a state where they contain the whole spectrum of culture, i.e. culture exists in the media. The other side of the coin appears to be, that culture exists *only* when it is situated in the media: we live in a mediated culture, and reality is only real when it is present in the electronic media. In my present view, therefore, the operative connections between media and liturgy can be visualized as in **figure 5**.

Figure 5.

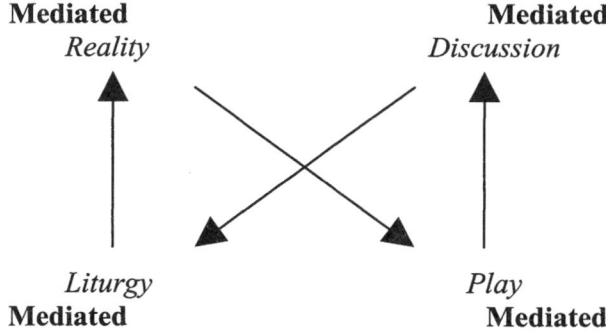

The situation is, in my view, comparable to the modern times (still today) when the culture is dominated by scripture. In our world this has been the case from about the time of the Renaissance.[17] In modern times the whole culture is dominated by its scriptural reproduction. It is a culture in which texts refer to texts, and in which one could suspect that there is not a reality 'outside the text'. In the present day, faith in the scripture is disappearing; we now tend to believe in the image, or icon, or idol. This means that images refer to images, and that there is no 'hors-image'.

5. The Interference of Liturgy and Media in the Mediated Celebration

Liturgy in the electronic media must indeed be approached as an image of liturgy. The image, however, is not a dead thing, but can be conceived of as a mediated liturgy. It is a genuine liturgical celebration *in the media*. Now the first question that comes up may be about the relation between the original celebration and its mediated form. This question will be answered, hopefully, after an investigation of mediated liturgical celebrations. The original liturgy, then, is the reality (first position in the square) and the mediated liturgy is its double denial in the fourth position of the square. As an example, I will now describe an observation of a woman reading from the Scripture in a celebration and in a broadcast celebration. In the celebration she is reading slowly and clearly with a sober voice, standing still, looking at the book and every now and then at the congregation. The soberness of her voice can be interpreted as the

---

17. In musical history, for example, *notation* caused a revolution in music, for it enabled musicians to stop the flowing of time by simple writing the music down on a piece of paper. This gave them the ability to think two or more melodies at one time. Polyphonic music could be imagined, and indeed was written, because the scripture, and not the human body, dominated the music.

lending of her voice to the divine: she is speaking, but not only she, it is *not not her*, it is God in her voice. In the broadcast celebration there is no difference, except one: she looks into the camera every now and then. How is this to be interpreted? Is the congregation extended, including the people who watch the broadcast? Probably, but what interests me here is *her* awareness of the camera. She is not looking as a news-reader (who looks into the camera constantly), and she is not looking as an actress (who does not look into the camera at all). Her looking into the camera *and* to the congregation and to the Bible says that her congregation there in that church is celebrating *and* lends her celebration to the media (so that other people may join them): we are celebrating, but not only we, it is *not not us*. This double denial, it is not not a liturgical celebration, governs her acting. Of course, there are many observations of things that go wrong, such as the girl in the congregation looking straight into the camera and then immediately looking away from it with eyes that say: "Oh dear, the director told us *not* to look into the camera, now everybody has seen me watching."

A second question concerning mediated liturgy may be to what reality the image, the mediation of the celebration, is pointing? According to our model, it points at a true reality or a real truth. But this truth is governed by the *mediated* nature of our culture: it is mediated truth, a mediated reality. The liturgy in the electronic media points at the affirmation of the medial culture. The question is if we should be content with the mediated reality. And I tend to answer this question in the affirmative. The church has the obligation to an inculturation of her faith.[18] The faith of the church must match the culture in which the church has to bring the Gospel. She is assigned to fill the mediated reality with a promise, with faith, hope and love. She has the task to mediate Gods blessing in this mediated culture. And moreover, the mediated liturgy transcends the reality she affirms. As we pointed out earlier, there is a difference between *starting* at the top-left position in the logical square and *arriving* at it ('fifth' position). The mediated liturgy does not stop with the affirmation of mediated culture, but transcends it; the sacramental message goes beyond the reality of which she is a part. Finally, the sacrament says that humans have to break out of this reality and reach toward the ultimate. The ultimate is not an ideal reality. In Christian faith the ultimate is a material reality, in which the word has become flesh, in which we will bodily be resurrected, in which Christ is *vere, realiter et substantialiter* present with the church.

---

18. Congr. de Cultu Divino et Discipl. Sacramentorum, *De Liturgia romana et inculturatione*. Instructio quarta "ad executionem Constitutionis Concilii Vaticani Secundi de sacra Liturgia recte ordinandam," in *Notitiae* 332 (1994) 3, 80-115.

6. Breaking of the Light

We have seen, that mediated liturgy reaches at a point beyond the mediated culture of which it is a part. And I would like to find the words with which we may describe this transcendence. In our search for a model of description, we should not forget that both the liturgy and the electronic media are *media*: they do not exist without the human being in which they have their ground. Media are grounded in us. We *are* liturgical and medial orientations. And thus, in search for an understanding of the processes of the mediation of liturgy, we need to bring our own bodily being into service.

Now then, bearing in mind that we are involved in the interference, what will the interference between liturgy and the media look like? At first, the media will indeed swallow the liturgical celebration and turn it into a program, or as I said earlier, mediated liturgy is an image. But due to the fact that liturgy is radically different, it may very well work like a metaphor, a strange body entering the isotopy and breaking it. The interference then of liturgy and electronic media may be a process in which we, the faithful, jump from one position to another in a 'square-dance', travelling through different constructions of reality.

a. *The imagination of the reality* (from truth to illusion). We live in an imaginative world already. And we realize that this reality is potential: it could have been and can be otherwise. On the one hand, such imagination has liberated us from the factual. We may get the idea that liturgy can be anyway we want it to be. On the other hand, the imagination has no ground, and can make our liturgy as it were homeless. But is not liturgy essentially at home where it *is* homeless indeed? And cannot the church play an important role here, in this desert? Should she not be present there were she is needed the most?[19] We may need to learn to celebrate a liturgy without a home, develop a liturgy which is *in* this mediated, imaginative world without being *from* this world. We may need to become aware that liturgy is at the same an image and more than an image. It is a gathering of people in a mystical and real body.

b. *The sanctification of the image* (unmasking the illusion). In Eastern theology they say that only when an icon contemplates an icon, the reality behind the icon becomes visible. In some way, it takes an image to unmask an image and see the reality behind it. This means that the mediated liturgy as an image is perfectly capable of interpreting the

---

19. E. Henau, "Over de aanwezigheid van de kerk en religie in de media," in *Jaarboek voor Liturgie-onderzoek* 16 (2000) (forthcoming)

imaginative reality of the media and see the truth it intends to tell us. We know that the illusion is an illusion, and we are able to look at the reality it intends to connect us with. People who do not understand the nature of the imagination, who do not see that it is an illusion intending to connect us with reality, want to break the image in an iconoclasm. But the image must not be broken. In a medial liturgy, we may break the rules of the omnipotent media,[20] and start a ritual radio and a ritual television.[21] The newly developed ritual media are capable of breaking the invisible light in visible colors.

c. *The transfiguration of the image* (from falsehood to sacrament). In order to receive the truth to which the imagination intends to connect us, we need to put our own bodies at stake. On our physical presence the transparent reality can be grounded. We become aware of this task: when the media make us aware of the inhuman; when photographers stop taking pictures and start to help; when recipients stop watching and engage themselves with the reality they have seen. Here the image is grounded and reflected in a transfiguration. In a transfiguration *the image watches the recipient*, so that the recipient sees his or her body reflected in the image.

d. *The realization of the image* (from sacrament to a new truth). When a human being devotes his or her physical presence to the truth of the sacrament, the sacrament is becoming real. What was imagined in the image is becoming real in one's body, until it is being born and goes out into the world.

The electronic media show an idea, and do not bring us in contact with reality. But we do not need the media to give us the real world, for we *are* the real world. What we need is the electronic media bringing us beyond the illusion and moving us to a liturgical form of attending the mystery of our own reality. This is not a postmodern iconoclasm, but a breaking of the mediated light in colors. The colors do not show but affirm, in a tangible presentation, the being of the true light.

National Raad voor Liturgie Willem Marie SPEELMAN
Liturgical Council of the Dutch Bishops Conference
Amerfoortseweg
NL-3705 GJ Zeist
The Netherlands

---

20. G. Aschenbach, "Die Lage der Religion in der mondernen Gesellschaft und die Medien – Eine Expertise," in *Religion und Fernsehen in den neunziger Jahren*, ed. E. Bieger et al. (Köln: KIM, 1994) 95-120.

21. W. M. Speelman, "Het ware licht" (footnote 7).

SECTION THREE

RE-IMAG(IN)ING SACRAMENTAL CONTOURS

AN INCARNATIONAL APPROACH TO EUCHARISTIC PARTICIPATION: ANGLICAN REFLECTION ON THE REAL PRESENCE OF CHRIST IN THE EUCHARIST

Anglicanism, when allowed to be what it was conceived to be in the latter sixteenth century, has a vast wealth to offer western sacramental theology. Intermingled within its sacramental thought is a theological anthropology able to worship God in a sacred dance of participatory union.

Anglicanism is capable of thinking in such a way for two basic reasons. One, its objective reality expects the true presence and grace of God when invoked. What allows for such an expectation is the clear distinction made between objective reality and objective literalism. Said differently, Anglicanism's theology is shaped and formed by an era when theologians did not try to describe the indescribable, and explain the inexplicable. Secondly, healthy Anglicanism has been nourished from a epoch when the Doctrine of the Trinity offered the foundation for the shape of all theological exchange, not only about God but also about the human being.

1. Doctrine of the Trinity: Greek Patristic and Selected Contemporary Thought

Gregory of Nyssa, in the fourth century, characterized the status of theological exchange concerning the Doctrine of the Trinity in the following way:

> The whole city is full of it, the squares, the market places, the cross-roads, the alleyways; old-clothes men, money changers, food sellers: they are all busy arguing. If you ask someone to give you change, he philosophizes about the Begotten and the Unbegotten; if you inquire about the price of a loaf, you are told by way of reply that the Father is greater and the Son inferior; if you ask "Is my bath ready?" the attendant answers that the Son was made out of nothing.[1]

These questions from the 'old-clothes men', cashiers, bath attendants and bread merchants concerning the Doctrine of the Trinity were not questions only about the interior of the deity. Instead, they were exchanges about the purpose and role of the human being and life itself. Questions concerning the Christological issues of this doctrine were not limited to the metaphysical makeup of Jesus the Christ. Instead, such questions were concerned with how we, the human being, might become by grace what Jesus the Christ is by nature. And the exchanges concerning the Doctrine of the Eucharist were not exchanges actually mindful about the transformation of the substance of bread and wine, but instead, exchanges revealing the holy desire within the human being to become the ecclesial body of Christ, the real presence, the seer of God's vision, and the builder of God's kingdom, no longer called servant, but friend.

With this being the case, then where did Gregory's 'old clothes men', bread merchants and the like first learn to shape their deepest and most foundational thought into theological form? They learned it from the work they did as the people of God. They learned it in their worship of God, which was their participation in their sacramental liturgy. Liturgy, molded from the bedrock of the doctrine of the Trinity and within the framework of the sacraments, was the ground for theological all enterprise.

However, this liturgical grounding was not seen as an autonomy set apart from either the doctrine of the Trinity, incarnation, or other theological enterprises. In the same sense these worshipers did not view themselves as individual entities set over against the God they worshiped. Sacramental liturgy, particularly as it applies to baptism and eucharist, must again become this *relational ground* for all theological enterprise and human identity. What follows is an attempt to establish the groundwork for such an enterprise.

Gregory of Nyssa, Athanasius, Basil the Great and Gregory of Nazianzus each agreed that God the Father seeks union and reconciliation with that which has been created. They sought to express this

---

1. Gregory of Nyssa, "On the Deity of the Son," in Timothy Wares, *The Orthodox Church* (New York: Penguin Books, 1964) 43.

sacramentally and liturgically. They also agreed that the Second Person of the Trinity must be divine in order to reveal, unite, and redeem. Similarly, the Holy Spirit must be divine in order to sanctify and divinize. In this way and through such logic, the Greek patristic doctrine of the Trinity evolved. It was this doctrine of the Trinity that propelled the theology of the Early Church through its councils and formed its creeds.

Most contemporary theological studies in the West, even those attempting to speak of the nature of God, have not chosen to look seriously at the Doctrine of the Trinity. Therefore, to see such a classic theme as the Doctrine of the Trinity explored by a few premier, constructive theologians today is noteworthy. More significant is the type of trinitarian study being undertaken. Today in the West, the most important work in this area is conducted by those scholars who are actively using the aspects and concepts of the Doctrine of the Trinity best characterized as Eastern Orthodox in essence. These scholars use the work of the Greek patristics including Irenaeus, Athanasius, Basil the Great, and the two Gregorys of Cappadocia.

Some of the most significant contemporary work is done by Jürgen Moltmann, Leonardo Boff, Miroslav Volf and Catherine Mowry LaCugna. Selected for their unique contributions to contemporary discussion, these scholars, within various denominations and cultural settings of the Western Christian Church, help define current discussion boundaries regarding the Doctrine of the Trinity.

Underpinning much of this contemporary trinitarian work is the recovery of the social nature of the Trinity. This 'social Trinity' is then compared with other hierarchical or dominating portrayals of the relations of the Persons. Moltmann offers a description of his project:

> [I seek to]...develop a social doctrine of the Trinity, according to which God is a community of Father, Son and Spirit, whose unity is constituted by mutual indwelling and reciprocal interpenetration.[2]

Moltmann, Boff,[3] Volf,[4] and LaCugna[5] each incorporate a technical analysis of the dynamic and intimate relation of the Persons of the Trinity. Critical to early patristic thought and described as attraction, interpenetration and mutuality, this relational dynamic is termed

---

2. Jürgen Moltmann, *The Trinity and the Kingdom* (Minneapolis: Fortress Press, 1993) viii.
3. Leonardo Boff, *Trinity and Society*, trans. Paul Burns (Maryknoll: Orbis Books, 1988).
4. Miroslav Volf, *After Our Likeness: The Church as the Image of the Trinity* (Grand Rapids: William B. Eerdmans Publishing Company, 1998).
5. Catherine M. LaCugna, *God for Us* (San Francisco: Harper, 1991).

perichoresis. The perichoretic attraction is to such an extent that the Persons actually exist and indwell one another.

They each recover this significant aspect of early trinitarian thought and seek to draw conclusions regarding humanity and the church. However, applications of this mutual and dynamically relational Trinity are forced into difficult and disconnected dialogue when considered with Western conceptions of the human being. For example, Moltmann speaks about the work of the incarnation:

> In the incarnation of the Son God humiliates himself, accepting and adopting threatened and perverted human nature in its entirety, making it part of his eternal life.[6]

Similarly, Boff spends chapters accounting for humanity's evils. While going to great lengths to portray the life of the Trinity as passionate and loving, his account of the human has little capacity for participation in that life.

LaCugna comes closest to suggesting *sacramental relevance* in trinitarian discussion:

> Sacramental life gives us a new way of being who and what we are, not just with respect to ourselves but in relation to every other creature as well as to God.[7]

However, by defining all liturgy as the "ritual celebration of the events of the economy of redemption,"[8] LaCugna leaves the relationship between God and humanity primarily in soteriological terms. For her, incarnation is necessary in response to humanity's sin, rather than the incarnation being God's creating and unifying self-revelation.

Overall, contemporary scholarship regarding the doctrine of the Trinity provides a helpful account of God's relational nature and suggests some conclusions for that relationality for human society. Unfortunately, these scholars persist in Western understandings of the human which do not allow for the same dynamically perichoretical relationship between God and humanity as is described for the life of God. This is important because the ontology of the human being is, in the West, not communal but individual, autonomous and singular in nature.

Characteristic of their work is an inability to incorporate, in either a relational or ontological way, the Greek patristic understanding of the human being and the sacraments, particularly the Eucharist. This is because in the East, sacramental thought developed along with early Christian discussions regarding the Incarnation and the Trinity.

---

6. *Ibid.*, 121.
7. *Ibid.*, 404.
8. *Ibid.*, 405.

According to Greek patristic thinkers, it was the grace of God, as offered through the Eucharist, that rendered the human being capable of being emptied of finite desires and attachments in order to be filled with the desire to participate, as a relational being, in God and with God, and with all God's creation.

We may see here that even explicitly trinitarian scholarship does not undertake the correlative work regarding relational aspects of the human being. A return to the Greek patristic trinitarian and anthropological understandings, which developed simultaneously, will illuminate their inter-relatedness and offer a renewed anthropology for the 21st century.

1.1. God the Creator

The anthropological teachings of the early Greek and patristic scholars evolved within the context of the seamless doctrines of the Trinity, incarnation and sacramental theology. The general principle was the Doctrine of Creation. Therefore, within the realm of creation, it is through the will of the Father that the anthropological aspects of creation exist. It is in participation with the Son that the anthropological aspects of creation come into being. It is by the participation of the Holy Spirit that the anthropological aspect of creation is perfected. This 'perfecting' through the Holy Spirit takes place by the Holy Spirit. Here, the Holy Spirit is the source of God that is both the informing and the forming tenet of created matter.

Athanasius wrote that God is the sufficient and highest cause of the world, both in matter and in form. He and other Greek patristic scholars saw God creating out of nothing. This *ex nihilo* principle strengthened the idea that God did not create out of necessity. Instead, God created out of will and love. In creating the world, God acted within God's nature and free of any external limitations. God created in a free act, setting up a cosmic and eternal 'free' and mutual relationship between God and humanity.

It is important to note that these scholars did not see God becoming the creator of the world only when God created. Instead, the Greek patristic thinkers guided the Early Church to accept a strong distinction between the notions of God's will for creation, which included God's plan and design, and God's carrying out and realization of this plan, will, and design.

All this leads to a most important Greek patristic understanding of God; God is love, and the world is a 'logical' conclusion of a cause outside itself. Since the Early Church conceived of God as 'complete', the aim and purpose of the world is realized no place other than in God's own nature. The content of this end and purpose of God is regarded scripturally as the happiness of rational creatures, which at the end of time, is cited as in and with the glory of God.[9]

Key to understanding the rich anthropological implications in this thought is to realize that for the Early Church, the aim of redemption through the Christ is the perfection, deification or *theosis* of God's creation. In the New Testament, this was spoken of as the "foundation of the Kingdom of God to God's glory."[10] It is important to realize that the very purpose for the creation of the world is not to be seen as separate from the redemption offered in Jesus the Christ. Using this same logic, the end of the world is not seen in and of itself; but it is looked at together with creation and redemption as one unique and indivisible whole. The creation of the world is seen as good in relationship to the act of redemption and also the world's end. This is not to say that the world is either the 'best possible' or the only possible world, nor is it to say there is no evil. Because of humanity's free will there is evil, damnable evil. None-the-less, this evil is contrary to the will of God.

1.2. God the Son - The Incarnation

According to the Greek patristics, Jesus the Christ was the bringer of this revelation about God's ambition for the participatory destiny of the human being. Jesus the Christ was also the one who made God again approachable through relationship to the human being. Athanasius believed that the "Word" was not impaired in receiving a body, so that the Incarnate should seek to receive a grace; but rather, the Christ deified that which he put on, and more than that, gave it graciously to humanity. Through the Incarnation, this Jesus brought the human being and God into union. This was done, in part, by Jesus the Christ offering the full perfection of human nature in its completed, whole, and full destiny of union with God. This is to say that the Second Person of the Trinity would have still become incarnate even if humanity had not sinned. Here, the Incarnation was but the complement and necessary part of creation. Add to this that the human being was created in God's image, the argument is made that the human being, even without sin, was incomplete in his or her destiny of participating in the nature of God, short of the Incarnation.[11] Therefore, it is most important to keep in mind that the benefits of the Incarnation exceeded simply salvation from sin and its consequences. Instead, the Incarnation caused the sharing in the nature of God united with humanity on the human side. This is a glory far exceeding what was lost by the Fall.

9. Dt 10,21; Ps 19,1; Prov 16,4; Lk 2,14; Rom 1,19-20;11,36; Heb 2,10.
10. Jn 17,4; Eph 1,5-6; Col 1,16.
11. 2 Pt 1,4.

The Thomist and the twentieth century Catherine Mowry LaCugna, on the other hand, have reasoned that the purpose of the incarnation was salvation from sin and death.[12] God foresaw the fall and therefore the incarnation. However, the incarnation was not to be considered a necessary part of creation, even though it was needed to redeem humankind.

In contrast, the sixteenth century Anglican theologian Richard Hooker, though a student of the thought of Thomas Aquinas, was more Greek in his view of the incarnation. As will be explained following, God is not only transcendent but also imminent, offering both absolute and relative attributes. These attributes also lie in the nature and the aim of the human being who is created in the image of God. It is uncomfortable in Western Christian theology to suggest that in mutual union, or fellowship, with God, the human being might become like God who created him or her.

Now granted, both Greek and Roman thought concerning the Incarnation, allowed for the mutual relationship or fellowship between God and the human being. Also, both Greek and Roman thought regarded the Incarnation to be the result of God's energy or grace and human receptivity and cooperation. However, to determine whether the Incarnation of the Word of God was 'possibility' or 'necessity' depends upon one's understanding of God and the human being.

Hooker chose to read the Greek patristic scholars as offering a theology involving an understanding of the Incarnation where there would be both an imparting of divine truth, power and life, and a capacity for the human to receive this divine truth, power, and life. Therefore, as previously stated, the Incarnation of the Word of God would have been necessary for the perfection of the human being even without human sin.

The Greek patristic scholars wished to take nothing away from the truth concerning sin and the human condition. They were clear in offering that the Incarnation in Jesus the Christ, the Second Person in the Trinity, does speak to the shaken hopes of humanity. The Incarnation *does* reconstitute reverence to something beyond ourselves. It does offer to fill the void spoken of by Augustine of Hippo. And the Incarnation does satisfy the longings of the human spirit. It even awakens the political and moral life as the human being is lifted by God's grace from the 'wages of sin'. Yet, this is not the total story of the Incarnation. These early church writers chose to not only offer a restored and redeemed understanding of the human being; they also wished to point out that, with spiritual faculties darkened by sin, the human being had 'forgotten' his or her greatest destiny, which was union with God in this life.

12. 1 Jn 3,5.

God the Son took on all that was human. In doing so, his life upon this earth was the life of one who was pure human. When His subject self was tempted to develop and proclaim itself over against 'the other' this represented the same struggle that defines created order.[13]

1.3. The Holy Spirit and the Human Being

Similarly, Greek patristic Christian thought regards the human being as the merger between the spiritual and the material aspects of God's creation, belonging in body to the physical order and in true identity, regarded as soul or spirit, to the spiritual order. Again, this notion does not suggest a type of dualism; the human being is not to be seen as having two natures. A human being is a unity, incorporating both body and soul. It is the entirety of body and soul of the human being that is filled with the energy and grace of the Third Person of the Trinity, the Holy Spirit. It is through the Holy Spirit that *theosis* or deification occurs as the human being is illuminated, sanctified, and quickened in faculty and capacity.

The doctrine of God's kingdom is very much a vision of this order of perichoretic relationship. The true dance of *perichoresis* can take place only when the divinity of the human being is taken seriously theologically.

Gregory of Nyssa builds upon these notions of human perfection found in the thought of Athanasius, Basil and Gregory of Nazianzus, as he summarizes, stressing both the ascetic and the ethical aspects of *theosis*. The human being, according to Gregory, is a great deal more than an imitation of the material world. The human being is to be appreciated because he or she has been created in the image of the Creator.

Here it is important to compare these Greek patristic ideas and positions with those of Roman and, later, Reformed thought. Roman Catholic teachings believed that original righteousness was part of a supernatural gift of God. They did not offer that these were part of the

---

13. It is most important to note that John Calvin's thought on how the two natures of Jesus the Christ make one person keeps closely to Chalcedonian orthodoxy. "... he who was the Son of God became the Son of man – not by confusion of substance, but by unity of person. For we affirm his divinity so joined and united with his humanity that each retains its distinctive nature unimpaired, and yet these two natures constitute one Christ." Calvin goes on to say, "Yet, neither is so mingled with the other as not to retain its own distinctive nature." Calvin then states that scripture refers to Jesus as man, other scripture to Jesus as God. However, a third form of scripture that refers to Jesus as pure God and pure man, "... comprehend both natures at once, very much of which are found in John's Gospel, set forth his true substance most clearly of all." See: John Calvin, *Calvin: Institutes of the Christian Religion*, ed. John T. McNeill, trans. Ford Lewis Battles (Philadelphia: The Westminster Press, 1960) II. xii.

nature of human beings, even in a potential way. Instead, this righteousness was in addition to the human endowments given at God's creation of the human being. This idea of *theosis* or deification would have seemed too magical and mechanical to be the grace of God.

Reformed thought re-instated aspects of Greek patristic thought. Yet, it did so by affirming the complete and perfect holiness and righteousness of the original state of the human being. This Reformed thought then assigned this endowment to the natural state of the whole human being independent of God's grace.

However, the Greek thinkers had already offered a middle way: Here the human being was potentially perfect and original righteousness was the result of the cooperation of the Spirit of God with human natural powers. This original righteousness was believed to be implanted in the human soul in creation.

2. Richard Hooker

6th Century theologian Richard Hooker sought to define Anglican theological boundaries within a complex setting. He returned to early struggles with the articulation of the faith and brought them to new clarity for the issues of his time. As a primary and formative voice in Anglican theology, and because of his insight into the specific application of trinitarian thought to the human being and the eucharist, Hooker's work is singularly significant.

Hooker worked in a context where a prevailing Western mindset regarding the nature of God and the human being saw an unbridgeable gap between what it meant to be God and what it meant to be human. Emerging and developing continental Reformation thought emphasized the depraved nature of the human, and therefore, a strictly soteriological aspect of the Incarnation. Rather than humanity participating in the gracious life of God, God must be humiliated in order to redeem humanity.

2.1. Anthropology

Richard Hooker's articulation of the human condition is consonant with the Greek patristic understanding. God created humanity and gave humanity the capacity to attain its potential. "And is it probable that God should frame the hearts of all so desirous of that which no one may obtain?"[14] This desire seeks that which it is like, humanity seeks God. Hooker's work represents a Western scholar's application of the

14. Richard Hooker, *Of the Laws of Ecclesiastical Polity*, Book I (Ellicott City: Via Media, Inc., 1994) 257.

intentional connection between the incarnational and anthropological thought offered through the thought of Greek patristic theologians such as Irenaeus, Athanasius, Basil the Great, Gregory of Nazianzus, Gregory of Nyssa and the like.

Refusing to adopt Western dualism and denigration of matter, Hooker writes not only of humanity being good, but, since it was created by God, all creation is good: "And because there is not in the world any thing whereby another may not some way be made perfecter, therefore all things that are, are good."[15]

Hooker uses terminology of desire to express the capacity for the human to participate in the life of God.

> Again, since there can be no goodness desired which proceeds not for God alone, ... all things in the world are said in some sort to seek the highest, and to covet more or less the participation of God [alone].[16]

How does Hooker express more clearly for his day this Greek patristic understanding of participation in God, or *theosis*? It is only when humanity is fully possessed *by* God, rather than possessing God as a commodity, theory or system, that *theosis* is possible.

> Then are we happy therefore when we fully enjoy God, as an object wherein the powers of our souls are satisfied even with everlasting delight; so that although we be [hu]m[a]n, yet by being unto God united we live as it were the life of God...Complete union with [God] must be according unto every power and faculty of our minds apt to receive so glorious an object.[17]

Like the patristic theologians, Hooker did not dismiss original sin, but for him it did not eradicate the created goodness of humanity. Hooker does not dismiss evil or humanity's horrible acts. Attributing departure from the will of God as "idolatry," Hooker gives both an account of free will and evil, while preserving the capacity of the human for *theosis*.[18]

2.2. Incarnation

In discussions of the Incarnation, Hooker brings together the categories of Trinity and humanity through the place where they intersect in Christ. Here the two natures mutually possess one another. Hooker emphasizes the eternal character of the Incarnation, rather than regarding the Incarnation as "later, in time," response to humanity's need for or experience of Christ as Savior. Hooker's incarnation thought, following the example of patristic theologians, instead, to an understanding of the

---

15. *Ibid.*, 215.
16. *Ibid.*, 215.
17. *Ibid.*, 255.
18. *Ibid.*, 235-236.

human being offering that "God became human being in order that human beings might become God." This was the most basic, fundamental and first principle of the human condition. This emphasis distinguished Hooker's work in his own day, and offers a unique perspective to contemporary theology in ours.

Humanity's understanding of the person of Christ is central to a consistent anthropology, consonant with a perichoretical understanding of the Trinity. Hooker affirms both the full divinity and full humanity of Christ:

> Christ is a Person both divine and human, howbeit not therefore two persons in one, neither both these in one sense, but a person divine, because he is personally the Son of God, human, because he ha[s] really the nature of the children of [humanity].[19]

It is in Christ that the perfection of human attributes was seen.

2.3. The Eucharist

Rather than re-establishing the Greek patristic formulation of the Trinity, Hooker uses their understanding of God as Trinity as a basis for moving to the *implications* of this dynamically relational and passionate communion of Persons. One of the main implications for Hooker was the meaning and purpose of the Eucharist.

Richard Hooker would move the discussion of Christ's presence in the Eucharist to one of discussing the participation of the communicant in the life of God. He expresses participation, or *theosis*, in this way:

> ....Our souls and bodies quickened to eternal life are effects the cause whereof is the Person of Christ, his body and his blood are the true wellspring out of which this life flow[s]. So that his body and blood are in that very subject whereunto they minister life ...by a far more divine and mystical kind of union, which make[s] us one with him even as he and the Father are one.[20]

Here again, Richard Hooker returns to the Greek patristic roots of theology in considering the Greek Father's understanding of the eucharist. Hooker notes:

> In a word it appear[s] not that of all the Fathers of the Church any one did ever conceive or imagine other than only a mystical participation of Christ's body and blood in the sacramental . . .[21]

---

19. Richard Hooker, *Laws*, Book V, 225.
20. *Ibid.*, 352.
21. *Ibid.*, 358.

Hooker shifts the arguments of his day to an area more relevant to an understanding of the human. Confronted on one side with Calvinists, and on the other with those who would staunchly defend transubstantiation, Hooker connects the two sacraments of Baptism and Eucharist in the following manner.

> If on all sides it be confessed that the grace of Baptism is poured into the soul of [hu]man[ity], that by water we receive it although it be neither seated in the water nor the water changed into it, what should induce [us] to think that the grace of the Eucharist must need be in the Eucharist before it can be in us that receive it?[22]

Hooker, as with most Anglicans, will not deny the presence of Christ in the elements, but he will insist that a more helpful place for the consideration of God's transforming grace through Christ's presence is in the communicant. He continues, "The fruit of the Eucharist is the participation of the body and blood of Christ."[23] Rather than contend with the manner in which Christ might be in the bread and wine, Hooker's understanding of the capacity for humanity's participation in God is central to his articulation of the Eucharist:

> [B]ecause our participation of Christ in this sacrament depend[s] on the co-operation of his omnipotent power which make[s] it his body and blood to us, whether with change or without alteration of the element such as they imagine we need not greatly to care nor inquire.[24]

Hooker connects humanity's union with God through the sacraments. He says,

> forasmuch as there is not union of God with [hu]man[ity] without that mean between both/ which is both [referring to Christ], it seem[s] requisite that we first consider how God is in Christ, then how Christ is in us, and how the Sacraments do serve to make us partakers of Christ.[25]

Hooker reminds his readers that the final work of grace in the eucharist belongs to God.

> because the sacrament being of itself but a corruptible and earthly creature must need be thought an unlikely instrument to work so admirable effects in [hu]man[ity], we are therefore to rest ourselves altogether upon the strength of [God's] glorious power who is able and will bring to pass that the bread and cup which he give[s] us shall be truly the thing he promise[s].[26]

---

22. *Ibid.*, 353.
23. *Ibid.*
24. *Ibid.*
25. *Ibid.*, 220.
26. *Ibid.*, 355.

Richard Hooker's sixteenth century thought offers contemporary theology the ability to build on his theological anthropology in conjunction with current trinitarian scholarship. Hooker's incarnationally based work provides a means for reconnecting western theological categories long separated by emphases on human depravity, God's impassability, and delayed eschatology.

3. Implications

As previously noted, 20th century scholarship regarding the doctrine of the Trinity, as reviewed in the beginning of this paper, provides a helpful account of God's perichoretic relational nature and suggests initial conclusions for that relationality for human society. Unfortunately, these scholars continue in their western understandings of the human individual. These understandings do not allow for the same dynamically perichoretical relationship between God and humanity as is described for the life of God.

While recent scholarship regarding the Trinity has returned to early church theological discourse for renewed inquiry, contemporary scholarship regarding the human has been largely left to non-theological disciplines such as sociology, psychology and philosophy. We offer to the field of theological anthropology an account of the human which reclaims and develops a theocentric understanding of the human and is consistent with significant contemporary trinitarian advances. Specifically, this paper suggests building an account of the Eucharist in which the human being is capacitated, through God's grace, in the Eucharist to desire and to participate in a dynamic relation with God, for the sake of the continued work of Jesus the Christ in the building of the kingdom of God.

A renewed theological anthropology could enhance the work of contemporary trinitarian theologians by placing the eucharist in a seamless context with ethics, ecclesiology, dogmatics, anthropology and liturgics. For example, Leonardo Boff's work could then incorporate the sacraments as a potential means of liberation, not solely as a means of oppression and unjust heirarchy. This theological framework would not allow social theory, including justice issues, to be optional for those undertaking other areas of theological inquiry. Questions of eucharistic participation become questions of life and practice, not only of ideology or concepts.

Other Anglican and Western work in related areas of this essay could further bridge Eastern Orthodox and Western ecclesial thought by continuing to utilize the idea of *perichoresis* and other relational aspects of the Eastern Orthodox doctrine of the Trinity. In a broader ecumenical scope, further study could focus upon a more expanded understanding of humanity's capacity for change. Here, an historical analysis would place the present dominant notion of change into the larger arena of transformation leading to *theosis* for the purpose of doing the will of God in this world. Such inquiry would aid in moving the anthropological focus in Western theology from solely that of soteriology to that of sanctification and the transformation of not only people and communities but also potentially idealogies and entire cultures. This approach could help free Western Christianity for more open and unrestricted interfaith dialogue.

Also, by using *perichoresis* as a basis for exploring human capacity for participation in God, *theosis* becomes the parallel human potential for dynamic and relational life. This participation is found in God's ongoing offering of Self in the Eucharist, and humanity's response in receiving God and offering self in return. Here humanity is restored to its dignity in creation rather than solely being acquitted from the consequences of original sin.

    Episcopal Church of the Redeemer   Eugene C. MCDOWELL
    502 West Sumter Street   Meghan F. FROEHLICH
    Shelby, North Carolina 28150
    USA

THE COSMOS AS PRIMARY SACRAMENT: AN ECOLOGICAL PERSPECTIVE FOR SACRAMENTAL THEOLOGY

Introduction

The ecological crisis, while it has been marginal to discourse in sacramental theology, is the single most critical event shaping the post-modern religious context. This observation is not meant to ignore social issues but to recognize the seamless character of socio-ecological decline. At its deepest level, the ecological crisis is a crisis of *meaning* in Euro-Western culture. It brings into question the dominant anthropocentric, dualistic worldview in the West that many scholars consider to be responsible for the ecological crisis and its related social upheaval.

There is evidence to suggest that the Christian tradition is implicated as one of the root causes of the ecological crisis.[1] As such, any solution will necessitate a religious response from Christians. Sacramental theology, especially in its relation to liturgy, has the potential to transform the consciousness of the world's practicing Catholics and thus influence their commitments and their behaviour. The essence of the sacramental principle, fundamental to sacramental theology, affirms the capacity of the created order to reveal divine presence. The underlying premise of this contribution is that sacramental theology ought to be more explicit in its commitment to reverencing the whole of creation by making the ecological crisis a central concern for its theological reflection. This contribution proposes that the work of Thomas Berry and Brian Swimme and their integration of the post-modern scientific perspective is a valuable resource for the construction of an *ecological* sacramental theology. They situate the findings of contemporary science as foundational to a worldview that can overcome anthropocentric bias and reorient Western consciousness to the earth and so to ecological wholeness.[2]

---

1. Lynn White Jr., "The Historic Roots of Our Ecologic Crisis," in *Science* 155 (1967) 1207-1212.
2. Thomas Berry, *The Dream of the Earth* (San Francisco, 1988); Brian Swimme, *The Hidden Heart of the Cosmos* (New York 1996). For examples of similar treatments of this theme, see Ted Peters (ed.), *Cosmos as Creation: Theology and Science in Consonance*

Physicist, Brian Swimme argues that the mystery and grandeur of such an "ongoing scintillating event" as the cosmos demands more than a scientific account, it demands a religious sensibility.[3] For Thomas Berry, like Swimme, the story of the universe is the overarching movement that encompasses all other stories.[4] The charge against this new universe story, by those sensitive to the postmodern critique, is its potential use as a meta-narrative that can attain, in their view, a totalizing tendency.[5] This however, this is to misread its intention. Rather, the universe story as told by Berry and Swimme is meant to contextualize the particular cultural narratives that give meaning to and direction in human life, within a *functional* cosmology, in order to contribute to the "development of [a] comprehensive ecological awareness."[6] For the most part, however, contemporary Christian theology has resisted the new universe story as the context for understanding its biblical-redemptive story and consequently has been inadequate in its response to the ecological crisis.[7]

In this contribution I argue for a relational construal of the term "sacrament," in keeping with the new cosmology that describes the universe as interdependent, alive, fecund and developing.[8] A relational view of sacrament, when ascribed to the cosmos, implies that the natural world not only reveals divine presence *in* the cosmos (as per the traditional view of the sacramental principle) but that the cosmos is an active participant in the working out of the divine will *for* the cosmos. Just as the sacramentality of Jesus is predicated on Jesus' own relationship to and involvement in God's transformative presence in and for the world, so too, the view of the cosmos as sacrament invites a broader interpretation of what sacrament means relative to the natural world.

This is not to say that the cosmos as sacrament is *equivalent* to Jesus as a sacrament of God. Obviously, Jesus' consciousness in terms of his free response to God's initiative bears a different quality that is not duplicated in cosmic processes. However, as a *product* of the cosmic process, Jesus' response is in part the response of the cosmos itself. Berry writes:

(Nashville, 1989); Larry L. Rasmussan, *Earth Community, Earth Ethics* (New York 1996).

3. Swimme, *The Hidden Heart*, 31.

4. Anne Lonergan and Carolyn Richards, *Thomas Berry and the New Cosmology* (Mystic, CT, 1991) 37-38.

5. For a discussion on this point see Heather Eaton, "A Critical Inquiry into an Ecofeminist Cosmology," Ph.D. dissertation, Toronto, 1996, 173-176.

6. *Ibid.*, 175.

7. Lonergan and Richards, *Thomas Berry*, 38.

8. Swimme, *The Hidden Heart*, 97-104.

Any human activity must be seen primarily as an activity of the universe and only secondarily as an activity of the individual. In this manner it is clear that the universe as such is the primary religious reality, the primary sacred community, the primary revelation of the divine, the primary subject of incarnation, the primary unity of redemption, the primary referent in any discussion of reality or of value.[9]

It is in this sense that the cosmos as the *primary* sacrament is affirmed. I will discuss this perspective under three aspects: 1) its potential for overcoming anthropocentric bias in sacramental theology, 2) its relationship to the hegemonic view of Jesus as primordial sacrament; and 3) its capacity for maintaining the unity of the creation-redemption motif.

1. Overcoming Anthropocentric Bias

I contend that the cosmos as primary sacrament advances the anthropological justification for the sacramental life while it overcomes the anthropo*centrism* that is inherent in the exclusive attention to human history that is endemic in sacramental theology. It does so by placing the human *within* the cosmic structures of reality, rather than above or beyond them, and accenting the tripartite quality of divine-earth-human relationships within that structure.

The cosmos as primary sacrament roots human experience in the unfolding processes of the cosmos. Berry's anthropological principles for a functional cosmology affirms the earth as primary and the human as derivative.[10] One of Berry's assertions is that the role of the human species is a celebratory one. He writes:

> The human is precisely that being in whom this total process reflects on and celebrates itself and its numinous origins in a special mode of conscious self-awareness. At our highest moments we fulfill this role through the association of our liturgies with the supreme liturgy of the universe itself.[11]

Relating sacramental life and the Christian liturgy in an analogous way to the liturgy of the cosmos is not new in Christian theology.[12] However, the

---

9. Lonergan and Richards, *Thomas Berry*, 38.
10. Berry, "The Cosmology of Religions," [unpublished manuscript], 41. There are thirteen principles which Berry gleans from the prevailing themes of postmodern science and he present them as attributes of a functional cosmology – one that can reorient cultural commitments towards a reverence for the earth and its processes. These principles are found throughout Berry's work. They are distilled in Brian Swimme's article entitled "Berry's Cosmology," *Cross Currents* vol. 37, 1987, 218-225. They also appear in Eaton's *A Critical Inquiry*, 85. See appendix for the complete list.
11. *Ibid.*, 37.
12. See Alexander Schmemann, *The World as Sacrament* (London, 1966) 16; Karl Rahner, "How to Receive a Sacrament and Mean It," in *The Sacraments: Readings in*

practice has usually been articulated from a hierarchical perspective in which the cosmos becomes absorbed into the human as the apex of its fulfillment.[13] Moreover, the Christian liturgy is presented, in teleological terms, as the fulfillment of God's plan for the *whole* world, marginalizing other cultures and their religious experiences of liturgy. Thus, the traditional association between the Christian liturgy and the liturgy of the cosmos has not only been anthropocentric but it has been totalizing in its *Christiancentrism* as well.

The cosmos as primary sacrament suggests the association of the Christian liturgy with the cosmos but gives *precedence* to the cosmos as the context for all liturgy. The cosmos is the primary event in which humanity is drawn into and participates in God's creative redeeming love (along with the rest of creation). The Christian liturgy is an efficacious moment but it is not the only moment nor the only mode of expressing eschatological hope and fulfillment. Such a perspective not only tends toward undercutting the anthropocentrism inherent in contemporary sacramental theology, but also creates a context for a postmodern approach to inter-faith dialogue.[14] Further, Berry's affirmation of the human as a celebratory species is not meant to absorb all of the natural world into the primacy of the human experience. Rather, it affirms the human gift of conscious self-awareness as *one* gift which, when put at the service of the whole cosmic community in conscious celebration, fulfills a necessary cosmic function. For Berry, what is central is to affirm that the human is a participatory reality in every aspect of its life.[15] He writes:

> Since the human in its religious capacities emerges out of this cosmological process, then the universe itself can be considered as the primary bearer of the religious experience.[16]

What is revealed by this expansion of horizon is the many ways in which the divine has been operative in the saving, creative movements of cosmic history. Berry's vision alerts the church to the need to incorporate this larger perspective in sacramental experience in a way that honours and centralizes these deep primordial truths. For Berry, liturgy is a privileged moment that could provide a way of "entering into the spiritual dimensions of the universe story."[17] In this larger context, sacramental experience that is expressive of an abbreviated version of cosmic history,

---

Contemporary Sacramental Theology (New York, 1981) 72-75 and "On the Theology of Worship," in *Theological Investigations*, vol. 19 (Baltimore, 1967); Teilhard de Chardin, "The Mass on the World," in *Hymn of the Universe* (London, 1965) 26.
  13. de Chardin and Rahner would be cases in point.
  14. Lonergan and Richards, *Thomas Berry*, 27-38.
  15. *Ibid.*, 25.
  16. *Ibid.*, 30.
  17. *Ibid.*, 37.

having to do almost exclusively with human salvation, seems to be a corruption of the anthropological vocation described by Berry.[18] Widening the horizons of sacramental theology to account for God's salvific activity in cosmic processes is a promising means of overcoming its anthropocentric bias without eliminating some of its important anthropological considerations.

1.2 In Relation to Jesus as Primordial Sacrament

Schillebeeckx original intention in *Christ the Sacrament of the Encounter with God* was to propose an anthropological-Christological foundation for the sacramental, ecclesial lives of Christians.[19] The question has to be asked whether an anthropocentric/Christocentric approach is no longer appropriate given the need to establish the claims of sacramental theology on a functional cosmology. That Jesus is a sacrament, is not under dispute. But, that Jesus is the *primordial* sacrament undermines the priority, both in regards to evolutionary time and to the efficaciousness of God's relationship in the whole of cosmic history. As American theologian Dennis Edwards' ecological construction of the Trinity points out, the inner theological connection between creation and redemption affirms the universe as the "self-expression of the *Trinitarian* God."[20] From this perspective, both the sacramentality of Jesus and the sacramentality of the church are derived from the sacramentality of the cosmos. The cosmos as the *primary* sacrament is proposed in order to make this reality more explicit in sacramental theology and to recover, in contemporary terms, the three-fold ordering of relations: God, the world and humanity.

This movement to contextualize the Christian story within the larger perspective of cosmic history, also addresses the concern of a postmodern

---

18. This anthropological vocation stands in contrast to David Toolan's anthropocentric rendering of the human task as "making the earth a sacrament." See David Toolan, "The Voice of the Hurricane: Cosmology and a Catholic Theology of Nature," in *"And God Saw That It Was Good": Catholic Theology and the Environment*, eds. Drew Christiansen and Walter Glazer (Washington, 1996) 94-99. Here, Toolan uses the scientific data as an apologetic for Catholic sacramental theology. His use of the strong anthropic principle positions humanity as nature's "ultimate black box" in which "nature's meaning – or meaninglessness hinges on us... If nature is to be sacred in our day, it will be by our fiat, by what we make of material things." (98) This position neglects the significance of the wisdom that issues forth from the natural world which always remains our teacher.

19. Schillebeeckx, *Christ the Sacrament of the Encounter with God* (New York, 1963) 3-6.

20. Denis Edwards, *Jesus the Wisdom of God: An Ecological Theology* (New York, 1995) 122.

theology. That is, it addresses the limitations of a theological approach that universalizes the Christian story which absorbs all of history into itself.[21] The cosmos as primary sacrament acknowledges the contingency of the Christian narrative within the framework of the larger narrative of the universe story. At the same time, it recognizes a universal relevance in the particularity of Jesus' life, death and resurrection as another paradigm "in which God's presence and action are felt."[22] It contextualizes the Christian story as one of the many places in which God's presence is revelatory and operative as creative, redeeming love. David Power's proposal for a postmodern appropriation of the Christian narrative he says, lies in relinquishing its overarching structure and contextualizing it within the "midst of events of suffering, hope, and loving triumph that are marked by their contingency."[23] The cosmos as primary sacrament would mark the appreciation of these events in the cosmic processes and envision them as inextricably connected to human history which has itself arisen out of the primordial struggle towards life.

Furthermore, the question of whether Christology has been too much the focus for sacramental theology is a valid one which has been raised by other theologians.[24] The Christological paradigm, characterized by Christ as the primordial sacrament, has done *more* than recover the anthropological basis of the sacramental life; it has also led to an anthropocentric focus in theological reflection and praxis. This narrow locus in sacramental theology has failed to give an account of the numinous wonder of the universe that beckons humanity to ponder the mysteries of life and the Absolute Mystery which is its relational ground.

The cosmos as primary sacrament offers a new opportunity to recover an aesthetic appreciation of the world in which humans move and have their being in a way that can reconnect them to the organic relationship between liturgy and their everyday lives in nature. It also invites a rethinking of the anthropological categories within the larger universe story and the meaning, for Christians, of the paschal mystery within this broader framework. Furthermore, the larger horizon provides a meaningful context for expressing the unity of creation and redemption theology. This will be the next point of discussion.

---

21. Roger Haight, *Jesus: Symbol of God* (New York, 1999) 352.
22. *Ibid.*
23. David N. Power, "Event Eventing," in *A Promise of Presence: Studies in Honor of David N. Power*, ed. Michael Downey and Richard Fragomeni (Washington, 1992) 291. See also Lieven Boeve, "Postmodern Sacramento-Theology: Retelling the Christian Story," in *Ephemerides Theologicae Lovenienses* 74 (1998) 337-343.
24. Theodore Runyon, "The World as the Original Sacrament," in *Worship*, 54 (1980) 495-511; Kevin Irwin, "The Sacramentality of Creation and the Role of Creation in Liturgy," in *"And God Saw That It Was Good,"* 105-146.

3. The Unity of the Creation-Redemption Motif

In light of the postmodern context, in which pluralism, the question of evil and the fragile state of the planet mark an urgency in theology, the concern to restore the unity of the creation-redemption motif is a common theme.[25] The cosmos as the primary sacrament opens up the horizon and sheds light on a Christian theology of God that is based on a metaphysics of relationality.[26] Such a theology discerns that the God, revealed in Jesus, who stands in solidarity with all those who suffer, describes the God whose "promise of resurrection, liberation and life" is already at work in the cosmos.[27] In American theologian, Edward Farley's words: "the empathetic suffering God of redemption is also the Creativity that disposes the world."[28] Farley's aim is to construct a theology of God that is consonant with Christian revelation and the world that humans actually inhabit. He writes:

> If we extrapolate the facticity of redemption to the whole processing world, we conclude that the *aim* of Creativity is something like redemption, the promotion of the reality, freedom and cooperative interrelation of entities ...[Divine] empathy is not simply what motivates the divine activity but is itself what is efficacious.[29]

In other words, the transcendent, mutually enhancing activities found in world processes are seen to be analogous to "the redemption of anxious, idolatrous human agents."[30] Farley interprets the struggle for life and well-being of other living entities as redemptive in their movement toward union and the mutual enhancement of the whole.[31] His judgement about the efficaciousness of God's interaction with natural entities affirms the sacramental principle at a deeper level. It describes a dynamic, relational view in which the cosmos is both active participant and respondent in God's creative, healing life with the world.

In this vein, the cosmos as primary sacrament offers a framework for a coherent theological understanding of how creation and redemption are inextricably linked as well as a new context for the celebration of liturgy.[32] As such, the incarnation of Jesus is relevant, not only with

---

25. See Haight, *Jesus*, 350-354; Anne Clifford, "Foundations for a Catholic Theology of God," in *"And God Saw That It Was Good,"* 20; Lucien Richard, *Christ: The Self-emptying of God* (New York, 1997) 127-128; Edward Farley, *Divine Empathy: A Theology of God* (Minneapolis, 1996) 134.
26. Edwards, *Jesus*, 125.
27. *Ibid.*, 123.
28. Farley, *Divine Empathy*, 301.
29. *Ibid.*
30. *Ibid.*
31. *Ibid.*, 305-307.
32. Berry, "The Cosmology of Religions," [unpublished manuscript], 34.

respect to his *human* nature but because Jesus is a product of the redemptive forces at work already in the cosmos. The human incarnation of Jesus can be interpreted as a concentrated moment of the divine activity that comes not from *on high* but from *within* the cosmic processes. Jesus' positive human response is an explicit cosmic response that advances the cosmic movement towards God's inclusive and redemptive love.

This perspective does not exclude the particularity of God's Word addressed in Jesus to human freedom. It is clear that the history of human freedom has directed itself against the forces of life in ways that the natural world has not. In terms of the reality in the world of both personal and collective sin, this misdirection of human freedom elicits a culpability in humanity that is not there for the rest of nature. As such, the Word addressed to humanity, in Christ, calls for a qualitatively different response. Nevertheless, the continuity that exists between world processes and the way God acts in and through Jesus Christ needs to be held to strict account.[33] Pertinent to this discussion is the movement in theology to recover an understanding of the Trinity which rescues it from a highly abstract theological approach and makes explicit links with how Christians understand God's presence in the world.[34] Denis Edwards' proposal for a Trinitarian approach to the doctrine of creation honours the intrinsic link between creation and redemption. A cosmological perspective provides a comprehensive context that supports such a retrieval.[35] In concert with these attempts and in recognition of the need to translate these concerns for sacramental theology, this contribution proposes the cosmos as primary sacrament to be an appropriate overarching metaphor for the construction of an ecological sacramental theology.

Elliot Allen Institute Dorothy MCDOUGALL
for Ecology and Theology
University of St. Michael's College
Toronto, Canada

---

33. Haight, *Jesus*, 357. Here, Haight concedes that any view of salvation in contemporary theology has to account for a contemporary scientific understanding of humanity within "the larger picture of reality of God's created cosmos" and the "negative impact human development is having on our life-support system."

34. Catherine Mowry Lacugna, *God For Us: The Trinity and Christian Life* (San Francisco, 1991) 2.

35. *Ibid.*, 115. See also, Leonardo Boff, *Cry of the Earth, Cry of the Poor* (New York, 1997) 154; Sallie McFague, *The Body of God: An Ecological Theology* (Minneapolis, 1993) 161; Yvone Gebara, "The Trinity and Human Experience: An Ecofeminist Approach," in *Women Healing Earth: Third World Women on Ecology, Feminism and Religion*, ed. Rosemary Radford Ruether (New York, 1996) 23.

Appendix A

There are thirteen principles which Berry gleans from the prevailing themes of postmodern science. He presents these as attributes of a functional cosmology – one that can reorient cultural commitments towards a reverence for the earth and its processes.

1. The Universe is the only text without a context. It is the great epic, the story from which all other stories depend and emerge.
2. The universe is the only self-referent mode of being in the phenomenal order. All other beings are universe referred.
3. We live in an emergent, time-developmental universe; an unfolding irreversible sequence of transformations, an evolving, integral, creative reality – a cosmogenesis.
4. The universe is the fundamental revelatory experience.
5. Everything in the universe is genetically related.
6. The three basic tendencies of the universe are differentiation, subjectivity and communion.
7. The universe is a community of subjects, not a collection of objects.
8. The primary intention of life is neither one of peace nor conflict, but creativity.
9. The earth is a one-time endowment.
10. The earth is primary, the human is derivative.
11. Humanity is a celebratory species. The universe reflects upon itself through the human. We cannot discover ourselves without first discovering the universe. Humans are a dimension of the earth and the universe.
12. The community of creatures on earth is of greater value than any particular part.
13. The earth is a single reality and cannot be saved in fragments.

BAPTISM: NEW THINKING FROM WOMEN-IDENTIFIED PERSPECTIVES

Most Christians, it is safe to say, cannot remember their own baptism. They may have looked at photographs, or heard the account from their parents or godparents, or may even have seen a video if they are still quite young. Most Christians therefore have no personal experiential point of reference for the actual sacramental event of their own baptism. For most, baptism happens to babies or, in the case of adult catechumens, to other people. Their lived personal experience remains second-hand, at a distance, limited to participation as parents or sponsors, or perhaps as the minister of the sacrament, or as the community gathered round as spectators. Yet baptism secures the person's identity as a Christian. Baptism is classically the first of the sacraments, not only chronologically in the order of administration but as the foundation of all other sacraments. Baptism is moreover the "matrix of all ministry"[1] and the basis and orientation-point for Christian identities and dignity, whether personal or collective.

For this reason a host of intriguing and often somewhat disorienting new questions raised from women-identified perspectives can be brought to bear on the theology and liturgical infrastructure of baptism, particularly as administered in its most distinctive liturgical setting at the Easter Vigil. Here the sacrament crowns an extended catechumenal process of discernment, spiritual growth, catechesis and insertion into a living faith community. To begin, however, we need to define what we mean by some basic terms – like women-identified, and indeed, baptism.

We will use the expression 'woman-identified' as a parallel and perhaps more precise and open term than 'feminism,' although the two are very close. Feminist theory is one form of postmodern thought which aims at an analysis of the structure and impact of gender relations, both descriptive and prescriptive. Feminist analysis systematically deconstructs naive assumptions about the nature of reality, specifically "how to understand and (re-)constitute the self, gender, knowledge, social relations and culture without resorting to linear, teleological, hierarchical

---

1. Gerard Austin, "Baptism as the Matrix of Ministry," in *Louvain Studies* 23 (Summer 1998) 101.

... or binary ways of thinking and being.² Feminist theorists participate in postmodernist thought by confronting static concepts of reason, knowledge and the atomized, individualized self which perpetuate deceptive notions of universality and objectivity which in turn favor androcentrism, the myth that what is gendered 'male' is normative and determinative for all persons. There are, of course, simpler definitions of feminism, such as "the belief that women are full human persons."

One problem from the outset has been that feminism also can take up a universalizing stance of its own, uncritically enshrining the social position, problems and priorities of Euro-american white middle-class women as a norm. This led to the emergence of (among others) womanist theory and theology which arises from lived experience and history rooted in the lives of African-American women, as well as *mujerista* theology among American Hispanic women of varying national origins. We will use more often the term 'woman-identified' to refer to concepts which arise from women's original efforts to think outside of dominative paradigms which exclude and demean women, in the understanding that in every case we are speaking out of multiple modalities of racial, cultural, economic and historically-shaped lived experience. Lived experience, after all, forms a primary *locus theologicus* for woman-identified theological reflections. Leaving intact a purportedly universalizing 'feminist theory'would simply result in another hegemony, this time of white middle-class Western women.

Ironically, this process of perceiving and testifying to one's own lived experience presumes a certain awareness that oneself is a subject – and not an object. One of the driving questions addressed at the 1993 conference of the European Society of Women in Theological Research which took place in Leuven had to do with the curious paradox that the dethroning of the sovereign subject has come about just at the historical moment in which sizeable groups of the globally marginalized and disenfranchised have barely begun to see themselves as the subject of their own lives, thoughts and perceptions, and have begun to acknowledge and identify with their own ideas. For women this means a systematic effort to move beyond the cognitive hegemony of androcentric categories and presuppositions.³ The background specific to some of the new issues in baptism arises precisely from an upsurge in the active

---

2. Jane Flax, "Postmodernism and Gender Relations in Feminist Theory," in *Revising the Word and the World: Essays in Feminist Literary Criticism*, ed. Vèvè Clark, Ruth-Ellen Joeres and Madelon Sprengnether (Chicago: University of Chicago Press, 1993) 67-89, 68.
3. Kristin De Troyer and Susan K. Roll, "Voicing Identity: Women and Religious Traditions in Europe," in *Bulletin of the European Society of Women in Theological Research* 6 (December 1992) 2-5.

liturgical subjectivity of women: groups of women acting as agents doing liturgy on their own terms, no longer merely objects of what in Flemish is called "liturgical pastoral care" by the clergy. One needs a secure grasp of one's own identity and where one's best interests lie, in order to ask the touchstone question proposed by feminist liturgist Marjorie Procter-Smith for all aspects of ritual and worship, "Is it true *for us*?"[4]

Does this mean to suggest that women as a gender / power minority are, in a sense, betrayed by postmodernism, to the extent that the now-dethroned subject is not sufficiently identified in its character as an androcentric, privileged entity, as distinct from the subject as a full human person of whatever race, class or gender within an interrelated network of relations? Why should the concept of the subject self-destruct when extended to large categories of heretofore marginalized persons, unless the subject were ultimately defined, explicitly or not, with reference to a non-subject category of persons which served as its negative identity? Perhaps just as pernicious in the long run, however, would be to dethrone the atomized individual subject by shifting the emphasis to the group. The strengthened role of the worshipping assembly, the community, forms one of the recognizeable strands in contemporary thinking about the sacraments in general; yet in uncritically focusing on the community, however defined, one might fail to question to what extent unjust, even exploitative hegemonies might be left intact and unquestioned due to the unthinking use of 'unitary' language and thought in liturgy.[5] Are unjust dominative structures or self-interested ideologies shaping the ritual event in question, disguised in universalizing language?

Another form of betrayal of women would result from failing to confront the definition of diametrically-opposed, mutually-exclusive absolute dualisms, such as the distinctions between sacred and profane, transcendent and immanent, body and spirit. This line of questioning could upset much of traditional sacramental language as well as classical theological presuppositions. A defined dualism never results in an evensided value-free split: the model 'tips' because of the inherent valuational duality. Dualisms have never been particularly friendly to women, nor indeed to any groups of persons identified on the downside

---

4. Marjorie Procter-Smith, *In Her Own Rite: Constructing Feminist Liturgical Tradition* (Nashville: Abingdon, 1990) 13.

5. Marjorie Procter-Smith, *Praying With Our Eyes Open: Engendering Feminist Liturgical Prayer* (Nashville: Abingdon, 1995) 26-27 and 30-31, defines unitary language as "authorized speaking, controlled prayer, one model of God and one model of address to that God" directed toward the maintenance of androcentrism and a patriarchal image of God. For a sketch of the potentially ambivalent results of feminism's "removal of the language of normativity" in opposing injustice, see Susan Frank Parsons, *Feminism and Christian Ethics* (Cambridge: Cambridge University Press, 1996) 188-197.

of the dominant culture, whether ethnic, social or economic minorities, other gender minorities, or those whose bodily or mental capabilities fall outside the mean. When the norm is defined from the perspective of androcentric hegemony, all traits and concepts which are assigned to females in a male/female dualistic split cannot help but end up effectively on the downside of the paradigm. This could apply as well to what we might call 'sequential dualism,' the idea of making a transition in a rite of passage from one state to another, presumably from a lower or lesser state to a more desirable or 'higher' state.

Newer thinking by Roman Catholic women theologians on 'sacrament' moves in several directions consistent with the above mentioned general trends. They broaden the concept of sacramentality itself considerably beyond the defined seven sacraments, and beyond the concepts of the church as *Grundsakrament,* a mystery,[6] and the theological position that Jesus in his human nature is the *Ursakrament,* articulated in the 1960s and 70s by Karl Rahner and Edward Schillebeeckx among others. Groups of women who come together as subjects to do liturgy for themselves often do not find their own persons, their female bodies, or the concrete realities of their daily lives reflected in the defined sacraments, and consequently seek a more authentic yet often diffuse sense of sacramentality as the living presence of God in a multitude of other mediators: a "'hidden' or 'implicit' sacramentality" according to Susan A. Ross.[7] Not merely 'complementary' to existing sacramental rites, new women's celebrations experiment with new ways not only to symbolize but to embody the living God,[8] as well as to articulate a vital relationship between liturgy and the making of social justice.

The administration of baptism at the Easter Vigil, in the explicit liturgical context of the dying and rising of Christ, follows a process of discernment, catechesis and spiritual growth, all taking place visibly among a living and supportive worshipping community, and presuming a

---

6. *Lumen Gentium* in the title of Chapter I, "The Mystery of the Church," and paragraphs 5, 39, 44, 63.

7. Susan A. Ross, *Extravagant Affections: A Feminist Sacramental Theology* (New York: Continuum, 1998) 23.

8. David N. Power, "Sacramental Theology: A Review of Literature," in *Theological Studies* 55 (1994) 657-705, especially 693-702 on Feminist Theology, with particular reference to Julia Kristeva on the semiotic and the symbolic. A wealth of material exists on new women's liturgies: see the two bibliographies by Teresa Berger in *Studia Liturgica* 19 (1989) 96-110, and 25 (1995) 103-117, as well as the bibliography of women authors in the field of liturgy in *Liturgy Digest* 1/2, 1994, 106-185. For an examination of symbols, including water, as used in some of these new liturgies see Susan Roll, "Traditional Elements in New Women's Liturgies," in *Questions Liturgiques* 72 (1991) 43-59.

relatively high degree of mutuality and cooperation. The promulgation of the *Rite for the Christian Initiation of Adults* effectively transformed how each of the sacraments may be conceptualized and provides a ritual context for women theologians to reexamine the lived sacramental experience with new eyes.[9] Infant baptism still represents the statistical majority of baptisms, but the RCIA draws on deep roots in the early history of the church's initiatory practice, as well as on a renewed baptismal theology of the post-Vatican II era which locates baptism at the foundation of the dignity of the people of God as a worshipping assembly, as well as the dignity of each baptized member of the Body of Christ. For these reasons we need to begin from the RCIA as normative Christian initatory model. Looking ahead to the future, this makes a good deal of sense in secularized and commercialized North Atlantic societies. It is not impossible to foresee that many persons who consider becoming members of the church will do so voluntarily as adults, and will need to come through a protracted and carefully guided process not only of instruction but of discernment, spiritual growth and integration. The early experiments with a proto-RCIA process in secularized postwar France point in this direction. In this case one could not presume much, if any, fluency in Christian culture, nor a foundation even of common ethical values and verbal concepts with which to communicate and understand religious ideas.

Five Issues Regarding Baptism

With these points in mind, we can identify five current areas of theological and pastoral ferment in which woman-identified theologizing is redefining or recasting some of the traditional theological and ritual underpinnings of the sacrament of baptism:

1. Baptism as "dying and rising with Christ" (Rom 6,3-4)[10] takes on a new coloration in view of emerging theological perspectives on the concept of embodiment and death. The *Rite of the Christian Initiation of*

---

9. Kathleen Hughes, *Saying Amen. A Mystagogy of Sacrament* (Chicago: Liturgy Training Publications, 1999) 33. See also Julia Upton, *A Church for the Next Generation: Sacraments in Transition* (Collegeville: Liturgical Press, 1990).

10. The metaphorical use of 'baptism' to mean death as in the death of Jesus can be found also in Mk 10,38-39 and Lk 12,50. While in Romans 6,1-14 Paul identifies baptism as a participation in the death of Christ, he does not speak of a resurrection already accomplished at the moment of baptism, but rather a future expectation of 'newness of life.' See Adela Yarbro Collins, "The Origin of Christian Baptism," in *Living Water, Sealing Spirit: Readings on Christian Initiation*, ed. Maxwell E. Johnson (Collegeville: Liturgical Press/Pueblo, 1995) 35-57 esp. 54-56; and Valerie A. Abrahamsen, *Women and Worship at Philippi* (Portland ME: Astarte Shell Press, 1995) 132.

Adults, at the lowering of the Paschal candle into the water at the Easter Vigil, employs the invocation, "We ask you, Father, with your Son to send the Holy Spirit upon the waters of this font. May all who are buried with Christ in the death of baptism rise also with him to newness of life".[11] The *Catechism of the Catholic Church* says, "... the 'plunge' into the water symbolizes the catechumen's burial into Christ's death, from which he [/she] rises up by resurrection with him, as a 'new creature'."[12] In the *Order of Christian Funerals* the coffin of the deceased is sprinkled with holy water accompanied by the words, "In the waters of baptism N. died with Christ and rose with him to new life. May he/she now share with him eternal glory".[13]

When a candidate for initiation steps into an immersion pool to be baptized at the Easter Vigil, that action of "dying and rising with Christ" shifts from a mere metaphor to a physical passage into and through a body of water, signalling a shift in the person's spiritual state and often her or his personal self-concept. The triumphal imagery attached to the resurrection of Christ in the Vigil liturgy reinforces the idea of victory over death as an enemy: "Christ has conquered! Glory fills you! Darkness vanishes forever"[14]. If baptism represents a self-identification with the death of Christ which took place by crucifixion, the inherent vulnerability, victimization and martyrdom of such a violent death contrasts sharply with death by drowning, a form of disintegration and dissolving[15].

Yet in contemporary woman-identified thinking, death is not a fearsome enemy to be forcibly crushed but rather a natural phase in the developmental process and the cycle of life. This in turn is linked directly to a new valuation of the inherent goodness of the human body, even given the fragility, tenuous health and strength, and eventual degeneration of the body. This contrasts strikingly with the paradigm of the female body as the 'Other' against which purity, cleanliness, rationality, control and holiness have been defined in androcentric thinking as polar opposites.[16] From a traditional gender perspective, the

---

11. *The Roman Ritual. The Rites of the Catholic Church vol. IA* (New York: Pueblo, 1988) 152 (paragraph 222).

12. Paragraph 1214, with reference to II Cor 5,17 and Gal 6, 15 as well as Rom 6,3-4 and Col 2,12.

13. Paragraph 185.

14. The Exultet.

15. Lucy Bregman, "Baptism as Death and Birth: a Psychological Interpretation of its Imagery," in *Journal of Ritual Studies* 1/2 (Summer 1987) 27-41, esp. 34-36.

16. Susan A. Ross, *'Then Honor God in Your Body' (I Cor 6,20) Feminist and Sacramental Theology on the Body*, in *Horizons on Catholic Feminist Theology*, ed. Joann Wolski Conn and Walter E. Conn (Washington DC: Georgetown University Press, 1992) 109-132.

female body has served as the image of the corruptibility and mortality of the body, that which must be conquered in order to secure eternal life. Theologians such as Maaike De Haardt have studied the body in theological discourse and found clear gender indicators relating to death:

> ... in Western culture, women's bodies represent the most dreaded of human characteristics – death, finitude and transience. Wasn't it Eve who brought sin and therefore death to the world? It is also gender specific in that feminist theologies continually stress the necessity of accepting finitude and mortality. Therefore, feminist theology argues that death is a 'natural' part of life. ... feminists regard the theological acceptance of finitude and death as a prerequisite not only for a life- and body-affirming theology, but a theology which tries to transform all kinds of hierarchical dualistic thinking as well. This gender specificity and dualistic thinking forms the root of the oppression, victimisation and death of so many bodies, according to the analysis of, among others, Carol Christ and Rosemary Radford Ruether.[17]

The type of dualistic thinking commonly found in pious literature would posit that death serves merely as a passageway to a 'better,' non-embodied, non-mortal, spiritual life, or at the least an eternal life in a glorified body (I Cor 15,42-46). This could be an (ultimately unsatisfactory) way of hedging our teachings: the Easter Vigil liturgy in particular in its often militaristic imagery presents resurrection as Christ's definitive triumph over death, yet human beings to this day can look forward to dying (so to speak) at the end of their lifespan. We do not in fact live on forever in this flesh, in spite of Christ's resurrection. Is the fear and hatred of death as the enemy reflective of a primarily androcentric focus on the singular individual's eternal survival in some recognizeable form? We can raise the question because up to now a preoccupation with personal survival after death with its loss of rational autonomy has not been characteristic of new woman-identified thinking on liturgy and sacrament. More likely women-identified believers will seek signs of the persistence of new life and hope in the cycle of the generations, in the affirmation of our profound connectedness, whether organic, spiritual or somewhere along the spectrum in between, with the ages and generations of those who have preceded us as well as the generations yet to come.[18] Can the ritualization and idealization of a passage from dying to rising provide a way to embrace our shadow side as a healing and healthy movement of the spirit and the emotions? Can

---

17. Maaike De Haardt, "Transience, Finitude and Identity: Reflecting the Body Dying," in *Begin With the Body. Corporeality, Religion and Gender*, ed. Jonneke Bekkenkamp and Maaike De Haardt (Leuven: Peeters, 1998) 13-14.

18. For an example of this thinking, see Carol Lee Flinders, *At the Root of This Longing* (San Francisco: Harper) 1998, 149.

women-identified theologizing find a less polarized, less aggressive metaphor to affirm life and healing? The work is already in progress.

2. The second primordial layer of meaning connected to baptism, in tandem with dying and rising with Christ, is that of (re-)birth to new life. Jn 3,1-10 recounts a dialogue between Jesus and Nicodemus which expresses the early church's understanding of baptism and gives gospel approbation to baptism as rebirth 'of water and the Spirit': 'What is born of the flesh is flesh, what is born of the Spirit is spirit.'[19] The theme appears repeatedly in the Easter Vigil initiation rites of the RCIA, coupled with the theme of dying and/or rising:

> By the power of the Holy Spirit
> give to this water the grace of your Son,
> so that in the sacrament of baptism
> all those whom you have created in your likeness
> may be cleansed from sin
> and rise to a new birth of innocence
> by water and the Holy Spirit. ...
> By the mystery of this consecrated water
> lead them to a new and spiritual birth.[20]

Only women give birth, not all women of course, but those who become mothers. Just as the waters break shortly before birth, and the child emerges from water into a new form of life, to be received and given a name, the baptisand emerges from baptism in an immersion pool (where this is available and customary) to a 'new life' in Christ. Yet the normative minister of baptism is a priest or deacon: rarely, and in practice only by way of exception in emergency situations or very understaffed localities would a woman, perhaps a nurse, hospital chaplain, or catechist, baptize. Some women theologians employ extensive anthropological data to highlight what is probably obvious: that some very foundational caretaking acts reserved to women – giving birth, serving meals, tending the sick – pass largely or entirely into the hands of male clerics as the human basis for sacramental ritual.[21]

Does the 'rebirth' of baptism imply a subsequent higher or better form of birth, a spiritual as opposed to merely bodily birth to supercede the

---

19. Jn 3,5, New Revised Standard Version.
20. "Prayer over the water," paragraph 222.
21. Christine E. Gudorf, "The Power to Create: Sacraments and Men's Need to Birth," in *Horizons* 14 (1987) 296-309. Gudorf states, "The cross-cultural perspective strongly suggests that the exclusion of women from sacred rituals is based in [sic] a fear of their power over life, and that this power over life is so central that men ritually claim it for themselves, simultaneously depriving women of it, at least within the sacred space and time," 301.

natural birth given by women, with all its pain, bleeding, danger of death, drama, and strong, highly ambivalent emotions? This could also be dualistic in nature and more clearly gender-inscribed. And if so, this profound and sustained meaning of the sacrament of baptism is obtained at the expense of women as a gender-category: women become the Other, the representative of the inferior former state out of which the baptizand passes into a nobler spiritual life mediated by male clerics.

Compare the overall ritual shape of baptism with the ritual action of the old rite of churching after childbirth, the former a sacrament, the latter a sacramental. In the rite of churching the new mother kneels usually at the church entrance with a candle, then after sprinkling with holy water and reciting a psalm the priest brings her into church for the first time since she has given birth, extending the left-side end of his priestly stole for her to grasp and literally leading her into church for a blessing. The ritual action mirrors the physical act of birth – the priest has induced a symbolic physical passage from a state of exclusion or uncleanness to one of inclusion and purity.[22] Up to the mid-twentieth century the mother was in all probability not present at the baptism of her child; some forty days following the baptism the mother is in turn, in this manner, 'reborn' in the church. Coupled with thinly veiled textual references to cleaning from impurity such as the use of Psalm 24,[23] the implication is that the woman is herself ritually retrieved from a state of marginality; at the hands of the priest – a 'clean' rebirth from the 'contamination' of the bloodshed of childbirth, a spiritual rebirth which restores her to access to the church building and to participation in the worshipping community.[24]

---

22. Grietje Dresen, "Het betere bloed. Heilige mannen en het bloed van vrouwen," in *MARA* 6 (1992/93) 28-40, 31, makes the point that when the new mother is led into the church as if on a lead or leash, the priest's stole functions ritually like an umbilical cord.

23. The pertinent verses are Ps 24, 3-4: "Who shall ascend the hill of the Lord? And who shall stand in his holy place? Those who have clean hands and pure hearts, who do not lift up their souls to what is false, and do not swear deceitfully." Some commentators claimed that verses 7-10 would create a parallel with the joyful entrance of God as the King of glory, however that interpretation is not supported by the ritual subtext. See Susan Roll, "The Churching of Women After Childbirth: an Old Rite Raising New Questions," in *Questions Liturgiques* 76 (1995) 206-229, 218.

24. Women in ancient times who had recently given birth were to sit with the catechumens as if their baptism had been temporarily negated, much like those in the order of penitents) See Roll, "Churching of Women", 210-211 and 219, and Susan K. Roll, "The Old Rite of the Churching of Women After Childbirth," in *Blood, Purity and Impurity: A feminist critique*, ed. Kristin De Troyer and Anne-Marie Korte (Edinburgh: Peter Lang, forthcoming). Interestingly, although the rite itself was in Latin, and in spite of theological explanations since the Enlightenment which generally stressed that it expressed the woman's own thanksgiving after a safe delivery, women themselves began to refuse the rite beginning in the 1940s, and by 1965 the rite had died out: see Roll, "Churching of Women", 220-226. The blessing of a new mother incorporated into the

3. The (rediscovered) process model of metanoia as the precursor to adult baptism in the RCIA is more congenial to many women's thinking than the more dramatic all-or-nothing conversion exemplified by Paul on the road to Damascus (Acts 9), or that of John Newton (+1807), the author of *Amazing Grace*.[25] Among women-identified liturgical theologians, Marjorie Procter-Smith finds the "sometimes lengthy and preferably rich and complex process of preparation, education, decision-making, 'conversion therapy', ritual participation and spiritual formation" of the ancient Christian initiatory process a promising model for a "feminist reclamation of baptism".[26] Some specific features of the process which offer particular potential for affirming women's lived realities and promoting a healthy gender/power balance include a component of women's history in the church within the instructional phase of the catechumenate, empowerment training through active involvement in social justice projects, the use of stories of women in Scripture as part of liturgies of the word, the adaptation of exorcisms to name structural evils such as racism, sexism and classism, and anointing as a way to give value to the body in the face of the degradation of women's bodies in popular culture and pornography as well as "the church's historical fear of women's bodies".[27]

Rosemary Radford Ruether stresses the social justice dimension of conversion inherent in the conscious choice which precedes adult baptism:

> Conversion is breaking free of the alienating and oppressive socialization that has distorted our consciousness into accepting the normalcy of victimization. Conversion is a leap to a new consciousness that renounces the ideologies that sought to justify these [patriarchal] systems of oppression and seeks an alternative world where truth and good relationships prevail.[28]

Kathleen Hughes concretizes the process of conversion, internal and external, in contemporary terms as a basis for her 'mystagogical' method of understanding the sacraments.[29]

Further questions are being raised based on anthropological research on women's initiation rites, more often than not undervalued or misinterpreted in the scholarly literature due to underlying assumptions

---

1972 Rite of Baptism was partially intended to replace it: "May he bless the mother of this child. She now thanks God for the gift of her child. ..."

25. "I once was lost but now I'm found, Was blind but now I see."
26. *In Her Own Rite*, 153.
27. *Ibid.*, 154-156.
28. Ruether, *Women-Church. Theology and Practice* (New York: Harper and Row, 1985) 126-127.
29. *Saying Amen*, 37-41.

concerning gender differences. Catherine Vincie surveyed research data on women's initiation rites for the Christian Initiation seminar of the North American Academy of Liturgy with an eye to its application to theological evaluation of the RCIA. She suggests that the term 'rites of passage,' while useful, may apply more to men's rites of initiation than women's; some women's rites can be better described as rites of confirmation and intensification. Men's initiation rituals more often involve spatial separation, nakedness, solidarity and peer bonding, a reduction in status followed by an increase in status, and often an emphasis on a sharp break with the past. Women's initiation on the other hand often involved spatial stability, different forms of temporary isolation from the community, clothing rather than nakedness, intergenerational bonding (between an older wise woman and a very young woman) rather than peer bonding, associating with women's activities, and continuity with the past. Ritual symbols or experiences may be interpreted quite differently by women than by men. Initiation rituals may either reinforce unequal social relationships between men and women, or serve to contradict and protest traditional values.[30]

A more theoretical issue is that of the ambiguity of directionality, or perhaps multi-directionality, inherent in initiation processes. We have already mentioned the question whether the classic model of conversion as a sudden total about-face is more typically gendered male. This does not mean that women as such never experience a sudden complete shift in their self-understanding and religious commitment. Women themselves may testify to the occurrence of both kinds of conversion in their own life histories: gradual or sudden, linear or polymorphous, a closed loop or a spiral, a journey which may end up at its anticipated destination, or someplace entirely different. A further question has to do with the directionality of the nature of affiliation with the community into which one is becoming initiated: if Christian initiation were to convey the impression that one has joined a closed fellowship or a secret society, it would be difficult to reconcile this with the idea that the Gospel impels believers toward mission, of which baptism marks the commissioning. In that sense, the Christian community is better compared to a circle in which participants join hands and face outward, not inward-looking only at themselves, a circle which incidentally is the most common spatial configuration in new women's liturgies.

---

30. Catherine Vincie, *Rethinking Initiation Rituals: Do Women and Men Do It the Same Way?* in *Proceedings of the North American Academy of Liturgy*, 1995, 145-170, esp. 166-167. See also Elisabeth Schüssler-Fiorenza, "Feminist Spirituality, Christian Identity, and Catholic Vision," in *Womanspirit Rising: A Feminist Reader in Religion*, ed. Carol P. Christ and Judith Plaskow (San Francisco: Harper and Row, 1979) 143-145.

4. If baptism is truly "the gateway to the sacraments... [by which] men and women are freed from sin, are reborn as children of God, and, configured to Christ by an indelible character, are incorporated into the Church,"[31] what are the ethical implications of initiating persons into a faith community in which some will face arbitrary role-definitions and restrictions based upon gender? There are in fact seven sacraments possible for men, but six for women.

Ironically, in the early church many women were attracted to a large extent because baptism promised women radical, prophetic equality in the face of the oncoming eschaton. The early church "did not practice gender-specific or gender-exclusive initiation," signaled in Gal 3,28, 'no longer male and female, for all of you are one in Christ Jesus'.[32] In the *Acts of Thecla* we can read a story of a woman converted to Christianity by the preaching of Paul, a woman passionately committed to mission who, when Paul refused to baptize her, baptized herself in a pool of water in the arena while facing martyrdom.[33]

How would responsible, honest prebaptismal catechesis for prospective Christians deal with the inherent ambivalence in Christian tradition and formal doctrine toward women's equal human dignity and human rights? How would credible catechesis reconcile the split between, for example, visionary statements such as Gal 3,28 and the essentialist perspective on women and men's nature embodied in, among other sources, *Mulieris Dignitatem* of John Paul II which identifies women's very being with specific sexual functions such as mother or virgin?[34]

Does this in effect amount to a two-track baptism – that some people are 'more baptized than others,' or that baptism does something different for female persons than it does for male persons, or that the 'gateway to the sacraments' which is baptism forms a more narrow passageway for females than for males? Perhaps, according to this argumentation, baptism admits of degrees – that females cannot be baptized 'enough' to become full human persons of absolute value and dignity since their identity as Christians is permanently relativized by their physical sexual

---

31. *Code of Canon Law* (1983) canon 849.
32. Teresa Berger, *Women's Ways of Worship: Gender Analysis and Liturgical History* (Collegeville: Liturgical Press, 1999) 32. Ruether, *Women and Redemption: A Theological History* (London: SCM Press, 1998) 32-33, points out that against a Hellenistic Jewish background the underlying theology had to do with the female 'becoming (spiritually) male' by renouncing all manifestations of her female sexuality, whether biological or cultural.
33. See Sheila E. McGinn, "The Acts of Thecla," in *Searching the Scriptures: A Feminist Commentary*, ed. Elisabeth Schüssler-Fiorenza (New York, Crossroad, 1994) 800-828 esp. 816-818.
34. *On the Dignity and Vocation of Women (Mulieris Dignitatem)*, Apostolic letter, 15 August 1988, esp. Paragraph 17.

status. On one level, the questions are absurd, yes, but in a literal sense perfectly logical.

5. Finally, new thinking emerging from ecofeminist theology promises at least to heighten awareness of the wider ethical consequences of the symbolic use of water as signifying cleansing and purification. An indicator of the primordial meaning of water is expressed in I Cor 10,2 "...our ancestors...all passed through the sea, and all were baptized into Moses in the cloud and in the sea ..." The directions for baptism in the *Didache* stress that the water should be cold and running; only by way of concession to circumstances could it be warm, or still, or poured on the head of the baptisand.[35] The contemporary rite of baptism for adults at the Easter Vigil elaborates on the primordial significance of water in salvation history, and repeatedly refers to its cleansing capacity: "... make holy this water which you have created, so that all who are baptized in it may be washed clean of sin and be born again to live as your children".[36]

In an earlier, less complex and less intensely interrelated world, it may have been easier to assume that using enough water would mechanically wash away any unwanted impurities and make them disappear permanently. Today, however, we know that impurities may simply be carried downstream to kill aquatic wildlife, or may contaminate the soil, or may have a very long radioactive half-life. We know that the world's supply of fresh potable water has diminished to the point that regions with large bodies of fresh water are under pressure to sell the water to arid, drought-stricken or polluted parts of the world. The ritual use of water as inherently cleansing and purifying may be presuming northern/western expectations of an infinite supply of clean water (which in fact is not really infinite), and which will continue to wash away all human-made contaminants, so the contaminating can go on with impunity. If in this case nature is merely an instrument serving human needs and desires, an argument could be made that this ritual use of water unthinkingly perpetuates a domination paradigm in which humanity freely exploits nature with impunity, and humans similarly make use of other classes of human beings to serve their needs. This domination model is exemplified in the classic question, is female to male as nature is to culture? If so, women and water / nature are here identified as the servant-element which exists only relative to, and for the sake of, the dominant entity.

L. Teal Willoughby points out several instances in which the use of water in new women's liturgies inadvertently employs this domination

---

35. James A. Kleist (transl.), *The Didache*, Ancient Christian Writers, 6 (New York: Paulist Press, 1948) paragraph 7.
36. RCIA paragraph 222.

model in assuming that nature will always 'clean up' after humanity.[37] Valerie Abrahamsen, on the other hand, finds in the ancient pre-Christian use of water a powerful healing and nurturing element whose significance persisted into the Christian era,[38] which might provide a basis for a revaluation of the human relationship to water. With the greatest respect for the significance of the cleansing properties of water to our ancestors in faith, and its symbolic significance deep in our own psyche, there may be a call here to greater ethical awareness of the consequences of human use of the elements of earth.

Conclusion[39]

So in keeping with the overall theme of this project, just what is 'sacramental presence' in baptism from the perspective of gender justice? The first question to pose is 'the presence of what, or whom?' And more trenchantly, 'who decides?' The presence of wisdom, of hope, of life-giving spirit, or perhaps the presence of the ages and generations of ancestors in faith whom we name the communion of saints. Perhaps a promise of hope for transformation, whether personal, familial, cultural, or national, which would embody resurrection as a paradigm for a hope-beyond-hope for a future of justice. This presence would not be one of a domineering, potentially threatening God which could be used diabolically to justify the domination of a few human persons over other humans, nor the exploitation of the common environment. Initiation would instead take place into a faith community – open, welcoming, outer-directed, passionately committed to prophetic witness and justice-making – marked by the sacramental presence of wisdom, hope and embodied transformation, a presence which engenders a dynamic and positive future.

Christ the King Seminary Susan K. ROLL
711 Knox Road, P.O. Box 607
East Aurora, New York 14052
USA

---

37. "Ecofeminist Consciousness and the Transforming Power of Symbols," in *Ecofeminism and the Sacred*, ed. Carol J. Adams (New York: Continuum, 1994) 133-148 esp. 134-135.

38. *Women and Worship at Philippi*, 134 and 138-140.

39. Some of the perhaps obvious stumbling blocks for a woman-identified analysis of baptism such as the masculine configuration in the Trinitarian formula (Father, Son, Holy Spirit where the last of these is named with a male pronoun), or androcentric assumptions embedded in texts and use of symbols in the Easter Vigil, have not been addressed here in order to concentrate on theological issues which lie somewhat deeper below the surface.

GOD'S CLOTHING
THE LIMITS OF POSTMODERNITY AND LIVING WATERS: GOD AS SOURCE, (DIS)SOLUTION, AND DELIGHT

One must obtain forgiveness for every essay in theology.[1]
Jean-Luc Marion

Although richly utilized in practice, waters – along with other common places of life such as light, earth, and trees – have largely been absent from Christian theological reflection.[2] This absence contrasts with the biblical record, with the extra-ecclesial experience of postmodern people, and with the contemporary ecological need for mindful practice in regard the environment.[3] Building on a central insight of Luther, namely that humans do not have access to a "naked God,"[4] this essay will critically apply selected aspects of the work of Sallie McFague and David Tracy to outline a postmodern theology that shifts the chronocentric paradigm of Christianity in the direction of what geographer Yi-Fu Tuan has called "topophilia" – the love of places.[5]

---

1. J-L. Marion, *God without Being*, trans. Thomas A. Carlson, foreword by David Tracy (Chicago: The University of Chicago Press, 1995) 2. It is especially the case that a *historian of religions*, like I am, must obtain forgiveness for aspiring to write an essay in theology as such. While I transgress disciplinary boundaries herein, I write as an amateur, a lay theologian, who is working on a book entitled *God's Clothing: A Theology of Places*, which combines cultural critique, biblical and historical theology, and autobiography in a constructive theology of places of water, light, earth, trees, and bodies.

2. P. McKenzie, *The Christians: Their Beliefs and Practices* (Nashville: Abingdon, 1988). Mountains have recently received some attention. See, for example, B. Lane, *The Solace of Fierce Landscapes: Desert and Mountain Spirituality* (New York: Oxford University Press, 1998) and J. D. Levenson, *Sinai and Zion: An Entry into the Jewish Bible* (Minneapolis: Winston Press, 1985).

3. A. Gore, *Earth in the Balance: Ecology and the Human Spirit* (New York: Houghton-Mifflin, 1992).

4. M. Luther, *Luther's Works, Volume 26: Lectures on Galatians, 1535, Chapters 1-4*, ed. J. Pelikan (St. Louis: Concordia Publishing House, 1963) 95. See also P. S. Watson, *Let God Be God!: An Interpretation of the Theology of Martin Luther* (Philadelphia: Muhlenberg Press, 1948) 76 and P. Althaus, *The Theology of Martin Luther*, trans. Robert C. Schulz (Philadelphia: Fortress Press, 1966) 20.

5. Y. F. Tuan, *Topophilia: A Study of Environmental Perception, Attitudes, and Values* (Englewood Cliffs, NJ: Prentice-Hall, 1974).

The postmodern condition is one of fragmentation, multiplicity, and pluralism. Any theology which does not recognize this condition is likely to replicate essentialist or foundationalist errors of the past.[6] Among the most profound of these errors has been the chronocentrism of Christian theology, which was more or less established by Augustine in his magisterial but misguided reaction to the sack of Rome.[7] Chronocentrism makes it difficult for humans to recognize the immanence or "real presence" of God, and denies the freedom of God to transcend the arbitrary human marking of moments.[8] More practically, chronocentrism disorients Christians, leading them to undertake all kinds of bizarre, if not debased, "pilgrimages" to places like Walt Disney World and the Mall of America.[9] A more modest, and organic, approach is necessary, recognizing (insofar as possible) the complex interweaving of space and time.[10]

Language simply cannot encompass time. Language can map space, but even then the danger of idolatry, of confusing map with territory, is high.[11] Three theses follow: First, theological language which inherently acknowledges its limits, its fabricated character as map, is least likely to lead into the idolatry that vainly fixes itself as the justification of human history.[12] Second, metaphors which direct human attention to the organic limits of experience further block the impulse to idolatry; the desire to turn language into more than it can bear. Finally, metaphors which "map" or "clothe" God's presence in the most common and ordinary phenomena of life can reorient Christian theology and practice in ways that avoid the vanity which blinds human beings to the excessive, indeed gratuitous,

---

6. D. Tracy, *On Naming the Present: God, Hermeneutics, and Church* (New York: Orbis, 1994). See also M. I. Wallace, *Fragments of the Spirit: Nature, Violence, and the Renewal of Creation* (New York: Continuum, 1996).

7. Augustine, *Concerning the City of God against the Pagans*, trans. Henry Bettenson (New York: Penguin Books, 1984).

8. See R. M. Hamma, *Landscapes of the Soul: A Spirituality of Place* (Notre Dame, IN: Ave Maria Press, 1998) and B.C. Lane, *Landscapes of the Sacred: Geography and Narrative in American Spirituality* (New York: Paulist Press, 1988).

9. See I. G. Zepp, *The New Religious Image of Urban America: The Shopping Mall as Ceremonial Center* (Westminster, MD: Christian Classics, 1986) and S. J. Fjellman, *Vinyl Leaves: Walt Disney World and America* (Boulder, CO: Westview Press, 1992).

10. The emphasis on an "organic" model for theology is from S. McFague, *The Body of God: An Ecological Theology* (Minneapolis: Fortress Press, 1992).

11. J. Z. Smith, *Map is Not Territory: Essays in the History of Religions* (Chicago: The University of Chicago Press, 1978).

12. This position reaches its apogee in Schleiermacher and his descendants. See most notably W. Pannenberg, *et al.*, *Revelation as History*, trans. David Granskou (London: Macmillan, 1968).

appearance of God's presence as love in *places*, among them, most notably for today, places of water.[13]

Meanders through the Metaphorical Thicket: Toward a Theology of Places as God's Clothing

Building upon the ancient apophatic tradition and postmodern awareness of the role of language in human cultures,[14] Vanderbilt Divinity School theologian Sallie McFague has argued in several influential books that a "metaphorical theology" is a helpful way to proceed theologically in an "ecological, nuclear age."[15] She writes:

> All talk of God is indirect: no words or phrases refer directly to God ... [A metaphorical theology insists that] our concept of God is precisely that: *our concept* of God – and not God ... How language, any language, applies to God we do not know; what religious and theological language is at most is metaphorical forays attempting to express experiences of relating to God.[16]

Here McFague identifies, without using the term, how idolatry begins. Language becomes reified and petrified as people (usually in the interest of power) confuse their language with the living God. Theology becomes theo-*logy*.[17] What follows, invariably, is violence.[18] Accordingly language which inherently acknowledges its limits, its character as map, is least likely to lead into idolatry that vainly fixes itself as the self-justification of human history.

Nevertheless, language is the theologian's medium, and therefore language which directs human attention to the organic limits of experience (and especially to finitude, as in a *theology of the cross*) is preferable to language which allows humans to arrogate to themselves a preferred place in the cosmos. Here David Tracy's conception of "limit-

---

13. I use here language of J-L. Marion, *God without Being*, trans. Thomas A. Carlson, foreword by David Tracy (Chicago: The University of Chicago Press, 1995) while also recognizing that I differ significantly with Marion on some issues of substance.

14. A central insight of ethnographers of religion in recent years has been the power of religious symbols to motivate behavior. See in particular C. Geertz, "Religion as a Cultural System," in *The Interpretation of Cultures: Selected Essays* (New York: Basic Books, 1973).

15. See especially, for the most succinct presentation of her argument, S. McFague, *Models of God: Theology for an Ecological, Nuclear Age* (Philadelphia: Fortress Press, 1987). The particular themes important for this essay are also developed in *Metaphorical Theology: Models of God in Religious Language* (Philadelphia: Fortress, 1982) and *The Body of God: An Ecological Theology* (Minneapolis: Fortress, 1993).

16. S. McFague, *Models of God: Theology for an Ecological, Nuclear Age*, 34-39.

17. J-L. Marion, 139.

18. R. Girard, *Violence and the Sacred*, trans. Patrick Gregory (Baltimore and London: The Johns Hopkins University Press, 1978).

experiences," as elucidated in his ground-breaking 1975 book, *Blessed Rage for Order*, is illuminating:

> Fundamentally, the concept [of limit] refers to those human situations wherein a human being ineluctably finds manifest a certain ultimate limit or horizon to his or her existence ... More exactly, limit-situations refer to two basic kinds of existential situation: either those "boundary" situations of guilt, anxiety, sickness, and the recognition of death as one's own destiny, or those situations called "ecstatic experiences" – intense joy, love, reassurance, creation.[19]

Tracy identifies limit situations in science, morality, everyday experience, and in religious life, and seeks to correlate these situations of human need with theological reflection.

Like Tracy, Sallie McFague seeks theological language which will address the conditions of postmodernity, and especially the ecological crisis. In contrast to the monarchical model of God, which she argues depicts God as distant and alternately dominating or benevolent, McFague proposes a metaphor of "the world as God's body" as a way to locate sacramental presence in a postmodern context. She writes:

> What this experiment with the world as God's body comes to, finally, is an awareness, both chilling and breathtaking, that we as worldly, bodily beings are in God's presence. It is the basis for a revived sacramentalism that is painfully conscious of the world's vulnerability, its preciousness, its uniqueness.[20]

Sacramental presence is found in and through the world, when we recognize the world as God's body.

This has been an influential model of God in the U.S.; the book in which it was first articulated won the award of the American Academy of Religion for the best theological writing of 1988. It deserved it, but like any experiment, McFague's central metaphor needs some refining. On the one hand, it goes too far and falls into the characteristic Protestant problem regarding the sacraments by making sacramental presence a matter of the intellect, dependent upon the "awareness" of the observer. McFague struggles to avoid this trap, but the metaphor of "body" for the world is invariably interpreted in an anthropocentric, individualistic, and, finally, intellectualist fashion: God is present insofar as one *recognizes* the world as God's body.[21] As with most Protestants since Zwingli, then,

---

19. D. Tracy, *Blessed Rage for Order: The New Pluralism in Theology* (New York: Seabury Press, 1975) 105.

20. S. McFague, *Models of God: Theology for an Ecological, Nuclear Age*, 77.

21. I have taught the book for ten years to undergraduates at Valparaiso; they consistently criticize the book for its elitism and idealism, although they might not use those words to describe the problem.

whoever controls the signs controls God, and whoever controls God controls the world and the environment. McFague's work perpetuates, in the end, an ideology of intellectual control that is as rigid in its own way as the metaphor of God as king. Her argument for "the world as God's body" thus at times replicates the pervasive Protestant moralism in the U.S. which seeks to use theology as a club or stick with which to beat humans into "awareness" regarding this or that political agenda. It goes too far and obliterates grace, the very power of love it seeks to invoke or marshal for environmental purposes.

On the other hand, the metaphor of "the world as God's body" does not go far enough. McFague supposes that God necessarily "expresses" God's self in and through God's "body," the world. In fact, God expresses nothing necessarily, and the world is even more mute than God.[22] We are the ones who use language who express things. It is our vanity which imagines that God speaks to us directly, or imagines that our "experiences" are in fact immediate encounters of "relating" to the living God[23]. Such enthusiasm erodes both transcendence – that is the usual charge against McFague's theology – *and* immanence. McFague repeatedly points out that language shapes reality, but then seems to forget that language of "the body" is no more likely than language of "king" to produce the sort of environmental "awareness" or "sacramentality" that she hopes, because language, and especially metaphor, can only express distance; it cannot create presence. More immediate encounters than with metaphor are needed for "sacramentality." And immediate encounters are not found with "a *metaphorical* body," but with a body, that is to say, with actual flesh and blood, bread and wine, all of which, of course, begin with water. Not the body alone, but its "places" may be the preeminent *loci* for theology in an ecological, nuclear age.

Ironically, then, McFague's metaphorical theology – for all of its provocation and promise – falls short by failing to recognize that theologies of "the body" are as fabricated as any other metaphors. We cannot jump back into the Edenic condition of nakedness, at least not in public. The uniquely human feature of our bodies is not that we have them, but that we clothe them, fabricating out of the elements we have been given covers that reveal more or less. As such, any theology reveals not a "naked" God, but God's clothing, i.e. God veiled. If we only have access to God theologically through metaphors, then we must use metaphors whose patent character *as* metaphor does not subtly tempt the

---

22. See the writings of A. Dillard, and especially *Teaching a Stone to Talk* (New York: Harper, 1982).

23. R. Knox, *Enthusiasm: A Chapter in the History of Religion* (Notre Dame, IN: University of Notre Dame Press, 1994 [1950]).

reader to forget that God's "real presence" is decidedly *not* metaphorical. Real presence is found in love, which indeed must be embodied to be real, but which also transcends the body as its "gift." Metaphors which "map" or "clothe" God's presence in the most ordinary, taken-for-granted places of life, then, might reorient Christian theology and practice in ways that can avoid the vanity which blinds human beings to the excessive, indeed gratuitous, appearance of God's presence as love in *places*, among them, most notably for today, places where we find the gift of waters.

Living Waters: God Clothed as Source, (Dis)Solution, and Delight

"I am haunted by waters." Norman Maclean saved those words for the last line of his novel, *A River Runs Through It*, but in the film Robert Redford moved the powerful poetry which immediately preceeds them to the beginning, because they offer the theme of the whole:

> Eventually, all things merge into one, and a river runs through it. The river was cut by the world's great flood and runs over rocks from the basement of time. On some of the rocks are timeless raindrops. Under the rocks are the words, and the words are theirs. I am haunted by waters.[24]

Less poetically, waters confront human beings with a limit situation. We need water. There is no substitute for it. Our bodies are mostly water: we sweat it out of our pores, and it cascades down our faces in moments of intense joy or unbearable grief. The surface of the Earth is mostly water: we drink it, wash and clean with it, bathe and swim in it. We are born in water. It takes endless shapes and forms: "There is mist, dew, droplet, rain, torrent; rivulet, brook, creek, river, whirlpool; there is lake and most of all the boundless depths of the sea."[25] Water teems with life; indeed, is a source of life. Its excess dissolves all in its path. Its presence can provide us with delight, joy, and pleasure. Water confronts human beings with a limit situation.

Not surprisingly, then, religions widely incorporate waters in their symbolic systems. There are sacred rivers, like the liquid *shakti*, or female energy, of the Ganges.[26] There are sacred lakes, like Texcoco, "our mother great water" to the Aztecs.[27] And there are the waters of creation. In Africa, Asia, the Americas, Europe, and the Middle East are

---

24. N. MacLean, *A River Runs Through It* (Chicago: The University of Chicago Press, 1983) 108.
25. M. E. Marty, *Baptism* (Philadelphia: Fortress Press, 1962) 8.
26. D. L. Eck, "Rivers," in *The Encyclopedia of Religions* ed. Eliade (New York: Macmillan, 1987) Vol. 12: 333-338.
27. R. F. Townsend, "Lakes," in *The Encyclopedia of Religions*, Vol. 8: 429-434.

found stories of waters from which life came.[28] The Bible practically drips. "Water" or "waters" appear 694 times in 620 verses, as seas, rivers, and streams, in wells, cisterns, jars, bodies and more.[29] Unfortunately, Christians have barely tapped this well of theological resources. There is no entry for "water" in the influential Protestant *A Dictionary of Christian Theology*,[30] it is little mentioned (except in relation to baptism) in *The Catechism of the Catholic Church*,[31] and water gets almost no attention in leading systematic or biblical theologies.[32] The chronocentric obsession of Christian theology has blinded us to an icon of grace, God "clothed" in the presence of water.

The sacrament of baptism is, of course, the most prominent way in which water appears in the Christian community, and can likewise serve as the starting place for a theology of water as a place in which God is "clothed." As the rite of initiation, baptism incorporates human beings into the Christian community through a new birth, and through the washing away of sin. But there is another dimension to the sacrament, less well-explored theologically. According to the apostle Paul, in the waters of baptism we "put on" Christ, as we put on a piece of clothing. Indeed, Paul makes the metaphor explicit:

> As many of you as were baptized into Christ have clothed yourselves with Christ. There is no longer Jew or Greek, there is no longer slave or free, there is no longer male and female; for all of you are one in Christ Jesus. (Galatians 3:27-28, NRSV)

A child of God who is washed in the waters of baptism is clothed with God as present in Christ. Luther interprets Paul in exactly these terms: "In Baptism ... Christ becomes our garment ... [as] the divine and inestimable gift."[33]

---

28. J. Rudhardt, "Water," in *The Encyclopedia of Religions*, Vol. 15: 350-358.

29. *Quickverse for Windows, v. 4.0c: NRSV* (Parson's Technologies, 1997).

30. A. Richardson (ed.), *A Dictionary of Christian Theology* (Philadelphia: Westminster, 1969).

31. "The Catechism of the Catholic Church Online,": <http://www.christusrex.org/www1/CDHN/ccc.htm>.

32. No listing for "water" is found in the index of *Summa Theologiae: A Concise Translation*, ed. Timothy McDermott (Westminster, MD: Christian Classics, 1989) and it is similarly absent from perhaps the two leading Protestant Old Testament theologies of a generation ago: Walter Zimmerli, *Old Testament Theology in Outline* (Atlanta: John Knox, 1978) and Gerhard von Rad, *Old Testament Theology.* 2 vols., ed. D. M. G. Stalker (New York: Harper and Row, 1962).

33. M. Luther, *Lectures on Galatians* 353.

I

Waters are a life-source. *Tanakh* is unequivocal on this matter, which should hardly be surprising when it is recalled that the people of ancient Israel lived in a more or less desert climate. Archeological evidence gives ample testimony to the creativity that the peoples of the ancient Near East used to collect and preserve water – pots, jars, pitchers, flasks, cisterns, fountains, and wells are among the common finds of biblical archeologists. The sharing of water was a key, if not essential, expression of hospitality in the biblical world.[34] A gift of water was like the gift of life itself.

Throughout the cultures of the ancient Near East, stories of creation from water were common.[35] Like their neighbors, then, the people of Israel imagined creation beginning in water. The very first verses of Genesis make the point:

> In the beginning, when God began to create the heavens and the earth, the earth was a formless void and darkness covered the face of the deep, while a wind from God swept over the face of the waters. (Gen 1,1-3)

Not an account of creation from nothing, as it has often been interpreted, this story asserts that creation was *from water*. In the second account, which begins at 2,4, the primeval waters are in the form of a "stream that would rise up from the earth, and water the whole face of the ground." The two creation accounts of Genesis agree on this point, which is by now well-established in biblical studies: the long-standing interpretation of the creation story which asserted that God created from nothing is incorrect.[36] The Biblical cosmogonies reveal a God who creates with waters, arranging them into new shapes that continually form a cosmos out of chaos.[37]

Now, waters as the source of life also have a spiritual, as well as a literal, sense in *Tanakh*. In his last vision, the prophet Ezekiel saw a river running from the temple, first ankle deep, then knee deep, then too deep to cross. The river ran out into the world, and brought life wherever it flowed. What was stagnant became fresh; every living creature flourished:

---

34. See the very helpful summary by P. A. Bird, "Water," in *Harper's Bible Dictionary*, ed. P. J. Achtemeier (San Francisco: Harper & Row, 1985) 1120-1121.

35. R. J. Clifford, *Creation Accounts in the Ancient Near East and in the Bible* – Catholic Biblical Quarterly Monograph Series, 26 (Washington: Catholic Biblical Association, 1994).

36. D. Tsumara, *The Earth and the Waters in Genesis 1 and 2: A Linguistic Investigation* (Sheffield: JSOT, 1989).

37. J. D. Levenson, *Creation and the Persistence of Evil: The Jewish Drama of Divine Omnipotence* (San Francisco: Harper and Row, 1988).

> "on the banks ... of the river, there will grow all kinds of trees for food. Their leaves will not wither nor their fruit fail, but they will bear fresh fruit every month, because the water for them flows from the sanctuary. Their fruit will be for food, and their leaves for healing." (47,12)

This is the river of life, these are the waters of Eden, now bringing new life to a parched people.

At the end of the Writings About Christ, in fact in the last chapter of the Christian *Bible*, the writer of Revelation sees the same image:

> Then the angel showed me the river of the water of life, bright as crystal, flowing from the throne of God and of the Lamb through the middle of the street of the city. On either side of the river, is the tree of life with its twelve kinds of fruit, producing its fruit each month; and the leaves of the tree are for the healing of the nations. Nothing accursed will be found there any more. But the throne of God and of the Lamb will be in it, and his servants will worship God; and they will see God's face. (22:1-4)

This vision is a loving one, an apocalyptic midrash on Ezekiel's vision which offers suffering people the hope that what we now see dimly, God veiled in the waters of creation, we will someday see clearly, bright as crystal: God's face, our source, the water of life. This water weaves us all together in what the late Joseph Cardinal Bernardin called "a seamless garment" between creation and redemption, with an ethic of environmental concern implied.[38] Sacramental presence, like everything else, begins with water.

II

Unfortunately, however, the experience of the Jews, like the experience of Jesus – was hardly one of a seamless garment. Therefore, the scribes of Israel also borrowed another plot-line from their neighbors: in some texts, God creates by enduring a battle with watery chaos. Psalm 74 and Psalm 104 both imply a cosmogony in which God creates order by vanquishing the primordial Leviathan; creation is order over chaos, the waters in their place. Here, waters are a threat – they drown, submerge, and dissolve.

Of course, *what* they dissolve is important. For the scribes of Israel, the waters invariably (dis)solved some humanly created problem. This is the point of the flood myth as recorded in Genesis 6–9:

> Now the earth was corrupt in God's sight, and the earth was filled with violence.... And God said to Noah, 'I have determined to make an end of all

---

38. J. Bernardin, *Consistent Ethic of Life*, ed. T. G. Fuechtmann (Kansas City, MO: Sheed & Ward, 1988).

flesh, for the earth is filled with violence because of them; now I am going to destroy them along with the earth.' (6,11-13)

The violence of the flood follows from the violence of humanity, and calls forth a change. The story reveals the way distorted desires, blind ambitions, and limited attachments produce violence whose chaos threatens to destroy us and the planet. That the story ends with a covenant, where God promises to respect life and asks the same of humans, only reinforces the point: waters can (dis)solve, and what they (dis)solve (textually, at least) are humanly created problems like the violence which stems from corrupted love.

If in *Torah* God renounced flooding as a way of doing business, the prophets nevertheless made rich use of water imagery as a way to induce people to change their evil ways. Amos put it most clearly, speaking for God:

> Because you trample on the poor, and take from them levies of grain, you have built houses of living stone, but you shall not live in them; you have planted pleasant vineyards, but you shall not drink their wine.

Without justice, there will be no true flow for anyone. Indeed, no amount of piety will replace the absence of justice. As is well known, Amos also has God say,

> I hate, I despise your festivals, and I take no delight in your solemn assemblies ... But let justice roll down like waters, and righteousness like an everflowing stream. (5:11; 21-24, NRSV).

The point is consistent with that of Genesis 1-11: waters (dis)solve some problem humans have created; in such a capacity they serve as an apt icon of God's grace which seeks a new world in which none are excluded. Love leads to justice, with fulfillment for all. No one should go thirsty.

The attachments of the prophets extend broadly – if they are not dissolved altogether in love – to strangers, gentiles, enemies, beasts, even the cosmos itself. The archetypal story is Jonah's. Jonah is commanded by God to call the people of the Assyrian city of Nineveh – Israel's enemy – to repentance. Instead, Jonah flees "from the presence of God" on a boat headed in the other direction. A storm comes up and Jonah is thrown overboard, where he finds himself in the belly of a sea monster. (1:1-17) We are back in the realm of Psalm 104 – the primeval waters again threaten to drown a human soul. Ironically, however, the chaotic waters bring Jonah closer to God. He prays, and God hears him. He gives thanks to God, for "all your waves and your billows passed over me." Jonah realizes, but only partially, that he is *now* – in the belly of the beast – in God's presence. God again calls Jonah to go to Nineveh. This time, having been released from the beast, he goes, and to his surprise, the people of Nineveh listen. The king proclaims:

> All shall turn away from their evil ways and from the violence that is in their hands. Who knows? God may relent and change his mind; he may turn from his fierce anger, so that we do not perish. (3,8b-9).

Surprisingly, at least to Jonah, God does change, the people are saved, and the story ends with the prophet, apparently having forgotten his experience in the waters, sulking and sitting outside the city in anger, baking in the sun.

Now the meaning of this story, which was probably addressed to an isolationist party within ancient Israel, has been kept clear among the Jewish people today, who read it on the Day of Atonement. Jonah's story is a story of change, of how he had to go through the waters to have his petty attachment to "his" people dissolved. It was only underneath the waters that Jonah found the presence of God; it is only *through the waters*, the story suggests, that one finds God-inspired change. Nineveh changes (for the better); Jonah changes (but not enough); even God changes. Waters can do that. They change everything in their path. Justice demands change. Fulfillment for all flesh does not imply a static state.

It is through the waters, then, that we find justice. Through the gift, available to all, we discover that love is not a possession (of individuals or nations) and justice is not retribution but both love and justice imply fulfillment for all flesh, even all creation. Paul puts it well: "We know that the whole creation has been groaning in labor pains until now." (Rom 8,22-23) There are no labor pains without water; no birth without love. The God clothed in living waters wants us to find the flow of justice. The flood story, Amos' call for justice, and the story of Jonah all seek to broaden our perspective, to loosen our attachment to our "possessions," and to heighten our responsibility to live without initiating violence. We are asked, in covenant with God, to care for the waters of creation in all forms, because they are one way in which God's all-inclusive grace is manifest to us. Water as a garment of God directs us not only to our source, but to a power which dissolves our petty attachments in a flow of justice.

III

Finally, though, water is our delight: a gift of God that in abundance or scarcity draws us with love. The living waters with which God is clothed provide humans with delight, joy, and pleasure. This aspect of God's clothing is most clearly revealed in the Song of Songs and the Gospel of

John. The explicit metaphors of the Song of Songs are frequently, as one would expect in an erotic ode to human sexuality, liquid, if not juicy. Thus the male figure in the Song of Songs, traditionally Solomon, describes his female lover as:

> a garden locked, a fountain sealed. ... Your channel is an orchard of pomegranates with all choicest fruits. . . . A garden fountain, a well of living water, and flowing streams from Lebanon.

His lover expresses her desire:

> Awake, O north wind, and come, O south wind! Blow upon my garden, that its fragrance may be wafted abroad. Let my beloved come to his garden, and eat its choicest fruits.

The man responds:

> I come to my garden, my sister, my bride; I gather my myrrh with my spice, I eat my honeycomb with my honey, I drink my wine with my milk.

Together, the couple exclaim:

> Eat friends, drink, and be drunk with love! (4,12-5,1)

Here, waters – streams of Lebanon, a garden fountain, living waters – merge with wine and honey in a sweet liquidity that is celebrated with all the passion – even unto drunkenness – that humans can muster. God, clothed in the waters of creation, gives us bodies flowing with water to experience some of God's own delight.

This theme returns in the Gospel of John. Jesus' dialogue with the Samaritan woman at the well of Sychar can be read as an extended midrash on the Song of Songs. It is the longest dialogue in the gospels, and in it Jesus breaks widely-accepted conventions of Hellenistic Jewish society. The sexual tension in the story is considerable. The woman, we learn, has been married five times and is currently living with a man to whom she is not married. Jesus, being a Jewish male, and a teacher, should not be talking with a woman, much less a Samaritan woman with loose morals. Yet, talk he does. He asks for a drink. She answers with surprise that he has addressed her. Jesus responds in turn with what is, in fact, a tease:

> If only you knew what God gives, and who it is that is asking you for a drink, you would have asked him and he would have given you living water.

John's Jesus here repeats the image from the Song of Songs, "living water," and asserts that the woman's problem is that she does not know what God *gives*. The woman plays along:

> Sir, you have no bucket, and the well is deep! Where do you get that living water?

She expresses her desire for what Jesus has to give. John has Jesus reply:

> Everyone who drinks this water will be thirsty again, but whoever drinks the water that I shall give will never suffer thirst any more. The water that I shall give will be an inner spring always welling up for eternal life. (4:8-15, NEB)

The dialogue continues for several more verses, and the two parties seem to enjoy the exchange: the woman leaves all but a convert, the first witness to the Messiah in the gospel.

John evokes in this dialogue themes implicit and explicit in the Song of Songs: a man and a woman discourse about intimate matters, in which topics of gift, desire, and pleasure appear, along with the rich (and rare) imagery of living water. That John was a master of metaphor goes without saying; that John here "clothes" the incarnate God in living water should also be obvious. The implications, however, may be less clear. John of course spiritualizes the erotic metaphors of the Song of Songs, while he does not thereby obliterate them. The truth of delight in living waters is true whether the waters are figuratively or literally interpreted. When one *knows* what God gives, *or* when one simply *enjoys* what God gives, one encounters living water that quenches thirst.

What then, does all of this suggest about sacramental presence in a postmodern context? If Christians truly are in some sense "clothed" in God's garments during baptism, then all waters (they eventually merge into one) are icons of the living God. Indeed, it may be only in the new millennium, as clean water again becomes scarce, and as we seek to find ways to protect it, that we can understand how the biblical writers could draw so fully and creatively from wells that connected God to waters. The God revealed in the Bible is present in living water, flowing as source like an inner spring through us, as a power which (dis)solves our petty attachments in a flow of justice, and as a garden stream which intimates to us deep, even eternal, joy.

To locate sacramental presence in this way has significant implications for pastoral practice, but to develop them fully would take more space than I have here. Briefly, however, the rich metaphors which relate God to water in the Scriptures imply that Christians have resources to develop a theocentric ethic which addresses the most basic policy decisions to be made regarding water usage.[39] Indeed, it may be that only such an ethic can keep us from treating water as a possession – and eventually (as some fear) going to war over it.[40] In any event, a theology which "clothes" God as "living waters" suggests that the church's

---

39. J. M. Gustafson, *Ethics from a Theocentric Perspective*. 2 vols. (Chicago: The University of Chicago Press, 1981-88).

40. A. Light and J. M. Smith (eds.), *Space, Place, and Environmental Ethics* (Lanham, MD: Roman and Littlefield, 1997).

reflection on issues of water conservation, usage, pollution, and purification should be moved from a peripheral to a central place in ethical reflection. A loving response to such an abundant-yet-scarce gift of love as we have been given in the beautiful blue blanket which wraps this planet must surely entail preserving it and caring for it. The Church can bring a significant and constructive voice to the global debate over environmental policies.[41]

On a local level, communities of Christians can incorporate water more fully into their common life, both liturgically and practically. In some cases, this will mean reviving practices recently abandoned, such as gathering Christians at bodies of living water like rivers and lakes. In others, it will involve creation of new rituals and practices. For instance, for the past three summers I served as spiritual advisor to the twenty-six member staff at Camp Arcadia, a Lutheran family resort on the shores of Lake Michigan. I wove water into our community life regularly. We began the season in late May with a baptismal reaffirmation in the (very cold) waters of Lake Michigan. We concluded staff orientation week with a pre-eucharist foot-washing, a ritual we repeated in a less intimate (and quicker) version several other times and with different groups during the summers as a "hand washing." About once a week we would "chrismate" each other with water during a meal-time devotion. Finally, we occasionally adapted a rite from the Jewish festival of Rosh Hashanah, known as "tashlich," which involved the "casting of sins" (in the form of stones) into the waters of the lake.

A number of everyday practices were also changed at the Camp over the course of my three-year tenure to make the common life of the Christian community there more water-friendly. We rebuilt an old well to increase its efficiency, installed low-flow shower heads and toilets, and designed a "request card" asking guests to reuse towels, if possible, in the interest of preserving water. That some of these changes were mandated by law made their implementation that much easier. That they were also motivated by economic concerns did not prevent them from functioning any less as reminders of sacramental presence. In caring for Lake Michigan, people intuitively understand that they extend loving care to a reality larger than themselves; a body of living water that is not unlike the waters in which they were clothed in baptism, if not in birth. It should go without saying that the people who visit the resort both love and respect the Lake. A theology which "clothes" God in living waters, then, might just form a framework for a community guided by loving policies,

---

41. R. B. Fowler, *The Greening of Protestant Thought* (Chapel Hill and London: The University of North Carolina Press, 1995). See also D. G. Hallman (ed.), *Ecotheology: Voices from South and North* (New York: Orbis, 1994).

practical rituals, and even a good theology – if the latter is not, in fact, an oxymoron.

The Lutheran Theological Seminary at Philadelphia   Jon PAHL
7301 Germantown Avenue
Philadelphia, Pennsylvania 19119-1794
USA